Bass Guitar

FOR DUMMIES®

A Wiley Brand

3rd Edition

by Patrick Pfeiffer

Foreword by Will Lee
Bassist, *Late Show with David Letterman*

Bass Guitar For Dummies,® 3rd Edition

Published by: John Wiley & Sons, Inc., 111 River Street, Hoboken, NJ 07030-5774, www.wiley.com

Copyright © 2014 by John Wiley & Sons, Inc., Hoboken, New Jersey

Published simultaneously in Canada

For general information on our other products and services, please contact our Customer Care Department within the U.S. at 877-762-2974, outside the U.S. at 317-572-3993, or fax 317-572-4002. For technical support, please visit www.wiley.com/techsupport.

Wiley publishes in a variety of print and electronic formats and by print-on-demand. Some material included with standard print versions of this book may not be included in e-books or in print-on-demand. If this book refers to media such as a CD or DVD that is not included in the version you purchased, you may download this material at http://booksupport.wiley.com. For more information about Wiley products, visit www.wiley.com.

Library of Congress Control Number is available from the publisher.

ISBN 978-1-118-74880-0 (pbk); ISBN 978-1-118-74894-7 (ebk); ISBN 978-1-118-74897-8 (ebk); ISBN 978-1-118-74874-9 (ebk)

Manufactured in the United States of America

10 9 8 7 6 5 4 3 2 1

Contents at a Glance

Foreword...*xiii*

Introduction 1

Part I: Getting Started with the Bass Guitar 7
Chapter 1: The Very Basics of Bass...9
Chapter 2: Gaining the Tools and Skills to Play 21
Chapter 3: Warming Up: Getting Your Hands in Shape to Play 57

Part II: The Bass-ics of Playing 67
Chapter 4: Reading, 'Riting, and Rhythm..69
Chapter 5: Understanding Major and Minor Structures 91

Part III: Making the Moves, Creating the Grooves....... 127
Chapter 6: Creating the Groove 129
Chapter 7: Going Solo: Playing Solos and Fills 167

Part IV: Using the Correct Accompaniment for Each Genre... 183
Chapter 8: Rock On! Getting Down with the Rock Styles 185
Chapter 9: Swing It! Playing Styles That Rely on the Triplet Feel 203
Chapter 10: Making It Funky: Playing Hardcore Bass Grooves 221
Chapter 11: Sampling International Flavors: Bass Styles from Around the World..237
Chapter 12: Playing in Odd Meters: Not Strange, Just Not the Norm 255
Chapter 13: Groovin' in a Genre: It's All About Style!.............................271
Chapter 14: Eight Degrees of Separation: The Beatles' Solution 287

Part V: Buying and Caring for Your Bass 307
Chapter 15: Love of a Lifetime or One-Night Stand? Buying the Right Bass 309
Chapter 16: Getting the Right Gear for Your Bass Guitar 319
Chapter 17: Changing the Strings on Your Bass Guitar 329
Chapter 18: Keeping Your Bass in Shape: Maintenance and Light Repair 339

Part VI: The Part of Tens 351

Chapter 19: Ten Innovative Bassists You Should Know 353

Chapter 20: Ten Great Rhythm Sections (Bassists and Drummers) 357

Appendix: Audio Tracks and Video Clips 363

Index 377

Table of Contents

Foreword..*xiii*

Introduction 1
    About This Book 1
    Foolish Assumptions...3
    Icons Used in This Book 4
    Beyond the Book 4
    Where to Go from Here..5

Part I: Getting Started with the Bass Guitar 7

Chapter 1: The Very Basics of Bass........................... 9
    Discovering the Differences between the Bass and Its High-Strung
        Cousins 9
    Understanding the Bass Player's Function in a Band 10
        Forging the link between harmony and rhythm 10
        Moving the song along 11
        Keeping time 11
        Establishing rhythms 12
        Looking cool 12
    Dissecting the Anatomy of a Bass Guitar 12
        The neck... 13
        The body 14
        The innards.. 15
    On a Need-to-Know "Basses": Gearing Up to Play Bass 15
        Coordinating your right and left hands 16
        Mastering major and minor chord structures 16
        Tuning your bass 16
        Combining scales and chords 16
    Playing Grooves, Solos, and Fills 17
        Creating grooves and riffs.. 17
        Treating yourself and your audience to solos and fills......... 17
    Experimenting with Different Musical Genres 18
    Stocking Up on Some Bass Gear 19
        Buying a bass 19
        Getting an amplifier 20
        Accessorizing your bass 20
    Giving Your Bass Some Good Ol' TLC.. 20

Chapter 2: Gaining the Tools and Skills to Play 21

Getting a Handle on Your Bass 21
Holding Your Bass 22
    Strapping on your bass: Strings to the outside.................23
    Voilà! Standing with your bass...24
    Sitting with your bass..25
Placing Your Hands in the Proper Position...........................26
    Positioning your left hand 26
    Positioning your right hand...27
Reading a Fingerboard Diagram 33
    The language of music: Scales and chords.........................34
    Viewing a diagram of the major and minor scales 36
    Playing open-string scales 37
    Finding the notes on the neck...37
    Identifying intervals: They're always in the same place....39
Tuning Your Bass Guitar 41
    Reference pitch sources to use when playing alone.........41
    Reference pitch sources to use when playing with others 43
    Tuning the bass guitar to itself 46
Playing a Song on Your Bass Guitar 53
    Making some noise with the open strings 54
    Closing the strings 55

Chapter 3: Warming Up: Getting Your Hands in Shape to Play 57

Understanding the Sound Your Bass Makes..........................57
Performing Right-Hand Warm-Ups 58
    Right-hand same-string strokes 59
    Controlling the strength in your striking hand:
        Right-hand accents 60
    Skating across the strings: Right-hand string crossing.........62
Coordinating Your Left Hand with Your Right Hand 63
    Doing finger permutations...63
    Muting the strings to avoid the infamous hum..................65
    Putting it all together...65

Part II: The Bass-ics of Playing *67*

Chapter 4: Reading, 'Riting, and Rhythm **69**

Reading Notation: No Pain, Much Gain...................................69
    Chord notation: The chord chart 70
    Music notation: Indicating rhythm and notes...................70

Tablature notation: Showing strings, frets, and sequence............71
The vocal chart: Using lyrics and chords for a
    singer or songwriter 73
Finding Any Note in Any Octave...73
Using the Metronome: You Know, That Tick-Tock Thing 78
    Setting the metronome..78
    Playing along 79
Dividing Music into Phrases, Measures, and Beats.........................79
    The quarter note...80
    The eighth note 81
    The sixteenth note..81
    The half note...81
    The whole note..82
    The triplet 82
    The dot 82
    The tie 83
    The rest 83
Discovering How to Read Music...84
    Rhythmic chunks 84
    Interval chunks..85
    What comes up must come down..86
Playing Your First Song While Reading Music 89

Chapter 5: Understanding Major and Minor Structures. 91

Building Major and Minor Scales...92
    Major scales...93
    Minor scales 94
Building Chords: One Note at a Time, Please 95
    Triads: The three most important notes of a chord 95
    7th chords: Filling out the triad 101
    Getting your kicks with boogie licks 102
Inversions: Down Is Up, and Up Is Down 103
    Major chord inversions..104
    Minor chord inversions..105
Spicing Up Your Sound: The Seven Main Modes (Scales)..............107
Using Chromatic Tones: All the Other Notes.................................113
    Chromatic tones within the box 113
    Chromatic tones outside the box 114
Bringing a Groove to Life with Dead Notes (Weird but True) 116
    Playing dead — notes, that is..116
    Raking dead notes...117
Sampling Accompaniments 118
    Using your accompaniments in a tune...122
    Keeping your groove gloriously ambiguous................................123

Part III: Making the Moves, Creating the Grooves 127

Chapter 6: Creating the Groove............................129

Anatomy of a Groove: Putting Together the Necessary Elements 129
    Getting your groove skeleton out of the closet 130
    Playing a song using only the groove skeleton.........................132
    Choosing the right notes for a groove 133
Creating Your Own Groove 136
    Covering the "basses": Creating dominant, minor, and
        major grooves..136
    Waggin' the groove tail 145
    Movin' and groovin' from chord to chord....................................146
    Finding the perfect fit: The designer groove...............................151
Grooving with a Drummer 154
    The bass drum 154
    The snare drum..154
    The hi-hat...155
Jammin' with Other Musicians 156
    Preparing your ear...157
    Listening for "the note"...157
    Pivoting the note..160
Getting Creative with Existing Grooves 162
    Altering a (famous) groove 163
    Simplifying a groove 165

Chapter 7: Going Solo: Playing Solos and Fills 167

Soloing: Your Moment to Shine 167
    Playing with the blues scale: A favorite solo spice 168
    Jamming with the minor pentatonic scale: No wrong notes........169
    Using the major pentatonic scale: Smooth as can be 173
    Moving from chord to chord...174
Creating Fills without Any Help from Your Dentist...............................176
    A match made in heaven: Connecting your fill to the groove......177
    Timing a fill 177

Part IV: Using the Correct Accompaniment for Each Genre 183

Chapter 8: Rock On! Getting Down with the Rock Styles 185

Rock 'n' Roll: It's The Attitude! 186
Hard Rock: Going at It Fast and Furious 191
Pop Rock: Supporting the Vocals 193

Blues Rock: Doin' What "Duck" Does and Playing
a Countermelody..196
Country Rock: Where Vocals Are King, and
You Take a Back Seat..199
One Rock Fits All: Applying a Standard Rock Groove to
Any Rock Song..201

**Chapter 9: Swing It! Playing Styles That Rely
on the Triplet Feel** **203**
Swing: Grooving Up-Tempo with Attitude.................................204
Jazz: Going for a Walk...205
Working the walk...207
Applying a jazz blues walking pattern.............................211
Blues Shuffle: Walking Like Donald Duck (Dunn, That Is)........214
Funk Shuffle: Combining Funk, Blues, and Jazz......................218

Chapter 10: Making It Funky: Playing Hardcore Bass Grooves **221**
R & B: Movin' to Rhythm and Blues.......................................221
The Motown Sound: Grooving with the Music of the Funk Brothers ...225
Fusion: Blending Two Styles into One.....................................226
Funk: Light Fingers, Heavy Attitude..229
Hip-Hop: Featuring Heavy Funk with Heavy Attitude...............233
Knowing What to Do When You Just Want to Funkifize a Tune...........234

**Chapter 11: Sampling International Flavors: Bass Styles
from Around the World**. **237**
Bossa Nova: Baskin' in a Brazilian Beat..................................237
Samba: Speeding Up with Bossa's Fast Cousin.......................239
Afro-Cuban: Ordering Up Some Salsa (Hold the Chips, Please)............240
Reggae: Relaxing with Offbeat "Riddims".................................242
Calypso Party Sounds: Dancing through the Groove.................245
Combining Reggae and Rock: The Distinct Sound of Ska.........246
African Grooves: Experimenting with Exotic Downbeat Grooves........248
Grooving on a steady beat, South African–style.................248
Checking out the bass groove styles from Cameroon...............249
Music without Borders: Grooving to the World Beat..................252

**Chapter 12: Playing in Odd Meters: Not Strange, Just
Not the Norm** **255**
An Odd-Meter Oldie but Goodie: The Waltz................................255
Beyond the Waltz: Navigating Beats in Odd Meter....................257
5/4 meter: Not an impossible mission...............................258
Take a groove you know and make it grow.........................261
7/4 meter: Adding two more beats.....................................262

Complex Simplicity: Syncopation and Subdivision 266
Syncopating in odd meter 267
Adding an eighth 267
Dealing with the rush 268

Chapter 13: Groovin' in a Genre: It's All About Style! 271
Playing Grooves in Each Genre: One Simple Song,
Many Genres Strong 272
Pop: Backing up the singer-songwriter 273
Rocking by the quarter or eighth note 273
R & B/Soul, with or without the dot 274
Feeling da funk 278
Layin' down some Latin grooves 279
When you're feelin' blue, shuffle 280
To Blend or Not to Blend: Knowing How to Fit In 282
Just blending in: How to do it 283
The bold and the beautiful: Creating a bold groove 283
Blending and bolding by genre 284
Signing off with a flourish 285

Chapter 14: Eight Degrees of Separation: The Beatles' Solution . . . 287
Playing Your Rhythm Straight or Syncopated 288
Pumping eighth notes 288
Syncopating the bass beat 289
Making Harmonic Choices 292
Feeling fine (with roots and 5ths) 292
Walking along Penny Lane 294
Coming together to move with the groove 297
Day-tripping in perfect agreement: Unison 297
Playing something to counter the melody with 301
Inverting while your bass gently weeps 302

Part V: Buying and Caring for Your Bass 307

Chapter 15: Love of a Lifetime or One-Night Stand?
Buying the Right Bass 309
Assessing Your Needs Before You Buy 309
Thinking long-term: Moving in together 310
Thinking short-term: Help me make it through the night 311
How many strings are too many? 311
To fret or not to fret 312

Needs Are One Thing . . . Budget Is Quite Another 313
A Trip to the Bass-Mint: Where to Shop for Your Bass Guitar 314
 Hitting the music stores...314
 Consulting newspaper ads...316
 Visiting online shops and individual online ads 316
When Money Is No Object: Getting a Custom-Made Bass 317

Chapter 16: Getting the Right Gear for Your Bass Guitar 319

Making Yourself Heard: A Primer on Amplifiers and Speakers 319
 Going with a combo or separate amp and speaker......................320
 Opting for solid state or tubes 321
 Picking a speaker size 321
 Setting the tone 322
Needs, Wants, and Nonessentials: Rounding Out Your Equipment......323
 Must-haves: Cases, gig bags, and more..323
 Definite maybes: Useful effects, gadgets, and practice items 325
 Extras: Effects pedals 327

Chapter 17: Changing the Strings on Your Bass Guitar 329

Knowing When It's Time to Say Goodbye 330
Off with the Old: Removing Bass Strings...330
On with the New: Restringing Your Bass..332
Ensuring a Long Life for Your Strings 338

**Chapter 18: Keeping Your Bass in Shape:
Maintenance and Light Repair 339**

Cleaning Your Bass, Part by Part..339
 The body and neck 340
 The hardware 340
 The pickups 340
 The fingerboard 341
 The strings 341
Making Minor Repairs to Your Bass...342
 The taming of the screw(s)..342
 Taking care of the finish...343
 Leaving the electronics to the experts..343
Adjusting the Bass Guitar 344
 Providing relief to the truss rod 344
 Raising and lowering the bridge 346
Assembling a Cleaning and Repair Tool Bag...348
Storing Your Bass 349

Part VI: The Part of Tens **351**

Chapter 19: Ten Innovative Bassists You Should Know **353**

Stanley Clarke 353
John Entwistle...354
James Jamerson...354
Carol Kaye 354
Will Lee 354
Paul McCartney...355
Marcus Miller 355
Jaco Pastorius 355
Victor Wooten 356
X (Fill in Your Own)...356

**Chapter 20: Ten Great Rhythm Sections
(Bassists and Drummers)** **357**

Bootsy Collins and Jab'o Starks...357
Donald "Duck" Dunn and Al Jackson Jr. 358
James Jamerson and Benny Benjamin.....................................358
John Paul Jones and John Bonham...359
Joe Osborn and Hal Blaine 359
Jaco Pastorius and Peter Erskine 360
George Porter Jr. and Zig Modeliste 360
Francis Rocco Prestia and David Garibaldi.............................361
Chuck Rainey and Bernard Purdie 361
Robbie Shakespeare and Sly Dunbar 362

Appendix: Audio Tracks and Video Clips **363**

Index **377**

Foreword

· ·

*F*or bassists or bass wannabes, *Bass Guitar For Dummies* takes you on a tour of the instrument and explores all avenues of bassdom. Of the myriad tools available for bassists, *Bass Guitar For Dummies* is at the pinnacle of them all. Never before has such a complete anthology been assembled. It's like having an unlimited ticket for all the rides at BassLand!

Patrick Pfeiffer, great communicator of bass guitar, has laid it all out for you to enjoy. *Bass Guitar For Dummies* can be read laterally, literally, or "loiterily." In other words, cover to cover, in order, or at your leisure; when you have a couple of minutes, just read a page, or a chapter. It's not too deep, not too heavy, but it's all good information and a lot of fun. So dig in, and enjoy *Bass Guitar For Dummies*!

All the Bass,

Will Lee, Grammy-award-winning bassist, *Late Show with David Letterman*

Introduction

. . . .

Shake the earth with deep, sonorous vibrations. Let your melodies swoop and soar like swallows over a meadow. Be the force that relentlessly drives the music with percussive, percolating emanations from your speaker. Rumble like the ominous thunder of an approaching storm. Whisper, growl, *roar* your grooves into the universe. For you, it's not enough just to be heard; you *will* be felt. You are . . . the bass player.

Imagine your favorite music without bass. It doesn't work, does it? The bass is the heartbeat of the music, the foundation for the groove, and the glue that holds together all the different instruments. You can hear the music sing as it's carried along by the bass groove. You can sense the music come to life. You can feel the vibrations of those low notes — sometimes subtle and caressing, sometimes literally earthshaking — as they propel the song. The bass is the heart of it all.

Leave center stage to the other musicians — you have more important work to do. The limelight may be cool, but bassists rule!

About This Book

You can find everything you need to master the bass in *Bass Guitar For Dummies,* 3rd Edition — from the correct way to strike a note to the way to play a funk groove in the style of Jaco Pastorius. It's all here.

Each chapter is independent of the others. You can skip the stuff you already know and go straight to the parts that interest you without feeling lost. To find the subject you're looking for, just check out the table of contents. You also can look up specific topics in the index at the back of the book. Or you can read from front to back and build up your bass-playing skills step by step. Whatever you choose, just remember to enjoy the journey.

I structure this book so you can decide for yourself how far you want to take your skills on the instrument. As I was writing, I checked out the entrance requirements for music schools and conservatories, and I included the information that fulfills those requirements (without getting too theoretical — after all, you don't want to spend all your time theorizing . . . you want to *play*). In fact, this book goes well beyond the minimum requirements and shows you how to actually *apply* all this information to real-life bass playing. I show you how to play in different styles and how to create your own grooves and solos so you don't have to copy someone else's bass line note-for-note.

No bass guitar? No problem. This book doesn't assume you have your own bass. If you don't, just head over to Part V to find out how to choose the right bass and accessories to get started. If you already have a bass, you can start with the maintenance section in Chapter 18 and find out how to set up your instrument so it's easiest to play.

You don't need to read music to figure out how to play the bass guitar. (You can unknit your eyebrows now . . . it's true.) So how can you get the information you need from this book? Here's how:

- ✔ **Look at the grids.** The grids are pictures of the notes you play on the fingerboard of the bass guitar. The grids show you where the notes are in relation to each other and which fingers you use to play them. They also provide you with an additional advantage: If you use the grid to finger a certain pattern of notes, you can then transfer the same pattern (fingering and all) onto any other section of the fingerboard to play the note pattern in a different key. That's why reading music isn't necessary. The notes on a page of regular music notation look completely different for each new key, but if you use the grid, you'll find that, as far as note patterns go, one size fits all.

- ✔ **Read the tablature.** *Tablature* is a shorthand notational technique that shows you which string to strike and where to hold the string down to sound a note. The short name for tablature is *tab* (just in case anyone asks).

- ✔ **Listen to the audio tracks.** You can hear all the exercises and grooves that are shown in the figures by simply going online to www.dummies.com/go/bassguitar and listening to audio tracks for each one. You can listen to the sound of a groove, take a look at the grid and the tab, put your hand in the proper position on the fingerboard, and then reproduce the sound. While you're there, you may as well check out the video clips that show you the details for playing certain figures.

  After you master a groove, you can pan to one side to remove the sound of the bass. Then you can play the groove in the example with just the drums and the guitar (in other words, with real musicians). Or you can create your own groove in the feel and style of the example.

- ✔ **As you improve, try reading the music notation.** As you get better, you can look at the notation and begin to learn to read music. After you figure out how to play a few phrases, you quickly discover that reading music notation isn't as difficult as it's made out to be. In fact, you'll realize that it makes your musical life easier.

I use the following conventions in *Bass Guitar For Dummies,* 3rd Edition, to help keep the text consistent and make it easy to follow:

- ✔ **Right hand and left hand:** Instead of saying *striking hand* and *fretting hand,* I say *right hand* for the hand that strikes the string and *left hand* for the hand that frets the note. My apologies to left-handed players. If you're left-handed, please read *right hand* to mean *left hand* and vice versa.

- ✔ **Up and down, higher and lower:** Moving your left hand up the neck of the bass means moving it up in *pitch* (moving your hand toward the body of the bass). Moving your left hand down the neck means moving it down in *pitch* (moving your hand away from the body). I use the same principle for the right hand. Going to the next *higher* string means playing the string that has a higher sound (the string closer to the floor). The next *lower* string is the string that has a lower sound (the string closer to the ceiling). Just think of whether the sound is higher or lower and you'll be fine.

- ✔ **Triple music notation:** In the figures, the music for the grooves and the exercises is printed with the standard music notation on top, the tablature below, and the grid next to them. You don't have to read all of them at the same time (good heavens — that would be worse than reading piano music). Simply pick the one you feel most comfortable with, and then use the others to double-check that you're playing the groove or exercise correctly. Of course, you also can listen to the audio tracks to hear what the music is supposed to sound like.

- ✔ **The numbers:** In the text, the numbers between 1 and 8 (1, 2, 3, 4, 5, 6, 7, and 8) represent notes in a chord or scale (for example, the number 3 represents the third note in a given scale). The designation 7th, on the other hand, refers to a particular chord, such as a major 7th chord. Finally, the distance between two notes (the interval) is called a 2nd, 3rd, 4th, and so on.

Foolish Assumptions

As I wrote this book, I made one assumption about you, the reader: I assume that you want to play the bass guitar. But that's it. I don't assume anything else. No matter what style you're interested in, this book covers them all. It doesn't even matter whether you want to play a four-, five-, or six-string bass. The grids featured in this book can be used for any bass guitar, and the shapes of the patterns never change. All you have to do is read this book with an open mind, and I assure you, you'll be playing bass . . . and quickly. Of course, you can master the bass even more quickly if you use this book in conjunction with private lessons from an experienced bass guitar teacher who can help you tackle specific weak spots in your playing. And any experience you've had playing another instrument won't go to waste, either.

Icons Used in This Book

In the margins of *Bass Guitar For Dummies,* 3rd Edition (as in all *For Dummies* books), you find icons to help you maneuver through the text. Here's what the icons mean:

This icon points out expert advice to help you become a better bassist.

Be careful! This icon helps you avoid doing damage to the instrument, yourself, or someone's ears.

Brace yourself for some technical facts and information that may come in handy some day. If you want, you can skip over this stuff — and still not miss a beat.

Certain techniques are worth remembering. Take note of the information that's highlighted by this icon.

This icon helps you better understand what you're hearing when you listen to the audio samples and watch the videos of the different techniques.

Beyond the Book

This book provides a solid foundation for learning bass guitar, but you can find many more resources on Dummies.com:

> ✔ There are more than 100 audio tracks that accompany the chapters of this book. I also give video demonstrations of more than 30 key lessons. You can download the audio tracks and watch the videos at www.dummies.com/go/bassguitar.

✔ You can download the book's Cheat Sheet at www.dummies.com/cheatsheet/bassguitar. It's a handy resource to keep on your computer, tablet, or smartphone.

✔ You can read interesting companion articles that supplement the book's content at www.dummies.com/extras/bassguitar. We've even included an extra top-ten list.

Where to Go from Here

Where do you go from here? Well, to Hollywood Bowl, of course! Maybe not right away . . . but, hey, never give up your dream. If you don't have a bass guitar yet, skip to Chapter 15 to see what's in store for you. ("What's in store for you" . . . get it? It's the bass shopping chapter.) If you're a beginner, you have a bass guitar, and you're ready to play, skip to Chapter 2 and start getting your instrument in tune (followed by getting your hands into shape). If you're already playing bass guitar, start reading Chapter 5 with your bass guitar in hand, and then enjoy playing your way through the rest of this book.

No matter how well you currently play, this book can help you improve your skills. If you're picking up the bass for the first time, remember that bringing music into your life may well be the first step in a lifelong journey of musical enrichment. If you want to delve deeper into this whole bass business, please visit me at www.PatrickPfeifferBass.com.

Part I
Getting Started with the Bass Guitar

In this part...

- ✔ Discover the different parts that make up a bass guitar.
- ✔ Get an overview of what your bass guitar can do.
- ✔ Figure out how to position your hands.
- ✔ Prepare to warm up and coordinate your hands.

Chapter 1

The Very Basics of Bass

In This Chapter

▶ Differentiating between bass guitars and other guitars

▶ Understanding the function and parts of the bass

▶ Getting ready to play bass

▶ Trying your hand at grooves, solos, fills, and different musical genres

▶ Picking up gear and taking care of your bass

*T*he bass is the heart of music. Its unique qualities set up a gravitational field that draws you in — perhaps it's the rich, deep, mellow sound or the hypnotic rhythms. In the right hands, the bass is a tremendously powerful tool, because it gives a band its feel and attitude. But what exactly is the bass? What makes the bass so powerful? And how does it contribute to giving music that irresistible feel? Whether you're a raw bass recruit or a seasoned veteran, this chapter helps you answer these questions.

Discovering the Differences between the Bass and Its High-Strung Cousins

Bass guitars differ from other guitars in several significant ways:

- ✔ **Traditionally, basses have four strings, while guitars have six.** In the 1970s, some bassists started adding strings. Nowadays, you can find five- and six-string basses (and beyond), but four-stringers are still considered the norm.

- ✔ **Nearly all bass guitars are electric.** Other guitars come in all flavors: electric, acoustic, or a combination of the two. You do encounter some beautiful acoustic bass guitars, but they're generally not loud enough to be of much use in a band (unless your band consists of just one or two acoustic guitar players who join you in your music-making endeavor).

✔ **The bass strings are an equal distance musically from each other.** The sound of each bass string is tuned an equal distance from the string above it, making the instrument perfectly symmetrical. So if you play a scale starting on one string, you can use the same fingering to play that same scale starting on a different string. This type of tuning makes playing the bass quite different from playing the guitar, where the second-highest string is tuned differently than the others.

✔ **The bass has a lower pitch than the guitar.** The deep notes of the bass fill the lower end of the sound spectrum. Think of these notes as the "bass-ment," or foundation, of music.

✔ **The bass's neck is longer than the guitar's, thus making its strings longer.** The longer the string, the lower the pitch; the shorter the string, the higher the pitch. Think of a Chihuahua and a Saint Bernard, for example. The Chihuahua has short vocal chords, and a rather high-pitched bark; the Saint Bernard . . . well . . . you get the idea.

✔ **The bass player and the guitarist serve different functions.** I won't bore you with the guitarist's job description, but the bass player's makes for fascinating reading, as the next section shows. By the way, if you *do* happen to want to know more about the guitarist's job description, you can check out *Guitar For Dummies,* by Mark Phillips and Jon Chappell (Wiley).

Understanding the Bass Player's Function in a Band

As the bassist, you play the most crucial role in a band (at least in my opinion). Everyone in the group follows your subtle (and sometimes not-so-subtle) lead. If the guitarist or saxophonist makes a mistake, hardly anyone notices, but if the bassist makes a mistake, everyone in the band and the audience instantly knows that something is wrong (in which case you may want to throw an accusatory glance at one of your bandmates).

Forging the link between harmony and rhythm

You're responsible for linking the harmony (chords) of a song with a distinctive rhythm (groove). This link contributes to the *feel* (mood) and *genre* (general style) of the music, which together determine whether a song is rock, jazz, Latin, or anything else. Chapter 6 tells you exactly what you need to do to establish excellent grooves, and Part IV discusses the different musical genres you're likely to play. The goal is to be able to emulate any bassist's style in any genre and, at the same time, to be creative — using your own rhythms, notes, and ideas!

Moving the song along

Every song is made up of chords (harmony) that are particular to that song, and all the notes in the song relate to the sounds of those chords (see Chapter 5 for more about chords). Some songs are based on only one chord, from beginning to end, and so all the notes relate to that one chord sound, making such songs easy to play. The chords of most songs, however, change as the song progresses. In these cases, the first group of notes in the tune relates to the first chord and has one kind of sound, the next group of notes relates to the next chord sound, and so on throughout the song.

By playing notes that are related to the chords of a song, one note at a time and in a precise rhythm, the bassist propels the music along. You set up each chord for the other players in your band by choosing notes that lead smoothly from one chord sound to the next.

Good music creates a little tension, which then leads to a satisfying release of that tension (a resolution). For example, you can feel the tension and release in as simple a tune as "Twinkle, Twinkle, Little Star." The tension builds as you sing the first line: "Twinkle, twinkle, little star." Can you end the song right there? No, because you want to hear how it ends. That's the tension. When you finish singing "How I wonder what you are," you feel a resolution to the tension, a sense of coming home. You can end the song there; in fact, that's how it does end. The bassist plays an important role in creating and releasing tension. You're pretty much in the driver's seat!

Keeping time

Keeping a steady beat, or *pulse,* is one of the bassist's primary functions. I refer to this function as *locking in with the drummer,* because you work closely with the drummer to establish the rhythm. So be nice to your drummers. Listen to them carefully and know them well. And while the two of you are on such cozy terms, spend some time together reading what Chapter 4 has to say about rhythm.

Nothing works better than a *metronome* to help you develop an unfailing sense of time. The steady (and sometimes infuriating) click that emanates from this device provides an ideal backdrop for your own precise note placement, be it on or off the beat. You can find out more about the metronome in Chapter 4.

Establishing rhythms

As a bassist, you need to have a clear understanding of exactly how the rhythm relates to the beat. Not only do you need to know where to place the notes for the groove in relation to the beat, but you also want to make your grooves memorable (see Chapter 6 for more about how to create memorable grooves). If you can't remember them, no one else will, either — including the listener (who, of course, makes the trip to hear you play).

Looking cool

While the guitarists move through their aerobic exercises on stage, dripping with sweat and smashing their guitars, you get to be cool. You can join in with their antics if you want, but have you ever seen footage of The Who? John Entwistle was cool. And if you ever get a chance to see U2, check out their bassist, Adam Clayton. He's one cool cucumber. Great bassists are just too busy creating fabulous bass lines to join in the antics of their bandmates.

Dissecting the Anatomy of a Bass Guitar

You can call it a bass guitar, an electric bass, an electric bass guitar, or just a bass. All these labels crop up in discussions of music and musical instruments, and you may encounter individuals who believe that only one of these labels is correct. But it doesn't matter which term you choose, because they all refer to the same instrument.

Figure 1-1 depicts the bass guitar (or whatever you prefer to call it), with all its main parts labeled.

The bass consists of three sections: The neck, the body, and the innards. The different parts of the neck and body are easy to see, but the innards aren't so obvious. You'd have to remove the cover (or covers) to get at the innards, but knowing why they're there is important.

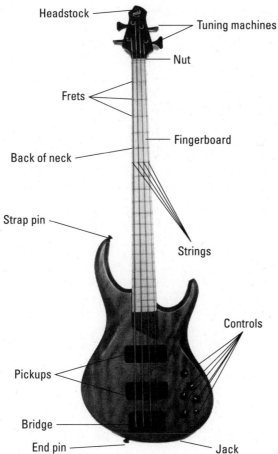

Headstock

Tuning machines

Nut

Frets

Fingerboard

Back of neck

Strap pin

Strings

Controls

Pickups

Figure 1-1:
The bass
guitar in all
its glory.

Bridge

End pin

Jack

The neck

The neck of the bass guitar falls under the dominion of the fretting hand
(usually the left hand). The following list describes the function of each part
of the neck:

- The **headstock** is the top of the neck. It holds the tuning machines for
  the strings.

- The **tuning machines** (also called *tuners* or *tuning heads*) hold the ends
  of the strings. (The other ends are anchored at the bridge on the body;
  see the next section for more info about the body of the bass.) By
  turning the individual tuning heads, you can increase or decrease the
  tension of the strings, which raises or lowers the pitch (sound).

✔ The **nut** is a small piece of wood, plastic, graphite, or brass that provides a groove (in this case, a small indentation) for each string. It establishes one end of the vibrating length of the string.

✔ The **fingerboard** is attached to the front of the neck and is the flat side of the neck, beneath the strings, that holds the frets. The neck and the fingerboard usually are two separate pieces, but not always. The frets are embedded in the fingerboard.

✔ The **frets** are the thin metal strips that are embedded, perpendicular to the strings, along the length of the fingerboard. They determine the pitch of the note that's played. Frets are arranged in *half steps* (the smallest unit of musical distance from one note to the next). When a string is pressed against a fret, the string's vibrating length, and thus its pitch, is changed.

✔ The **strings**, strictly speaking, aren't part of your bass, because you remove and replace them periodically. However, your bass would be absolutely useless without them (except maybe as a "bass-ball" bat). The strings are connected to the tuning machines at one end and to the bridge at the other. The vibration of the strings produces the sound.

✔ The **back of the neck** refers to the part of the neck where the thumb of your fretting hand rests.

The body

The body of the bass guitar falls under the dominion of the striking hand (usually the right hand). The following list describes the function of each part of the body:

✔ The **pickups** consist of magnets embedded in a plastic bar that lies underneath and perpendicular to the strings. You may have two magnets for each string or one long magnet for all the strings. The magnets form a magnetic field, and the vibration of the string disturbs (or *modulates*) that field. This modulation is then translated into an electric signal, which in turn is converted into sound by the amplifier and speaker.

✔ The **controls** are the knobs used for adjusting the volume and tone (bass and treble) of the pickups. They're located toward the end of your bass.

✔ The **bridge** attaches the strings to the end of the body; it holds one end of each string. Modern pickups, such as piezo pickups or lightwave pickups, are sometimes installed inside the bridge. These pickups read the vibration of the string at the bridge.

✔ The **strap pin** is the metal knob on the body near the neck, where you attach one end of your shoulder strap (usually the thick end).

✔ The **end pin** is the metal knob on the bottom end of the body (by the bridge) where you attach the thin end of your shoulder strap.

✔ The **jack** (also called the *input jack*) is the socket used for connecting the cord from your bass to the amplifier (for more on amplifiers, see Chapter 16).

Well, there you are — who says you don't know jack?

The innards

The innards, sometimes referred to as the *guts,* aren't visible to the eye (they're hidden in the cavity of the instrument and covered with plates), but they're essential to the sound and feel of the bass guitar. The following list describes the innards of the bass guitar:

✔ The **truss rod** is an adjustable metal rod that runs the length of your bass guitar's neck. The truss rod controls the curvature of the neck and fingerboard and keeps them stable. If you need to make adjustments to it, you can reach it through the top or bottom of the neck.

✔ The **electronics** of a bass guitar are a collection of wires, "pots" (short for *potentiometers,* or electronic capacitors, the round devices connected to the inner side of a volume knob), and other important-looking electronic items that help convert the vibration of the string into sound. The cavity for the electronics usually is located under a plate on the back of your bass guitar's body. It also may be located under the control knobs on the front of your bass.

✔ The **batteries** are an option. If your bass has *active electronics* (electronics with their own power source), you have one or two 9-volt batteries attached to the electronics (via some wires). These batteries are located in the same cavity as the electronics or in an adjacent cavity on the back of the body, and you need to replace them periodically. If your bass has *passive electronics* (electronics with no batteries), you don't have to worry about replacing batteries.

On a Need-to-Know "Basses": Gearing Up to Play Bass

Getting yourself ready to play — both physically (with technique exercises) and mentally (with theory) — is essential to being a good bass player. You also have to prepare your instrument by tuning it and playing it correctly. When you play the bass guitar correctly, your fingers can move with ease from note to note.

Coordinating your right and left hands

Because you play the bass with two hands — one hand striking and the other fretting (no, it's not worried!) — both hands have to be well coordinated with each other. With the exercises in Chapter 3, you can warm up your hands on a daily basis (just like an athlete warms up before a sporting event).

Mastering major and minor chord structures

Two basic tonalities prevail in music: major and minor. Each tonality has a distinctive sound. Major sounds somewhat *happy* or *bright,* whereas minor sounds *sad* or *dark.* Musicians use these sounds to express the mood of the song (or themselves, for that matter).

As a bassist, you have a unique advantage: The bass is perfectly symmetrical, and all the fingering patterns remain intact no matter where you play them on the neck. Any major or minor chord will always *feel* the same to your fingers, because the pattern of notes doesn't change. Each fret on the neck equals one half step, the smallest *musical interval* (distance between two notes). The sound of each string is exactly five half steps from the sound of the next lower string . . . no exceptions! Chapter 5 tells you all about these patterns.

Because all your chords and scales fall into consistent patterns that you can play anywhere on the neck, the question becomes, "Where do you start the pattern?" Chapter 4 guides you through this process with ease.

Tuning your bass

Tuner and *bass* . . . reads almost like a fishing expedition, but fishing for the right note is the last thing you want to do when playing your bass. Your bass needs to be in tune with the other instruments as well as with itself. Chapter 2 explains several different methods for tuning your bass just right.

Combining scales and chords

Scales and chords form the backbone of music. Here's a brief rundown on each of these:

✔ *Scales* are groups of notes (usually seven) used to create tunes.

✔ *Chords* are three or four specific notes within a scale that form the harmonic (musical) content.

As a bassist, you use scales together with chords to form your bass lines (or grooves). Using both scales and chords gives you flexibility to express your individuality (see Chapter 5 for details). You often can spice up your bass lines by choosing from several corresponding scales.

Playing Grooves, Solos, and Fills

Playing grooves is an essential art to being a good bassist. After all, the grooves you play determine the harmonic *and* the rhythmic content of a song. Is it any wonder that good bassists are the most sought-after musicians?

Creating grooves and riffs

Grooves and riffs contain several basic elements (Chapters 6 and 7 tell you all about them). Grooves have a rhythmic content (groove skeleton) and a harmonic content (a chord and scale). *Riffs* are a short melody that you can play to fill a space in the music.

A bassist will often play a groove in the lower register and then add a riff in the higher register to give the bass line variety and to keep listeners interested. Creating grooves and riffs isn't just a matter of divine inspiration (although that never hurts); it's actually dictated by science and can be practiced.

Treating yourself and your audience to solos and fills

As a bassist, your job is to play the groove. But that doesn't mean you have to restrain yourself from playing tasty solos and fast-fingered fills. As long as your solo or *fill* (miniature solo) relates to the groove and is indeed part of it, you can play them to your heart's content.

When you need a very cool solo, or you need to fill some space with bass *flash* (a fancy mini-solo to show off your skills), the blues scales and pentatonic scales are hard to beat. Whether you're playing blues, rock, jazz, or anything in between, these scales, when properly applied, will never let you down. You benefit from the symmetry of the bass: One fingering fits all! (Refer to Chapter 7 for the lowdown on these scales and on fills and solos.)

Experimenting with Different Musical Genres

Defining the genre of a tune is your primary function as a bassist. You define a genre by the notes and rhythms you choose — and you have to do this while locking in with the drums! In this section, I show you some of the common genres plus some tips to make you feel comfortable playing outside your genre of specialty.

A musical *genre* is an overall type of music, such as world beat. A musical *style* is a subcategory of a genre, such as reggae or West-African music (both of which are considered world beat styles).

The following list defines the genres you'll encounter most often:

- ✔ **Rock** styles are generally played with a steady eighth-note pulse (two eighth notes per beat) tightly locked with the drums, which drives the song. A lot of styles are part of this encompassing genre. Among them are pop, rock, rock 'n' roll, fusion, and even country. I provide a broad selection of *templates* (note and rhythm suggestions for each style) for you to choose from, and I hope that you expand on them for your own playing — just take a peek at Chapter 8 and rock on!

- ✔ **Swing** styles are based on the triplet feel. With the *triplet,* a single beat is subdivided into three equal units, not the usual two or four. The styles in this genre are somewhat lighter than the rock styles, and they include the shuffle (which is common for most blues styles), as well as the walking bass lines, which are associated with jazz. Shuffle off to Chapter 9 to find out more about swing.

- ✔ **Funk** styles rely heavily on the sixteenth note, the smallest rhythmic subdivision commonly used in music. For bassists, this is the busiest genre. You may have quite a few notes to play and need to lock in firmly with the drums to keep the groove tight. This genre focuses a lot of attention on the bass and is usually a technical challenge. So check out Chapter 10 and get your fingers ready to play some intricate stuff.

✔ **World beat** is a widely recognized category in almost any music store. I use this term to describe styles that aren't native to North American music but are relatively common, such as South American, African, and Caribbean styles. This book prepares you for the most common world beat styles, but bear in mind that many other international styles are out there waiting to be explored. For more on the world beat genre, see Chapter 11.

✔ **Odd meters** aren't part of the regular four-beat patterns you may be used to. Meters that use five, six, or seven beats (and beyond) are part of the odd meter family. Although unusual, odd meters can sound quite natural when played correctly. In fact, the waltz (three beats to the measure) is an odd meter style that arguably feels very natural because it's so common. Chapter 12 tells you how to play odd meters smoothly.

✔ **Beatles** styles are about one thing: What would Sir Paul do? That's the question to ask yourself when you're faced with a song and you're not quite sure how to approach your bass part. Paul McCartney is probably the most famous of all bass players, and with good reason. He developed eight distinctive styles of bass accompaniment that apply to just about every contemporary song out there, be it a pumping eighth note, a walking line, or a countermelody. Chapter 14 has your bass covered.

Playing in a specific genre is an important skill to develop. For example, say that you're used to playing jazz, but your friends want to play rock 'n' roll. How do you create a bass groove that sounds authentic and fits the bill? Chapter 13 shows you the ins and out of the main musical groove genres so you can satisfy any requirements your bandmates impose on you without sounding like a jazz head *trying* to play rock 'n' roll.

Stocking Up on Some Bass Gear

So many basses, so little time. Well, maybe you have a lot of time, but the fact remains: You have a lot of different basses to choose from, and new ones are coming onto the market all the time. You need to know what to look and listen for. You also should know what other gear you need to fulfill your *bass* desires.

Buying a bass

Some basses offer a specific sound, and others offer an array of different sounds suitable for many different styles of music. Of course, you want to choose a bass that you can play comfortably. Okay, your bass should also look cool, but remember: Looks are only varnish deep. Chapter 15 helps you with the entire bass-buying (or is it *bass-adoption?*) process.

Getting an amplifier

How much power do you need? How is the sound? Can you carry everything yourself, or will you need half a dozen burly roadies to budge the amp and speaker? Check out Chapter 16 for help with these questions. Oh, and speaking of "budge" . . . how big is your budget? How much money you have to spend is another consideration when thinking about purchasing an amp.

Accessorizing your bass

You need to carry some items in your bass bag at all times, such as a strap, tuner, and cables. Other items are optional, such as a chorus unit or fancy stickers for your fans. Chapter 16 helps you determine which accessories you need and which you don't. Think about whether you can perform without an item. If you can, it's optional; and if you can't, it's a necessity.

Giving Your Bass Some Good Ol' TLC

Even though your bass requires very little maintenance, certain parts need an occasional adjustment or periodic replacement. You can do a lot of maintenance yourself, with a minimal complement of basic tools. Check out Chapters 17 and 18 to guide you through this process.

Changing the strings is the most common maintenance you perform on your bass. How often you change the strings depends on how clear you want your sound to be — the newer the strings, the brighter the sound. Whatever you do, *please* don't listen to the stories about bassists who change their strings every 25 years (and then only because one broke).

Change your strings *at least* every three to six months (more often if you play a lot). And be sure to wash your hands before you play (sounds funny, doesn't it?) to keep dirt from your hands off your strings. For more info on changing your strings, see Chapter 17.

Chapter 2

Gaining the Tools and Skills to Play

In This Chapter

▶ Holding your bass properly

▶ Positioning your right and left hands

▶ Finding out how to read a fingerboard diagram

▶ Getting your bass in tune

▶ Practicing your first song on your bass

▶ Access the audio tracks and video clips at www.dummies.com/go/bassguitar

*I*n this chapter, you tackle the basics of playing the bass: how to hold your instrument, how to position your hands, how to read a fingerboard diagram, how to tune your bass, and how to play a song. So roll up your sleeves and dive in.

Getting a Handle on Your Bass

Before getting started, let me clarify some terminology. I refer to *right hand* and *left hand* in this book, but what really matters is what each hand does:

✔ The right hand is your *striking* hand; that is, it strikes (or plucks) each string and puts it into motion to produce a sound.

✔ Your left hand is your *fretting* hand; it presses the strings onto the fret to settle on a pitch.

If you're left-handed and you decide to play your bass as a lefty, apply the instructions for your right hand to your left and vice versa.

Frets are the small metal strips embedded in the fingerboard of your bass, underneath the strings. You usually have 20 to 24 frets on your bass. To fret a note, you press the string onto the fingerboard between two frets with your left hand. For example, to play a string at the 3rd fret, you press your finger between the 2nd and 3rd frets, closer to the 3rd. Doing so shortens the string so when you strike it, the string vibrates beginning at the 3rd fret. Take a look at Figure 2-1 to see the proper way to fret a note on the 3rd fret. Note that the string doesn't have to touch the wood of the fingerboard between the frets, just the frets (in this case, mainly the 3rd fret).

Figure 2-1:
Fretting a
note.

Photo by Steven Schlesinger

Holding Your Bass

In this chapter, you finally get to wear your bass, which, after wading through the preliminaries in Chapter 1, is a welcome change.

If you watch other bass players, either live or on television, you may notice an array of ways to hold a bass. Some definitely look cooler than others, but you may have difficulty playing with a proper hand position when the instrument is either scraping along your ankles or creeping up around your chin. Compromise is the name of the game here.

Strapping on your bass: Strings to the outside

When you strap on your bass for the first time, I recommend that you sit down to do it. Adjusting the strap is easier this way. Ideally, the strings of the bass should cross over your belly button at a slight angle upward (up on the neck end). This position ensures optimum right- and left-hand coverage, and it works well regardless of whether you're standing or sitting. Oh, and, yes, the strings should face the outside!

Strapping on and adjusting a bass eventually becomes as natural as riding a bike, but when you first start out, you have to follow some basic instructions to get it right. If your *left* hand is strained when playing, try raising the height of the bass. If your *right* hand feels uncomfortable, try lowering the bass.

You can achieve the ideal compromise position for both your left and right hands by following these steps:

1. **Attach the thick end of your strap to the *strap pin* (the little metal knob) on the body at the neck end of the bass.**

2. **Attach the thin end of your strap to the bottom strap pin (also called the *end pin*) of the bass.**

3. **Hold your bass solidly by the body or the neck with your left hand, and pull the strap over your head and right shoulder, putting your right arm through as well.**

   Allow the strap (with the bass attached) to rest on your left shoulder and continue across your back until it connects with the bottom strap pin of the bass just below the right side of your rib cage.

4. **Adjust your strap in length until the strings are crossing the area over your belly button, and then fine-tune it from there.**

   You can find your own personal preference, but you want your bass to rest in this general area. Take a look at Figures 2-2 and 2-3 and note that the general position of the bass is the same whether you're standing or sitting.

Voilà! Standing with your bass

And now, get on your feet! The time has come to take a stand with your bass. Here's how:

1. **Make sure your strap is securely attached to the strap pins.**

   Also, make sure your strap is straight, not twisted from one end to the other.

2. **Let your bass hang loosely from your shoulder.**

   Keep your left hand underneath the neck, but don't clutch it. Some basses are a little neck-heavy and others are perfectly balanced. No matter what type of bass you have, you need to get used to the feel of it.

3. **Position your hands on the bass.**

   Your left hand should be free to roam the neck from top to bottom without having to hold the bass. Your right hand should be able to reach all the strings comfortably.

The standing position will most likely be your live or performance position (see Figure 2-2).

Figure 2-2:
Standing
with your
bass.

Photo by Steven Schlesinger

Sitting with your bass

During those endless hours of practice, you may want to sit down to play (see Figure 2-3). When you do, try to sit so your thighs are higher than your knees. I recommend using a stool or a tall chair without armrests. That way, the position of your bass is similar whether you're standing or sitting.

After you sit down, keep the strap on. You may feel a slight slack in the strap when the bass touches your thighs, but it should still hold the bass stationary. Your left hand needs to be free to roam across the neck without your having to worry about holding the bass in place, and your right hand must be able to reach all the strings comfortably.

Figure 2-3:
Sitting with
your bass.

Photo by Steven Schlesinger

Placing Your Hands in the Proper Position

The secret to getting your hands into position is simple: Keep them loose and relaxed. You want to strike and fret the strings with the least amount of effort possible. The proper position enables you to play at great speed and with great accuracy. It also helps you control your tone.

Check out Video 1 to see me demonstrate the left- and right-hand positioning.

Positioning your left hand

You want your left hand to cover one fret per finger without causing any undue stress. By using one finger per fret, you set up your hand to execute almost any musical figure without *shifting,* or moving your hand position to reach a note. (A *figure* is an independent and self-contained musical phrase, sort of like a sentence when you're speaking.)

When you do have to shift your hand, a move of one fret in either direction usually suffices.

Check out Figure 2-4 for the proper left-hand position, and follow these steps to accomplish it:

1. **Hold out your left hand with your outstretched arm in front of you.**

   Keep your wrist and hand limp.

2. **Without changing the angle on your wrist, turn your hand so your palm faces up and your fingers are slightly curved.**

   Position your thumb so it faces your index finger (or the area between your index and middle fingers).

3. **Bring in your elbow to the side of your rib cage (without moving your hand) until the neck of your bass is in the palm of your hand.**

   Remember not to close your hand!

4. **Place the tip of your thumb on the middle of the back of the bass neck.**

   Make sure that your fingertips are pointing upward.

5. **Gently spread your fingers onto the strings, with each finger close to an adjacent fret.**

6. **Curl your fingers until your fingertips are on one of the strings.**

   Be sure to keep the tips of your fingers close to the frets.

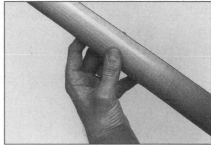

Figure 2-4:
Position
of the left
hand.

Now you're just about ready to press the string to the fret to play a note. Even though you can now fret the desired note, something still has to set the string in motion to produce the actual sound. This is where your right hand comes in. Read on for details.

Positioning your right hand

You may see several popular right-hand techniques; so many, in fact, that they could fill a book all on their own. In this book, I concentrate on the *finger-style* technique, which is the most diverse and widely used among them, accommodating virtually all styles of music. This technique also allows you to work more efficiently with *dynamics* (accenting certain notes). In this section, I also show you the proper positions for the *pick* and *slap* (thumb) techniques.

I refer to the right hand as the striking hand rather than as the plucking or pulling hand. The other terms are technically correct, but I prefer the term *striking* because *plucking* and *pulling* imply that you should pull the strings away from the body of the bass, which produces a thin sound. Instead, you need to strike the string *into* the body of the bass, not *away from* it. Think of it as if you're trying to touch the pickup underneath the string with your fingertip after you strike the string.

Finger-style playing

The name *finger-style* refers to your striking the strings with the index and middle fingers of your right hand. You can hear this style in country, rock, jazz, and funk — and just about any other type of music. Jaco Pastorius, James Jamerson, and Francis Rocco Prestia are only three of the multitude of bassists who use this technique. Take the following steps to set up your hand properly. Then compare the position of your hand to Figure 2-5.

Figure 2-5:
Right hand in the proper finger-style position.

1. **Bring your right arm up, as though you're pointing to something in the distance, while keeping your wrist, hand, and fingers relaxed.**

   Keep your wrist at a 45-degree angle (approximately), keep your thumb facing your index finger, and keep your fingers gently curved, with your fingertips pointing to the floor.

2. **Start bending your elbow slowly, keeping it just slightly away from your rib cage.**

3. **Let your hand approach the instrument until your thumb settles onto the *thumb rest* (a small plastic or wood bar for resting your thumb on) or the edge of the *pickup* (the magnetic bars that pick up the string vibration).**

   Keep your elbow next to your body, not behind it.

4. **Settle the weight of your arm onto your thumb.**

   This position may take some time getting used to, but it keeps your hand and shoulder in their most relaxed state. The thumb acts as a measuring device for your fingers and the individual strings. In this position, you can feel which string you're playing instead of having to look to see where you are.

5. **Reach for your high string (the one closest to your feet) with your index or middle finger (see Figure 2-6).**

Figure 2-6:
Hand
reaching
for the
high string.

Your thumb has to bend a little, and your hand must pivot out on it to reach the highest string.

The terms *high string* and *low string* refer to the sound of the strings, not the position of your hand. Your high string is actually the string closest to your feet, whereas your low string is closest to your head.

6. **Reach for your low string (the one closest to your head).**

Your thumb is now straighter. Your hand pivots on the resting thumb toward your body, and your palm is closer to the body of the bass, as shown in Figure 2-7.

Pick-style playing

Some players prefer to use a *pick* (a small triangular plastic piece, about the size of a quarter) rather than their fingers to produce a note. Because the strings on a bass are much heavier than those on a guitar, your bass pick needs to be heavier as well.

Photo by Steven Schlesinger

Figure 2-7:
Hand
reaching
for the
low string.

You can hold the pick in one of two ways: closed or open. To set your hand properly for closed-hand pick playing, follow these steps:

1. **Hold your pick between your index finger and thumb.**

2. **Make a light fist and rest your thumb on top of your index finger.**

3. **Slide your index finger along the bottom of your thumb until it reaches the first knuckle of your thumb.**

   This is where the pick goes, with only the tip of it showing. See Figure 2-8.

You also can try playing with an open hand (see Figure 2-9). The pick still goes between your thumb and index finger, but you leave a space between your fingers and your palm, and you rest your ring finger and pinkie against the body of the bass. You may like the increased control you get from using this method. Both styles require you to make a twisting wrist movement with your picking hand.

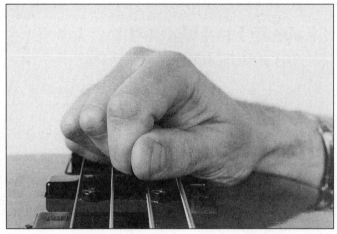

Figure 2-8: Holding the pick in a closed-hand position.

Photo by Steven Schlesinger

With a pick, you can strike the string from either above or below. Some players prefer only downstrokes; others use only upstrokes. Still other players combine the two for an even faster technique. Feel free to experiment and find out which technique suits your musical style.

Pick playing isn't an *aural* (acoustic) necessity anymore. Technology has caught up, and I assure you that your bass will be heard equally well without a pick. However, in the age of music videos, pick playing is preferred for its visual impact. You can really see the bass player working when he or she is using a pick.

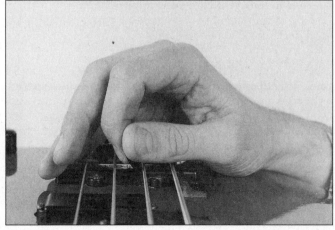

Figure 2-9: A pick in the open-hand style.

Photo by Steven Schlesinger

From Carol Kaye to Paul McCartney: A brief primer on famous pick players

Pick-style playing was a popular technique in the early days of the bass guitar (the 1950s and '60s). Many first-generation players switched from guitar to bass and brought the pick along with them. Joe Osborn and Carol Kaye, two Los Angeles studio musicians, are examples of former guitarists who continued to use a pick to play their bass guitars. The sharp attack of the pick brought new levels of clarity and definition to the notes they played. In the process, it also shattered the belief (previously held by producers and engineers, who were used to the upright bass) that the bass should be felt and not heard. This helped the bass guitar gain worldwide acceptance. Joe Osborn can be heard on many of The 5th Dimension's hits, such as "Aquarius/Let the Sunshine In." Carol Kaye played on a lot of The Beach Boys' hits, including "Good Vibrations."

If you search the Internet for info on these two famous bassists, you'll find that they both played some great bass lines on a lot of famous tunes. I have links for these and other great players on www.PatrickPfeifferBass.com for you to explore. A great *bass line* is a bass part that propels and builds the tune, has a unique quality that defines the tune, and doesn't get in the way of the melody and vocals. Think about "Come Together" by one of the most famous pick players, Paul McCartney, the bass player for The Beatles. Paul single-handedly (actually, he used both hands and a pick) brought the bass to the foreground in popular music, inventing some of the most memorable bass lines along the way. When you listen to his bass lines in "Penny Lane," or "Day Tripper," or the incredible "Something," you become more aware of the crucial role the bass plays in modern music.

Slap-style playing

The technique of playing *slap-style* or *thumb-style* is to strike a low string with the side of your thumb, giving it a *percussive sound* (a sharp attack and decay of the note, like a drum), and then to *snap* (or pop) a high string with your index finger. Here's how you do it:

1. **Make a light fist with your right hand.**

   Lift your thumb away from your fist as though you were hitchhiking.

2. **Loosen up on your index finger and create a hook.**

   Your index finger should look like it's pulling the trigger of a gun.

3. **Rest your forearm on the body of the bass so your right hand hovers above the strings.**

4. **With a sharp twist of your wrist, flick your thumb against one of the low strings, striking it at the very end of the fingerboard.**

   This flick creates the slap sound. You need a lot of wrist movement for this style. Figure 2-10 (see left side of figure) shows you how to do it correctly.

Popular slappers and thumbers

Slap-style became popular in the 1970s and '80s. Larry Graham (Sly and the Family Stone, and Graham Central Station) was one of the first slappers, and players such as Stanley Clarke and Louis Johnson continued to expand the technique. Marcus Miller, Flea (Red Hot Chili Peppers), and Victor Wooten (Béla Fleck and the Flecktones) are some of today's popular thumbers.

Figure 2-10:
Thumb striking the string (left), and index finger snapping the string (right).

Photos by Steven Schlesinger

5. **Hook your index finger under a high string, and with an opposing twist of your wrist, pull the string away from the fingerboard, and then let it snap against the frets.**

   Make sure your thumb continues *past* the string and onto the fingerboard so the string is free to vibrate and the note rings. Figure 2-10 (see right side of figure) shows you how to do it.

   Don't pull too hard on the high string, or you may break it. Only a small amount of force is required.

Reading a Fingerboard Diagram

In some situations, musicians are required to read music and even play the exact note written on a chart or page of music. (I give you the basics of reading music in Chapter 4.) However, most bassists prefer to create their own accompaniment for a tune, if given a chance. They think of the selection of notes as a picture. Using a fingerboard diagram (or grid) is a great way to see such pictures.

The language of music: Scales and chords

Musicians choose notes from a *scale,* an orderly ascending or descending sequence of notes, to create their music. The most commonly used scales have seven notes, beginning with the *root* (the first note). The eighth note (the *octave*) in the sequence sounds similar to the root, but it's a higher root. A *chord* is a combination of three or more notes taken from a scale. (I cover both scales and chords in more detail in Chapter 5.)

You don't have to read music to play bass; music isn't a visual art — it's an aural art. You hear it. Some of my favorite bassists can't read a note and still manage to come up with incredible bass parts. Most bass players, however, find that reading music is a useful skill when playing with other people. Some band leaders require you to read music.

Music often is written on paper so it can be communicated to others; the same note can appear on paper in several forms. One form is the *fingerboard diagram,* or *grid,* which is simply a picture of the fingerboard (in an upright position). It's the clearest way to show you how to space your fingers along the fingerboard for playing the different scales and chords. Check out Figure 2-11 for a picture of the two grids I use in this book.

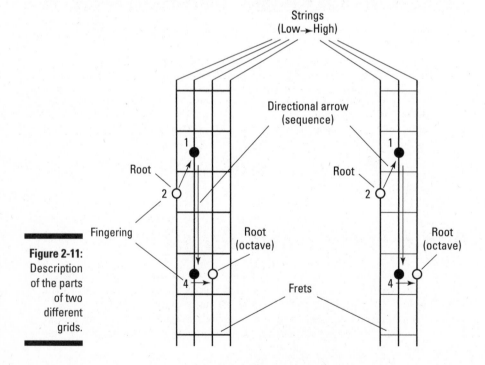

Figure 2-11: Description of the parts of two different grids.

A grid is composed of the following elements:

- ✔ **The vertical lines on the grids represent the strings, from low (left) to high (right).** The first grid shows four strings. The second shows only three, even though your bass has at least four, because on almost all parts of the neck, you can play one complete scale (one octave) or chord using only three strings. The beauty of indicating finger positions on grids is that you can superimpose the grid onto any part of the bass, as long as you have enough strings and frets to work with.

- ✔ **The horizontal lines in the grid represent the frets.**

- ✔ **The solid black dots and the open circle represent notes to be played.** The open circle is the *root,* or *tonal center.* The root is the most important note in a scale or chord, and it's usually the first note you play. (I cover these terms and concepts in detail in Chapter 5.)

- ✔ **The numbers next to the dots tell you which finger you use to play the note, as follows:**

  1 = index finger (the pointer)

  2 = middle finger (well, never mind)

  3 = ring finger

  4 = pinkie (little finger)

- ✔ **The arrows from dot to dot indicate the sequence of the notes to be played (if there is a specific sequence).** On the bass, you almost always play one note at a time.

The four-finger technique I describe in the preceding list can help you play everything with the least amount of effort, the fewest shifts, and the greatest level of consistency. Using the same fingering time after time when playing the same scale or chord is essential for developing speed and accuracy and for smooth playing. In other words, keeping your fingering consistent helps your hand become familiar with the moves and builds muscle memory so you can occupy your mind with other things (like fending off overly excited groupies).

The major scale starting on the root C, called the *C major* scale or the *key of C,* looks and feels exactly like the major scales that begin on any other root. For example, it looks exactly like the major scale starting on D (which, you guessed it, is called the *D major* scale, or the *key of D*). Both scales have the same structure and are played with the same fingers in the same sequence; the D scale just starts two frets above the C scale.

When you memorize a pattern for playing a scale or chord in one key, you can play the same pattern for that scale or chord in every key, anywhere on the neck of the bass.

Viewing a diagram of the major and minor scales

The major and minor scales are the two primary scales in music. Both are constructed in half-step and whole-step combinations. A *half step* is the distance from one fret to the next on the bass. A *whole step* skips one fret. I cover the exact construction of major and minor scales in Chapter 5.

In Figure 2-12, you see grids that indicate the notes of both the major and minor scales.

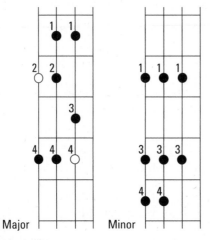

Figure 2-12:
Grids showing a major scale (left) and a minor scale (right).

To play one complete scale, you start on one note (such as C) and play an ascending scale up to the same note C but higher, as you can see on the grids in Figure 2-12. The notes of the scales fit on three strings, and you can play them without shifting your left hand. One complete scale is an *octave*.

You can play any of the major and minor scales without shifting the position of your hand.

You can see me demonstrating both the major and minor scales in Video 2.

Playing open-string scales

Playing an open string means striking a string without first pressing down on a fret. Playing scales that include open strings involves a slightly different pattern from all the other scales. You play *open-string scales* without pressing down on a fret for some of the notes. In two keys, E and A, the open string itself is the root. See Figure 2-13 for some sample grids.

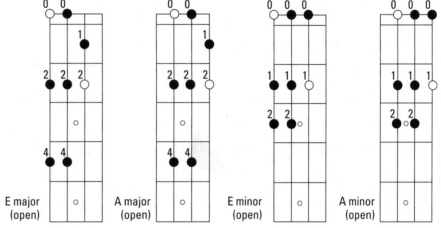

Figure 2-13: Grids showing open-string scales.

E major (open)   A major (open)   E minor (open)   A minor (open)

Finding the notes on the neck

Any of your patterns (except for the open E and A scales described in the preceding section) work in all keys. Because you can transpose these patterns to any key, all you have to do is nail the root with the proper finger of the left hand (usually the middle finger for the major patterns and the index finger for the minor patterns), and you're in position. Only one question remains: How do you find a certain key when someone asks you, for example, to play in C?

The sides, and sometimes the top, of your bass's neck are marked by dots. These dots are your landmarks for determining where a note is located. After you find a note, use the dots as a reference to find the note again. The notes are organized in a sequence of half steps, which are the smallest step in music (at least in music of the Western hemisphere). Each half step is one fret. The order of notes in half steps is: C, C♯ (pronounced "C sharp") or D♭ (pronounced "D flat"), D, D♯ or E♭, E, F, F♯ or G♭, G, G♯ or A♭, A, A♯ or B♭, B, and C. Notice that some of the notes have two names. For example, C♯ and D♭ are the same note. (It's a half step above C or a half step below D.)

The notes on the open strings of your bass are tuned (from low to high) E, A, D, and G (the thinnest string). You can start from any open string and count the half steps to find a specific note. For example, to find your C on the A string (see Figure 2-14), your 1st fret on the A string is A♯ or B♭, the next fret is B, and the one after that is C (the fret with the first dot).

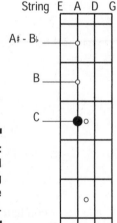

Figure 2-14:
Grid
showing
C on the
A string.

If a note is raised by a half step (one fret), it has a ♯ (sharp) symbol next to it. For example, if you take the C that's played on the 3rd fret of the A string (the second thickest string) and raise it a half step to the 4th fret, it becomes C♯. If a note is lowered by a half step, it has a ♭ (flat) symbol next to it. For example, if you want to lower the B that's on the 2nd fret of the A string by a half step, press the string to the 1st fret and the B becomes B♭.

Your bass has two dots on the 12th fret. These dots are your octave marker for the open strings. By pressing down any string at the 12th fret and striking it, you produce the same note you get when playing the open string, but the note is an octave higher. If you want to find your C on the E string (see Figure 2-15), you can start on the E-string octave marker and go backward: E, E♭ or D♯, D, D♭ or C♯, and C. The C note is four frets below the octave marker, between the third and fourth dots of the E string.

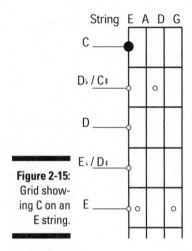

Figure 2-15: Grid showing C on an E string.

Identifying intervals: They're always in the same place

An *interval* is the distance between two notes. For example, in the scale of C, the distance from the root C up to F is four notes (C, D, E, F), so the interval is called a 4th. When you identify an interval, you count the original note (C in this example) as well as the final note (F).

Musicians communicate with interval terminology: "Hey, try a 4th instead of the 5th on the G chord," which means: Play the G with a C (an interval of a 4th) instead of the G with a D (an interval of a 5th). So recognizing intervals clearly is important. The intervals are always in the same configuration; a 4th, for example, always looks and feels the same, regardless of what key it's in.

Figure 2-16 shows the names and configurations of each interval. The open circle is the note you're measuring the distance from; the small black dot is the interval. You can find them on your own by feeling them with your hand (again, covering one finger per fret). When you get comfortable with how they feel, you'll have an easier time applying them to your playing. You can cover all the intervals with only three strings at your disposal.

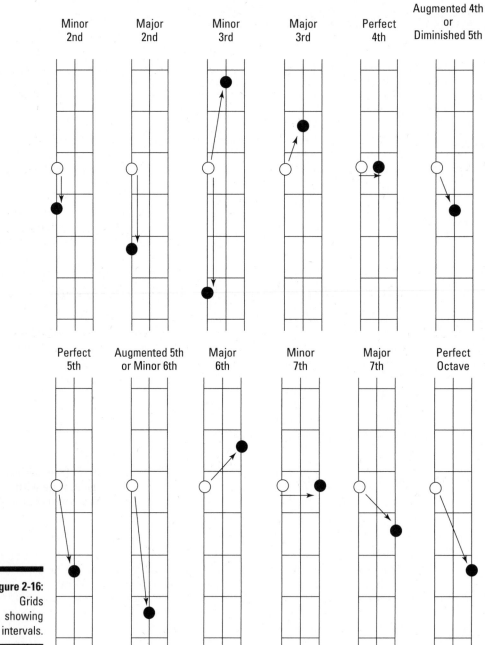

Figure 2-16: Grids showing intervals.

Tuning Your Bass Guitar

After you strap on your bass, tuning it is the first item on your to-do list, which you can do in several ways. The following sections lead you through the different tuning techniques. It may take you a little time to get used to hearing the low frequencies of the bass notes, but with practice and a few tricks, you'll be able to tune a bass in no time.

On Track 1, I play the open strings of a four-string bass, one at a time. Get used to the sound of those strings so you know how a correctly tuned bass sounds. You can use this track for tuning your own bass. However, you need to be familiar with some other useful techniques for tuning your bass.

Whether you're playing alone or with others, you need to use an aural reference source, called a *reference pitch,* for tuning your strings. A reference pitch is a note you use as the basis for tuning the strings on your bass. It's to tuning what the North Star is to ship navigation. The piano is an excellent source for a reference pitch because its tuning is very stable. But you're not limited to the piano — many other sources are available as well.

When you play alone, you can use any of the methods described in the following sections for finding a reference pitch to tune your bass. But if your guitar- and piano-playing friends come over to jam, stop what you're doing and get your bass in tune with everyone else's instruments.

Reference pitch sources to use when playing alone

When you're playing alone, it doesn't matter whether you're in tune with the rest of the universe, but you do need to have all your strings in tune with each other if you want your music to sound harmonious. You can use any of the sources in the following sections to tune your bass.

A tuner

Using an electronic tuner is by far the easiest way to tune your bass. The modern tuners have a display that lets you see exactly where your string is, in terms of pitch, whether it's sharp (too high) or flat (too low), and what note it's closest to (in case your bass gets knocked around, and the G string is now closer in sound to F than G).

To get your bass into tune with a tuner, follow these steps:

1. **Buy a tuner.**

   Okay, okay! Maybe that goes without saying, but keep in mind that you want to use a tuner that can register the low bass frequencies. Not all tuners can hear bass notes. You can get a tuner that connects to your bass via a cable, or you can get a clip-on tuner.

2. **Plug your bass into the tuner via the cable (an electric cord that connects your bass to your amplifier) or clip the clip-on tuner onto your headstock.**

   You can see a picture of the cable in Chapter 16.

3. **Strike an open string and let it ring.**

   Low frequencies travel slowly, and the tuner needs time to read the note.

4. **Tune the string until the needle (or light) of the tuner is in the middle of the display, indicating that the string is in tune. (I tell you how to adjust the tuning heads in the later section "Tuning the bass guitar to itself.")**

   Make sure to check that the pitch indicator shows the correct note for the string (E, A, D, G), or you may find that the G string is in perfect tune with G♯, which is way out of tune with what the G string is supposed to sound like.

Tuning with a tuner works even when you're in a noisy environment. Make sure you have a spare battery for your tuner, though. Otherwise, the only way you can see motion in the tuner's needle is by watching it jump as you fling it against the wall in frustration.

You don't want to depend entirely on a mechanical device. You need to know how to tune the bass by yourself in case a garbage truck backs up and crushes your tuner as you're loading your gear into your car.

Your own strings

When you play alone, you can tune your bass relative to itself, which is referred to as *relative tuning*. For relative tuning, you use one string, usually the low E, as a reference pitch and adjust the other three so they're in tune with it. (I explain how to get the strings in tune in the later section "Tuning the bass guitar to itself.")

When you use relative tuning, you may not be in tune with anyone else's instrument, because the E string you used as a reference for tuning the other strings may not be a perfectly tuned E. But if you're not playing with anyone else, who cares?

A tuning fork

The tuning fork gives you one reference pitch only. It corresponds to the sound of the open A string, the second-thickest string (although several octaves higher). The tuning fork gives you an excellent way to tune your bass, provided you follow these steps:

1. **Strike the tuning fork against a hard surface and place the handle of it (without touching the two prongs) between your teeth.**

   You can now hear the note A resonating in your head. ***Note:*** You may not want to share your tuning fork (other than with that special someone), and you may want to keep it reasonably clean; otherwise tuning with the tuning fork could leave a bad taste in your mouth.

2. **Tune your A string to the A of the tuning fork.**

   Refer to "Tuning the bass guitar to itself," later in this chapter, for complete details on carrying out this step.

3. **Tune the other strings to the A string.**

   The later section "Tuning the bass guitar to itself" explains the basics of the tuning process.

Reference pitch sources to use when playing with others

When you play with other musicians, you need to get your bass in tune with their instruments. You can tune all your strings by comparing them individually with the appropriate note of the same pitch from an instrument that's already in tune, such as a piano. However, I strongly urge you to get just one string in tune with the reference pitch and then use your tuned string as a reference pitch for tuning your other strings. Read on for two common reference-pitch sources.

A piano

Because the tuning of a piano is very stable, it serves as an excellent source for a reference pitch. Figure 2-17 shows the keys on the piano that match your open strings. You may find it easiest to use a reference pitch (on the piano) that's one octave higher than the note you want to tune on your string.

A guitar

The lowest (thickest) four strings of a guitar correspond to the four strings of your bass (see Figure 2-18): Going from low to high (thick to thin), the strings are E, A, D, and G. Bear in mind that the guitar strings sound one octave higher than your bass strings. They're the same note, only higher.

Figure 2-18 shows which guitar strings correspond to your bass strings.

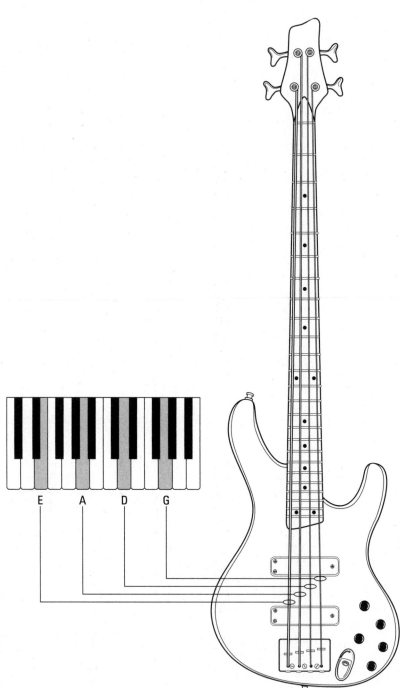

Figure 2-17:
Piano keys
that match
the open
strings on
the bass.

E   A   D   G

Figure 2-18:
Guitar
strings that
match the
open strings
on the bass.

G
D
A
E

Tuning the bass guitar to itself

Eventually, it always comes down to this: First, you tune one string of your bass (usually the E string) to a reference pitch, and then you tune your other three strings to that tuned string.

To tune a bass string (usually the E string) to a reference pitch, listen carefully to the sound of the reference pitch you've chosen (for reference pitches, see the previous sections). If you choose E as a reference pitch, strike the open E string of your bass with one of the fingers of your right hand. If the note from your bass doesn't match exactly with the reference pitch, you hear a wavering sound. As you turn the tuning head, the wavering gets slower as your E string's pitch approaches that of the reference source. When you reach the exact match — the perfect E — the wavering stops. If the wavering gets quicker, you're turning the tuning head in the wrong direction. Restrike your E string and turn the tuning head the opposite way.

You can tune the rest of your bass guitar strings in one of three ways: With the 5th-fret method, the 7th-fret method, or the harmonics method.

In all cases, if the notes don't match exactly, you hear a wavering sound. As you turn the tuning head, the wavers occur at wider intervals as they approach an exact match. When you find the exact match, the wavering stops.

The 5th-fret tuning method

The 5th-fret tuning method is the most common method for tuning bass guitars.

If you're playing with other people, be sure to get a reference pitch for the E string (the lowest and thickest string) from one of the other tuned instruments, and then tune that string before tuning the others.

The following steps explain how to tune your bass by using the 5th-fret method (see Figure 2-19):

1. **Using one of the fingers on your left hand, press the tuned E string down at the 5th fret.**

   Touch only the E string, because the open A string needs to vibrate freely. The place to press is actually between the 4th and 5th frets, slightly behind the 5th fret.

2. **Strike the fretted E and the open A strings together with your right-hand index finger and let them ring.**

While you're comparing the sounds of the two strings, keep your left-hand finger holding down the lower string at the 5th fret. Get used to turning your tuning heads with your right hand (by reaching over your left hand) when using this method. The notes should be a perfect match. If they're not (which is usually the case), follow these steps:

> a. **Listen to whether the sound of the A string is lower (flat) or higher (sharp) than the E string.**
>
> You hear a wavering sound if the strings aren't in tune.
>
> b. **If you're not sure whether the A string is sharp or flat, lower the pitch of the A string until you can hear that it's clearly flat.**
>
> c. **Restrike both strings, and then slowly raise the pitch of the A string by turning its tuning head with your right hand until the sound matches the pitch of the E string at the 5th fret.**
>
> If you go too far, you can hear that the A string is sharp (too high). In that case, lower the pitch of the A string by turning its tuning head in the other direction. When the A string is in tune with the E string, you're ready to tune the D string.

3. **Press the tuned A string down at the 5th fret (touching only the A string).**

4. **Strike the A and open D strings together and let them ring.**

   Listen to whether the D string is sharp or flat, and then turn the tuning head for the D string accordingly until the pitch of both strings matches perfectly. When the D string is in tune with the 5th fret of the A string, proceed to tuning the G string.

5. **Press the tuned D string down at the 5th fret (touching only the D string).**

6. **Strike the D and open G strings together and let them ring.**

   Listen to whether the G string is sharp or flat, and then turn the tuning head for the G string accordingly until the pitch of the 5th fret of the D string matches the open G string perfectly.

Your bass is now in tune. If you tuned the E string to a reference pitch, you're now ready to play with anybody who's in tune with that same reference pitch.

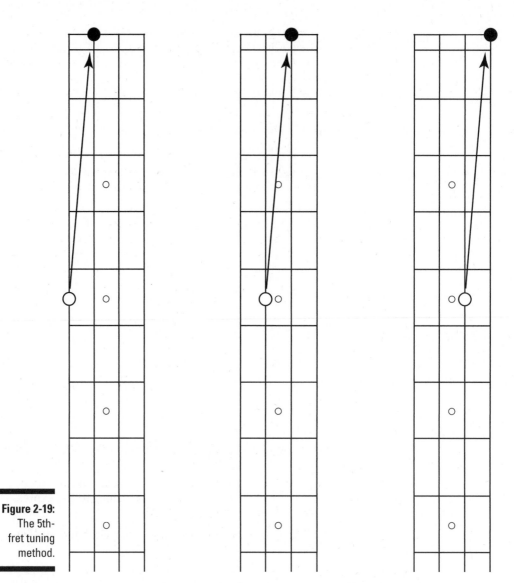

Figure 2-19:
The 5th-
fret tuning
method.

The 7th-fret tuning method

The 7th-fret method is similar to the 5th-fret method, but it works in reverse (from high to low). You need to tune your G string (not your bathing suit, but the highest, or skinniest, string on your bass) to a reference pitch from a tuned instrument (if you're playing with others).

When you have the G string in tune, press it down at the 7th fret. The note you get when you strike the G string, with the 7th fret pressed, is D, but it's an octave higher than the next lower (thicker) string. (See Figure 2-20 for a picture of the 7th-fret tuning method.)

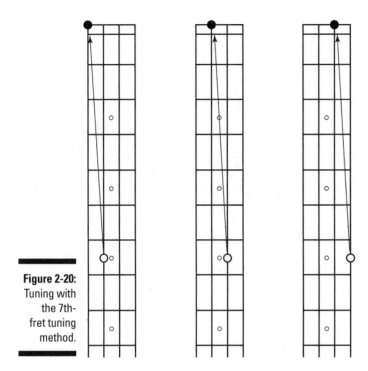

Figure 2-20:
Tuning with
the 7th-
fret tuning
method.

Here's a step-by-step description of how to tune your bass with the 7th-fret method:

1. **Using a finger on your left hand, press the tuned G string down at the 7th fret.**

   Make sure you don't touch the adjacent (lower) D string; both strings should vibrate freely. (This brings a whole new meaning to the expression of fretting about your G string, doesn't it?)

2. **Strike the fretted G and open D strings with your right hand and let them ring together.**

   The pitch is an octave apart, but it's the same note. Listen to whether the D string is sharp or flat, and then turn the tuning head for the D string accordingly until the strings are in tune with each other.

3. **Press the tuned D string down at the 7th fret without touching the next lower string (the A string).**

4. Strike the D and open A strings and let them ring together.

The pitch is an octave apart, but it's the same note. Again, listen to whether the A string is sharp or flat, and then turn the tuning head for the A string accordingly until the A string is in tune.

5. Press the tuned A string down at the 7th fret, making sure you don't touch the E string.

6. Strike the A and open E strings together and let them ring.

As with the other strings, the pitch is an octave apart, but it's the same note. Listen to whether the E string is sharp or flat, and then turn the tuning head for the E string accordingly. When the E string is in tune, your entire bass is in tune.

The harmonics tuning method

Harmonics are notes that sound naturally on a string when you lightly touch it at certain points and then strike it with your right hand. Because the bass strings sound so low, the higher harmonics are much easier to hear. The strongest and clearest harmonics can be found at the 12th fret, the 7th fret, and the 5th fret.

Take a look at Figure 2-21 for the main harmonics.

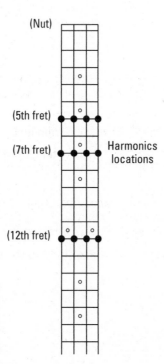

Figure 2-21: The main harmonics.

(Nut)

(5th fret)

(7th fret) — Harmonics locations

(12th fret)

The sounds of the harmonics are crystal clear, which makes them a great tuning tool. However, to use the harmonics, you must first develop a solid technique for making them ring. To play harmonics, follow these steps:

1. **Lightly touch the desired string at the 12th, 7th, or 5th fret with one of the fingers on your left hand (the middle or index finger is best, but any will do).**

   Don't press the string to the fret, and make sure only one finger is touching the string. Leaving your left-hand finger resting on the contact point (12th, 7th, or 5th fret), strike the string with your right hand, as I explain in Step 2.

2. **Place your right hand close to the bridge and strike the string (that you're touching with your left hand) with either the index or middle finger of your right hand.**

   The closer your striking (right-hand) finger is to the bridge, the clearer your harmonic will be.

3. **When the harmonic rings out, you can remove your left-hand finger from the string.**

   The harmonic will continue to ring out as long as you don't touch the string.

The harmonics tuning method is the most difficult and most precise tuning method you can use to tune your bass without a tuner. But if you follow these steps, you'll quickly get the hang of tuning your bass to itself using harmonics.

1. **Using the pinkie of your left hand, lightly touch the tuned G string at the 7th fret. (The G string should already be tuned to an outside reference source.)**

   Strike the string and let it ring. This sounds the harmonic.

2. **Using the middle finger of your left hand, lightly touch the D string at the 5th fret.**

   Strike the harmonic and let it ring *together* with the previous harmonic. Adjust the tuning head of the D string until the wavering stops.

3. **Using the pinkie of your left hand, lightly touch the D string at the 7th fret.**

   Strike the harmonic and let it ring.

4. **Using the middle finger of your left hand, lightly touch the A string at the 5th fret.**

   Strike the harmonic and let it ring *together* with the previous harmonic. Adjust the tuning head of the A string until the wavering stops.

5. **Using the pinkie of your left hand, lightly touch the tuned A string at the 7th fret.**

   Strike the harmonic and let it ring.

6. **Using the middle finger of your left hand, lightly touch the E string at the 5th fret.**

   Strike the harmonic and let it ring *together* with the previous harmonic. Adjust the tuning head of the E string until the wavering stops.

Check out Figure 2-22 for the relationships between the harmonics.

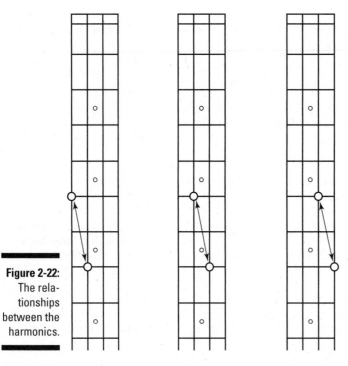

Figure 2-22: The relationships between the harmonics.

The following list gives you the most important harmonics for tuning:

- ✔ The 7th-fret harmonic on the G string (the thinnest string) is exactly the same note as the 5th-fret harmonic on the D string (the second-skinniest string).

- ✔ The 7th-fret harmonic on the D string is exactly the same note as the 5th-fret harmonic on the A string (the second-thickest string).

- ✔ The 7th-fret harmonic on the A string is exactly the same note as the 5th-fret harmonic on the E string (the thickest string).

Most of the notes that are offered to you as reference pitches (such as from a guitar) are in a higher octave. If you tried to match the higher note exactly, the string you're tuning would snap and whip around your ears. Comparing notes that are an octave (or two) apart is easiest using harmonics.

When you strike a harmonic on a string that isn't in perfect tune, you can hear a beating or wavering sound. Let the harmonics ring, and slowly turn the tuning head of the string you're trying to tune. If the wavering gets faster, you're turning in the wrong direction. If the wavering gets slower, you're turning in the correct direction. Turn the tuning head until the wavering stops. When the tone is even, your string is in tune. If the wavering gets slower and then speeds up again, you've turned the tuning head past the correct pitch. In this case, slowly turn the tuning head in the other direction until the wavering stops.

Playing a Song on Your Bass Guitar

Ladies and gentlemen, it's time for your very first song! What? Already? You bet! You may not be ready to tour, but you can certainly play along with the song on Track 2. In fact, you can do it with one hand tied behind your back. All you need to do is play the open strings on your bass . . . and break out some attitude.

Tracks 2 and 3 are play-alongs of two songs, the first using the open strings and the second using closed strings. I cover both scenarios in detail in the following sections. When you're comfortable with the songs, eliminate the bass on the recording by panning to one side so you can play along without any help. You can see me playing these songs in Video 3.

Making some noise with the open strings

Let your striking hand become comfortable with the individual strings on your bass. The thickest string, the one closest to your head, is the E string. Strike it a few times to get a feel for it. Careful! Don't strike it too hard. You get plenty of sound by striking the strings with a light touch, and quite frankly, the bass sounds at its best with a light touch.

The next string, the second-thickest, is the A string. Same deal here: Strike it a few times until you're comfortable and it sounds good. Next to the A string is the D string. Go ahead, you know what to do. Finally, the fourth string, the skinny one closest to your feet, is the G string (to bass players, it's more than a fashion statement). Make it sound good and get ready to rock and roll!

When you look at Figure 2-23, you see the letters that correspond to your open strings. Strike the appropriate string, in tempo with the song, each time you see its letter. Listen to Track 2 a few times before playing along.

Figure 2-23: Song played on open strings.

Closing the strings

Ready for another rousing performance? If you've really followed my instructions up to this point and tied one hand behind your back, please untie it now. You need it for this next song.

Looking at the fingerboard of your bass, you see the frets and the dots (*inlays*) between some of the frets. Find the 3rd fret. In the space between the 2nd and 3rd frets, you can see a dot. Press down on the E string with a finger (not the thumb) of your fretting hand in that space so the string is now touching the 3rd (and 2nd) fret. You have just "closed" the E string. While holding the string in place with your fretting hand, strike the same string with your other hand and listen to the sound. Instead of an E, you're now playing a G.

Find a balance in strength and coordination with both hands. If you don't press strongly enough with your fretting hand, the string will buzz; if you press too hard, it will hurt. If you strike too hard with the other hand, the string will rattle; if you don't strike it hard enough, you won't get much sound. Keep experimenting and have fun. Repeat this process with all the strings and get your hands used to what each string feels and sounds like.

Use your newfound skill in the song on Track 3. To keep things clear, the song in Figure 2-24 is written descriptively rather than in musical notation. When you see "E string, 3rd fret"; it means that you press the E string to the 3rd fret and strike it evenly in time with the music. When you see "A string, 3rd fret" you do the same with the A string. Ditto for "D string, 3rd fret" as well as "G string, 3rd fret." Only the 3rd fret is being used right now so you can acquaint yourself with the sound and feel of the closed strings.

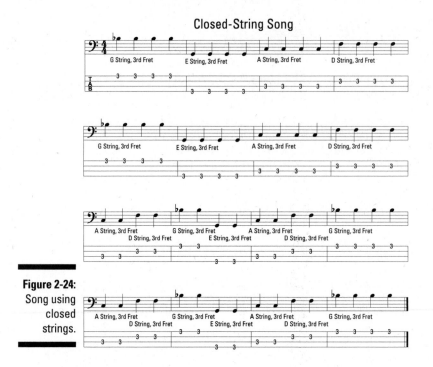

Figure 2-24:
Song using
closed
strings.

You're now well on your way to being a full-fledged bass player.
Congratulations!

Chapter 3

Warming Up: Getting Your Hands in Shape to Play

In This Chapter

▶ Recognizing how your bass produces sound

▶ Strengthening your right hand for striking

▶ Conditioning your left hand for fretting

▶ Access the audio tracks and video clips at www.dummies.com/go/bassguitar

Ready to jam? Strap your bass safely around your shoulder. Place it at the proper angle and height (see Chapter 2), put your hands in position, and get ready to play your heart out.

Wait a minute! Not so fast. Keep that bass strapped on, but before you start playing, it helps to know what makes your bass tick — or, um, sound. In this chapter, I explain how you produce sound on the bass and how you can strengthen your hands and coordinate them to produce that sound. That's right: One hand needs to know what the other is doing.

I highly recommend doing all the right- and left-hand exercises in this chapter every day before you play. The more familiar you become with these exercises, the quicker you can cruise through them. Just keep doing them. Nothing warms you up better, except maybe a warm hug on a cool night.

Understanding the Sound Your Bass Makes

When you strike a bass string, it vibrates. This sustained vibration is what you hear as the *pitch,* or *tone* (it's also referred to as a *note*). Each note vibrates at a different speed (called *frequency*). To give you an idea of how fast this vibration is, the open A string vibrates at a frequency of 55 times per second when properly tuned. The *pickup* (the magnet underneath your strings that I talk about in Chapter 1) on your bass translates this string vibration into an electrical charge, which in turn is converted to sound by the amplifier and speaker. (Chapter 16 provides more about amplifiers and speakers.)

Both tension and length determine the pitch of a string. The more tension a string has (that is, the tighter the string is), the higher its pitch; the less tension it has, the lower its pitch. (Just think about how your voice gets higher and higher when you get tense.) Similarly, the shorter a string is, the higher its pitch; the longer a string is, the lower its pitch.

When a string is tuned at the proper tension, you need to change only the length to alter its pitch. You change the length by fretting the string (no, you don't make it nervous). *Fretting the string* means that you place a left-hand finger on the string and press it down onto a fret on the fingerboard, in effect, shortening the length of the string. To get the desired bass note, hold the string down on that fret, and with a right-hand finger strike the string (causing it to vibrate). Voilà! The string is shorter, and the pitch (or note) is higher.

Performing Right-Hand Warm-Ups

Just as with any other physical activity, you need to prepare your body for bass playing. Without proper exercise, your hands simply won't be strong enough or coordinated enough to endure long hours of playing. A few minutes a day with the proper exercises go a long way.

Start the exercises in this section by positioning your right hand on the bass. (If you have any questions about your hand positions, check out Chapter 2 for a thorough description.) To avoid any confusion, I use letters for the fingers of the right hand and numbers for the fingers of the left hand. The letters are as follows:

- ✔ Index finger = *i*
- ✔ Middle finger = *m*

For now, your left hand gets to take a break while your right hand is working out. (To see the numbers I use as substitutes for your left-hand fingers, refer to the later section "Coordinating Your Left Hand with Your Right Hand.") Feel free to use your left hand for scratching various body parts — preferably your own rather than someone else's and never on stage!

Check out Video 4 to see me demonstrate the techniques in the following sections.

Right-hand same-string strokes

When you play notes on the same string, you need to be able to alternate between your index and middle fingers so you can play notes in rapid succession and with an even tone. The following steps show you how to practice these same-string strokes:

1. **Using the index finger (*i*) or middle finger (*m*) of your right hand, strike the lowest string.**

2. **Alternate between your *i* and *m* fingers (striking the string with one finger at a time). Keep the sound even as you alternate.**

   Don't lift your fingers really high and slap them down. If you slap the string, you'll create a lot of unwanted fret noise. Don't pluck the string up (like a classical guitar player), either. If you pluck the string up, it will vibrate over the pickup in a certain way that produces a very thin sound. Instead, your angle of attack (your strike) should be *into* the instrument, making the tone full and round.

Take a look at Figure 3-1 for the proper strike angle for the right hand. This technique gives you an authoritative and punchy sound, which is exactly what you want as a bass player.

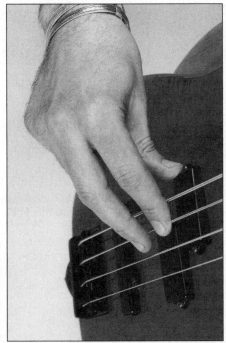

Figure 3-1:
Angle of attack for right-hand strike.

Photo by Steven Schlesinger

A word about terminology: I personally say *strike* rather than *pluck* because the word *pluck* is used extensively for guitar playing. Guitar players and bassists *attack* their strings differently, and I simply want to differentiate between the two. But don't be surprised to find *pluck* or similar terms in other books about bass playing.

Play evenly on each string, alternating between your *i* and *m* fingers. Aaaaaah . . . can you feel those calluses building up? You want those calluses; believe me. You better make your fingers tough and hard so you can strike the string all day long without any pain (or blisters).

As you play, you'll probably notice that your striking fingers are coming to rest on the next lower string when you play the adjacent higher string. This technique is correct; it helps mute the strings that aren't being played. When you play the lowest string (the E string), your fingers should come to rest against your thumb (which, of course, is firmly anchored to the thumb rest or the pickup, right?). Check out Figure 3-2 for the proper striking sequence.

Figure 3-2:
Sequence
of fingers
striking the
string.

Photos by Steven Schlesinger

Controlling the strength in your striking hand: Right-hand accents

This section takes you one step closer to creating music and introduces accents into your playing. No, I'm not talking about a German accent for a polka or a French accent for a chanson; I mean making some of the notes you play stick out from the rest.

Accenting a note means making it slightly louder than the others. To accent a note, just strike the string slightly harder. Being able to control the volume of each note allows you to accent some, which makes your bass line more interesting.

Don't accent a note too hard, though. If you strike a string too forcefully, the sound becomes distorted, and the tone leaves much to be desired. (It also quickly tires out your hands.)

Follow these steps to accent a note correctly with either striking finger:

1. **Start playing the E string with the alternating *i* and *m* fingers of your right hand.**

2. **Accent only the notes you strike with your *i* finger.**

3. **After you get comfortable using your *i* finger, accent only the notes you strike with your *m* finger.**

4. **Repeat this exercise on the A string, and then move on to the D string and G string.**

   You want to familiarize yourself with all the strings, because each string has a slightly different feel.

When you're comfortable accenting with either finger, put the previous instructions into exercise form by following these steps:

1. **Play evenly, alternating between your *i* and *m* fingers.**

   Think of this as a four-note sequence where you play *i m i m*.

2. **Accent the first note of each sequence (the underlined *i*), making it *i̲ m i m*, *i̲ m i m*, *i̲ m i m*, and so on.**

3. **When you have a handle on playing *i m i m*, start the sequence with *m*, making it *m i m i*.**

4. **Accent the first note again (this time, the underlined *m*), making the sequence *m̲ i m i*, *m̲ i m i*, *m̲ i m i*, and so on.**

5. **Repeat the preceding steps on all the strings.**

Check out Figure 3-3 for the notation for this exercise.

Figure 3-3: Right-hand accents.

Notice how the accented notes in Figure 3-3 are still within a certain range of volume; they aren't distorted. Listen to Track 4. Your notes should always sound clear and controlled. This exercise sounds the same using either finger, which is, of course, the idea.

Skating across the strings: Right-hand string crossing

The final stage of the right-hand warm-up is called *string crossing*. How do you cross the strings? It's very straightforward. Just remember the following rules:

- ✔ Alternate the middle and index fingers of your right hand when you're striking the same string. (Refer to the exercises in the earlier section "Right-hand same-string strokes.")

- ✔ Alternate your middle and index fingers when you're crossing from a *lower* to a *higher* string (that is, the lower to the higher string in terms of pitch). The lower string is closer to your head, and the higher string is closer to your feet. You also can think of it as crossing from the thicker to the thinner string.

- ✔ Rake with the same finger when you're crossing from a *higher* to a *lower* string. (*Raking* means striking a string with one finger and then letting it follow through, striking the next lower string with the same finger.) Again, keep in mind that going from high to low means going from the thinner string to the thicker string.

Take a look at your alternating fingers when you're crossing from a lower to a higher string to make sure you're doing it right. Remember that the lower string is the one on top (nearest your head).

A regular four-string bass is tuned from low to high: E, A, D, and G. Try the following exercise, in that order, for right-hand coordination:

1. **Strike the E string with *i*.**

2. **Strike the A string with *m*.**

3. **Strike the D string with *i*.**

4. **Strike the G string with *m*.**

Now strike the G string again, this time with *i* (alternating on the same string), and rake it all the way across the D, A, and E strings. Keep the rhythm and volume even by making sure your fingers strike the strings evenly.

After you play the E string with *i,* continue with the second half of the exercise:

1. **Strike the E string with *m*.**

2. **Strike the A string with *i*.**

3. **Strike the D string with *m*.**

4. **Strike the G string with *i*.**

Now strike the G string again with *m* (alternating on the same string), and rake it all the way across the D, A, and E strings. Again, keep the rhythm and volume even in both directions by making sure your fingers strike the strings evenly.

Listen to this exercise on Track 5. You won't hear a difference in the sound of the strings as the fingers alternate. Listen to the evenness of the volume of the notes and to the timing between the notes. The timing is identical whether you're going up or down on the strings.

Coordinating Your Left Hand with Your Right Hand

The job of your left hand is to press down on the string at the appropriate fret, which gives you the desired pitch, while the right hand strikes the same string simultaneously, producing the sound. You see bass players using a variety of left-hand positions, but without a doubt, the most economical position is the one that uses all four fingers on the frets (while the thumb remains on the back of the neck with as little pressure as possible). In this section, I show you how to train your left hand for some finger independence.

The left-hand fingers are numbered in the figures throughout this book as follows:

- Index finger = 1
- Middle finger = 2
- Ring finger = 3
- Pinkie (little finger) = 4

I demonstrate the techniques in the following section in Video 5.

Doing finger permutations

Get ready for one of the best exercises you'll ever find for bassists: finger permutations. The *finger permutation* exercise gives you a workout for every possible combination of finger sequences on your left hand. Here's how it works:

1. **Position your left hand on the neck of the bass so your index finger (1) is on low G (the 3rd fret on the E string).**

2. **Spread your fingers so each one covers one fret.**

   Try to keep your left hand as relaxed as possible as you're covering the frets. This way your hand doesn't tire, and you can move it more quickly.

3. **Press the notes under your fingers, one finger and fret at a time, in this order: 1 2 3 4.**

   Your right hand strikes the string to sound each note, and you can make little mini-shifts with your left hand to reach all the frets in a relaxed state.

4. **Repeat the process on the A string (the next string), the D string, and then on the G string.**

5. **When you complete this finger combination on every string, go back to the E string and do the next combination.**

Table 3-1 shows you the complete list of left-hand permutations (all the fingerings starting with 1, and then 2, 3, and 4). Practice one column at a time, and repeat the process until you do all the combinations (and I mean *every one*). These exercises give your left hand the desired coordination and strength in only a few short minutes to play all those hip bass lines I show you in Part IV.

Table 3-1	**Left-Hand Permutations**		
Starting with the Index Finger	*Starting with the Middle Finger*	*Starting with the Ring Finger*	*Starting with the Pinkie*
1 2 3 4	2 1 3 4	3 1 2 4	4 1 2 3
1 2 4 3	2 1 4 3	3 1 4 2	4 1 3 2
1 3 2 4	2 3 1 4	3 2 1 4	4 2 1 3
1 3 4 2	2 3 4 1	3 2 4 1	4 2 3 1
1 4 2 3	2 4 1 3	3 4 1 2	4 3 1 2
1 4 3 2	2 4 3 1	3 4 2 1	4 3 2 1

Figure 3-4 shows an example of the first combination of the left-hand permutations. You can try these exercises on any area of the neck of the bass. On the audio tracks, the exercises start on low G (with the index finger on the 3rd fret of the E string), but don't limit yourself to that area.

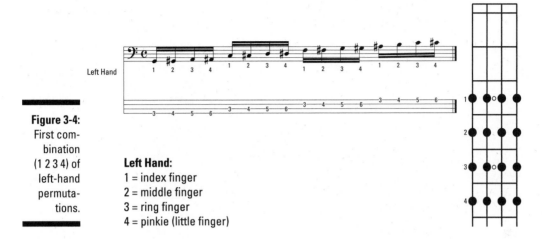

Figure 3-4:
First combination (1 2 3 4) of left-hand permutations.

Left Hand:
1 = index finger
2 = middle finger
3 = ring finger
4 = pinkie (little finger)

Listen to Track 6 to hear what the left-hand permutations sound like.

Muting the strings to avoid the infamous hum

When you play, you may find that some strings vibrate even though you didn't strike them. *Sympathetic vibration* (the official name for this hum) is a natural phenomenon. You can silence, or *mute,* any string by touching it lightly with either your left hand (preferably with more than one finger) or your right hand, or even with both hands. As you refine your muting technique, sympathetic vibration will become less and less of a problem.

For example, if you strike a low G on the E string, the open G string vibrates as well. Just keep your left-hand fingers in (light) touch with the strings, and you won't hear any vibration. Take a look at Figure 3-5 to see what muting with the left hand looks like. Notice how the undersides of the fingers touch the other strings, preventing them from vibrating.

Putting it all together

Try the simple exercise in Figure 3-6 that coordinates the fingering of the left hand with the striking of the right.

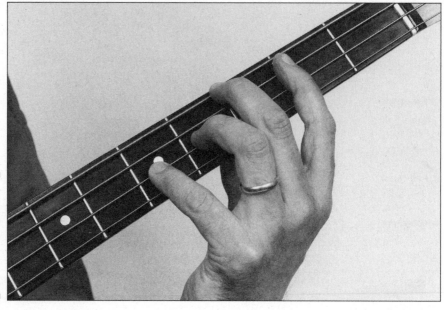

Figure 3-5:
Left hand playing low G while muting the other strings.

Photo by Steven Schlesinger

Figure 3-6:
Practice exercise for combining the right and left hands.

Left Hand:
1 = index finger
2 = middle finger
3 = ring finger
4 = pinkie (little finger)

Right Hand:
i = index finger
m = middle finger

Make sure your right hand alternates properly. You start this exercise with a different finger on each repetition (alternating the *i* and *m* fingers). As for your left hand, it doesn't have to shift for the entire exercise as long as you use all four left-hand fingers properly.

You can hear the very cool exercise from Figure 3-6 on Track 7. This exercise doubles as a hip groove. Who says exercises have to be boring?

Part II
The Bass-ics of Playing

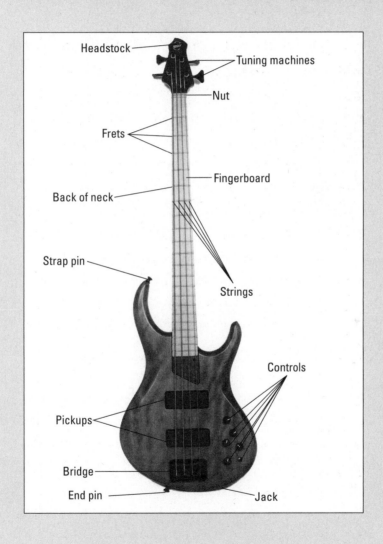

Visit www.dummies.com/extras/bassguitar for additional info on practicing with your bass.

In this part...

✔ Get the skinny on how to read different kinds of notation for your bass playing.

✔ Find all the different notes on your bass guitar.

✔ Work out how to keep time and develop solid rhythm.

✔ Understand major and minor tonalities and how to use them.

✔ Experiment with different inversions.

✔ Explore 7th chords and modes and how to use them to build grooves.

✔ Spice up your grooves with chromatic tones and dead notes.

Chapter 4

Reading, 'Riting, and Rhythm

In This Chapter

▶ Discovering different types of notation

▶ Finding notes in all octaves

▶ Playing with the metronome

▶ Understanding phrases, measures, and beats

▶ Reading music and playing while reading

*R*eading music isn't nearly as important for bass players as it is for classical musicians (who re-create someone else's music as they read it). A bassist usually creates his or her own bass lines for a tune by choosing notes from chords and scales (see Chapter 5). Sometimes, you may even come up with an idea for a bass part that's perfect for a tune, and you don't want to forget it, so you need to be able to write it down. Then, when you need it, you can read it.

In this chapter, I introduce you to some fast and easy ways for tackling the dilemma of reading music. And by the time you're finished with this chapter, you'll probably agree that reading music is pretty easy . . . and useful.

Reading Notation: No Pain, Much Gain

Reading music is nothing to be afraid of. You don't even have to read music to be a good (or great) bass player, but it certainly enriches your musical experience and opens doors that otherwise may remain shut.

When you solve the mystery of reading music and discover the joy in it, you may find yourself reading Bach preludes instead of a novel before going to sleep. In this section, I introduce four types of musical notation: chord notation, music notation, tablature (or tab), and the vocal chart (or lead sheet). For bassists, these are the most important notational systems.

Chord notation: The chord chart

Chords can evoke certain moods. For example, a major chord usually sounds happy and bright, whereas a minor chord sounds sad and dark. Just as a color on canvas may evoke a certain feeling, a chord works on the same principle, only acoustically instead of visually.

The *chord chart,* which is one form of musical notation, tells you in *chord symbols* what notes you can choose for playing a particular song and how many beats each chord lasts. Chord symbols name the *root* of a chord, such as E (see Chapters 2 and 5 for more info on the root), and the *color* of that chord, such as *m* for minor or *Maj* for major. You can choose to play any of the notes from the chord or scale that relate to the chord symbol. For more details on the happy mating of chord symbol, chord, and scale, check out Chapter 5.

A chord chart doesn't tell you exactly which notes to play. The style of the music and your (or your bandleader's) taste influence the sequence and rhythm of the notes you choose from the chord. Part of the fun of playing is choosing your own notes and developing your own creative style. Just keep an open mind . . . and open ears. If it sounds good to you, it usually is.

For more information about which notes are best, look at Part IV of this book, which discusses the many genres of music and tells you how to play different chords in different styles. Figure 4-1 shows you how to play four beats of music for the E minor chord in a rock style.

Figure 4-1:
Measure
of E minor
from a
chord chart
in chord
notation.

Music notation: Indicating rhythm and notes

Another form of notation spells out both the rhythm and the notes; it's known as *music notation.* Regular music notation is written on a musical staff. The *musical staff* consists of five lines and four spaces on which the notes are written. The *clef* (the first symbol you see at the beginning of the musical staff) shows whether the notes on the staff are low (bass) or high (treble). For bass players, the bass clef is the clef of choice. (We try to stay out of treble if we can.)

Music notation is much more exact than the chord chart (see the preceding section). Not only does it tell you what note to play, but it also tells you which octave to play the note in, how long to hold the note, which note to accent, and so on. In short, this method doesn't leave much room for creativity, but it does leave the embellishments up to you. Figure 4-2 shows the measure of E minor in music notation; it also shows the different parts of the staff.

You can hear *exactly* what Figure 4-2 sounds like when you listen to Track 8. Every note is accounted for.

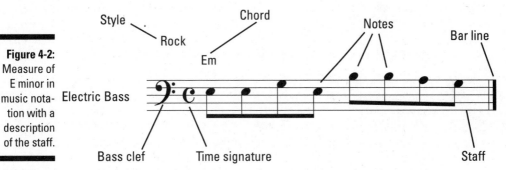

Figure 4-2:
Measure of
E minor in
music nota-
tion with a
description
of the staff.

The bass sounds one octave lower than the written note. Piano players, when reading from the same sheet as the bass player, play the same notes an octave higher (see Chapter 2 for a discussion of octaves).

Tablature notation: Showing strings, frets, and sequence

Tablature (or *tab*) shows you which strings to press and on which frets for the correct notes. Using this method, you can see the exact notes and their sequence, but you generally can't see the rhythm, which is why tablature usually is accompanied by music notation (see previous section).

When you rely on tab notation, bear in mind that the frets indicated may not be the only places on the neck where you can find those notes. For example, you can find the G of the open G string in these spots as well:

✔ The 5th fret of the D string

✔ The 10th fret of the A string

✔ The 15th fret of the E string

See Figure 4-3 for the different locations of the same note G.

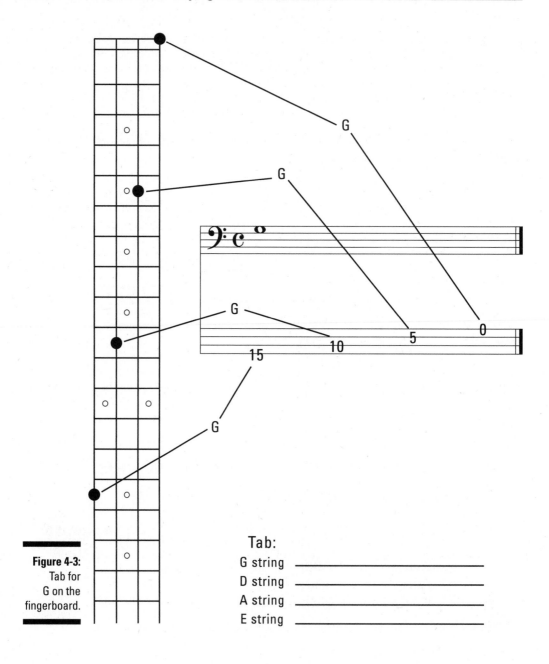

Figure 4-3:
Tab for
G on the
fingerboard.

Tab:

G string

D string

A string

E string

The best choice of note to play is determined by the position of the other notes in the pattern you're playing. Keep in mind that you want to avoid any unnecessary shifts in your left hand; whenever possible, play the notes of the chord in one area of the bass neck.

The vocal chart: Using lyrics and chords for a singer or songwriter

The vocal chart is a common form of notation (combining the lyrics of a song with its chords) that you use when you're working with a singer or songwriter. With this type of notation, you're getting only the most basic information for your accompaniment, which means that you're free to explore different ways of interpreting a song. In a vocal chart, the chord is simply written over the word that's sung when the chord is played.

For example, the song "Happy Birthday" would have a G over "Happy," a C over "birthday," and a G over "you." The line would look like this:

    G   C   G

Happy birthday to you

Vocal charts are an imprecise notation technique, but if you're familiar with the song, sometimes that's all you need. Just make sure all your bandmates are familiar with the same version of the song you're playing. And remember, in this particular case . . . follow the singer!

Finding Any Note in Any Octave

After you understand the four types of musical notation, the next step is to find out where the notes are located on the bass neck and what they look like on paper. Figure 4-4 gives you an illustration of this.

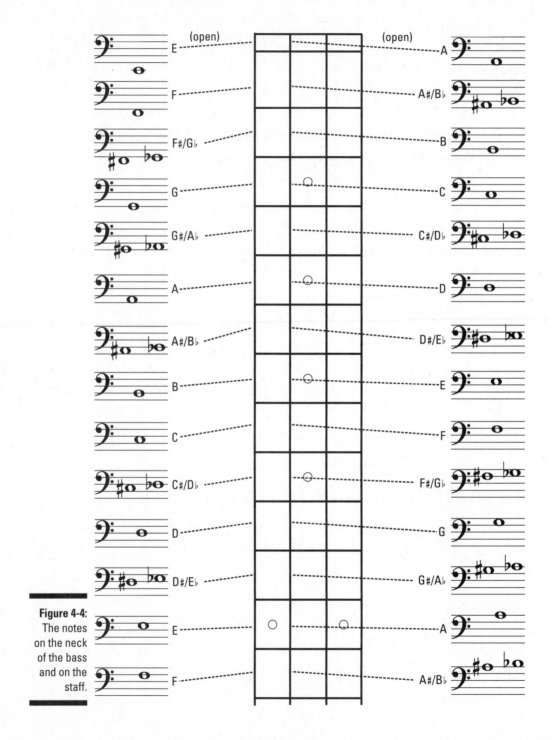

Figure 4-4:
The notes on the neck of the bass and on the staff.

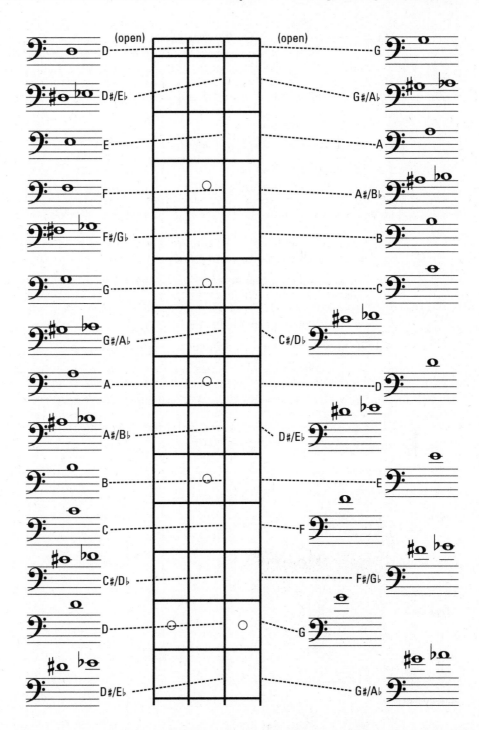

Finding notes over the entire bass range can be challenging (but not impossible), because each note occurs in at least two places on the neck of the bass. Knowing where the alternative notes are located allows you to play easily and efficiently anywhere on the fingerboard. You can use one of the three following methods to help you find the notes you want on any part of the neck:

✔ The octave method

✔ The handspan-plus-two-frets method

✔ The marker method

The *octave method,* also called the *two-strings/two-frets method* is the most common way to find the same note in a different place. Here's how to do it:

1. **Place your left-hand index finger on any note on the E string and strike it with your right hand.**

   You can find the same note an octave higher by letting your ring finger cross one string and land on the D string, the second string up. The ring finger naturally positions itself on the higher octave of the original note, two frets above the index finger.

2. **Press your left-hand ring finger down for the octave.**

   Your octave note is two strings and two frets above your original note. This method also works from the A string to the G string, and you can use your middle finger and your pinkie. If you have a note on the G or D string and you want to find its lower octave, just reverse the process. Figure 4-5 shows the relationship of the notes using the octave (or two-strings/two-frets) method.

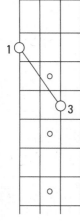
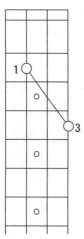

Figure 4-5: The octave, or two-strings/two-frets, method.

While the octave method helps you locate a note two strings away, the *handspan-plus-two-frets method* helps you locate a note on the adjacent string. Follow these steps:

1. **Press down a note on the A string with your left-hand index finger, and strike it with your right hand.**

2. **Shift your left hand two frets toward the bridge, and move your pinkie from the A string to the E string.**

3. **Press your pinkie down on the E string in the new position and play that note.**

You now have the same note in the same octave as your original note on the A string. This process also works in reverse. You also can use this method when going from the D to the A string and from the G to the D string. Figure 4-6 shows the relationship of the notes in the handspan-plus-two-frets method.

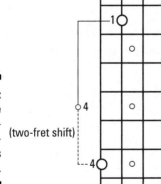

Figure 4-6:
The handspan-plus-two-frets method.

(two-fret shift)

If you need to locate a note on the same string, use the *marker method*. With this method, you simply use the markers (dots) embedded on the side and face of your bass neck. If you look at the neck, you can see one section — on the 12th fret — that has two dots in the space of one fret. This fret is your octave marker for your open strings. You can play the octaves for all the open strings (E, A, D, and G) at this fret.

For example, the octave of open E is directly at the double dot on the same string. If you want to play the octave of low F on the E string (the note on the 1st fret of the E string), you can find its octave one fret above the double dot (on the 13th fret). If you want to play the octave of low G on the E string (the note at the first dot of the E string), you can find its octave at the first dot past the double dot (15th fret) of the E string. The marker method applies to all the other strings as well.

You can practice all these methods of finding notes by choosing a note at random, such as C, and then locating all the instances of that note on your bass neck. When you're finished, move on to another note (A♭, for example). Repeat this exercise until you cover all 12 notes: C, C♯/D♭, D, D♯/E♭, E, F, F♯/G♭, G, G♯/A♭, A, A♯/B♭, and B. *Note:* A ♯ ("sharp") raises a note by one half step, and a ♭ ("flat") lowers it by one half step.

Later in this chapter, I show you how to put the different kinds of musical notation into practice, but first you need to understand rhythm, which is what the next section is all about.

Using the Metronome: You Know, That Tick-Tock Thing

A *metronome* is a device that helps you develop good rhythm. Metronomes come in many shapes and colors, but they all have one thing in common: They give you a steady clicking sound on which to base your timing. Like a very loud clock tick, the metronome produces a steady beat. You can adjust the speed of the click to suit your needs.

The old-fashioned acoustic metronomes have a small weight that swings back and forth. They need to be used on a level surface and must be wound up periodically. Electric metronomes need to be plugged into a wall outlet. The small battery-powered metronomes are the most common and the most user-friendly.

Just in case you don't have a metronome handy, but you have a computer hooked up to the Internet, you can find plenty of free metronomes online. There goes any excuse you may have for not using one.

Setting the metronome

The face of the metronome has a sequence of numbers (usually from 40 to 208). These numbers tell you how many clicks per minute you hear when you set the dial to a particular number. In other words, if you set your metronome to 162, you hear 162 clicks per minute at regular intervals.

Playing along

Don't be surprised if it takes some practice to regulate your playing to the ticking of the metronome. It's a challenge at first to get in sync with the clicks and not to rush or drag during the space between each one. The slower the tempo on the metronome, the farther apart the clicks are from each other and the more difficult it is for you to keep exact time.

Here's an exercise that may help you get used to playing with a metronome: Set the metronome to 80 and play a repeated note on your bass, matching the click of the metronome exactly.

Listen to Track 9 to hear a bass playing precisely to the click of a metronome set at 80.

Playing with a metronome enables you to keep a steady rhythm not only at tempo 80 but at any tempo. Set your metronome at different tempos and try playing along.

Dividing Music into Phrases, Measures, and Beats

Tunes are divided into *phrases*. You can recognize a phrase by listening to singers — they tend to take a breath between each phrase. Phrases are divided into *measures* (bars), and measures are divided into *beats* (or clicks of the metronome).

In most tunes, four clicks of the metronome equal one measure, and four measures equal one phrase. In other words, a musical phrase is 16 beats long, or 16 clicks of the metronome. The organization of phrases makes it easier to keep your place in the music and communicate with the other musicians. To see what phrases, measures, and beats look like, check out Figure 4-7.

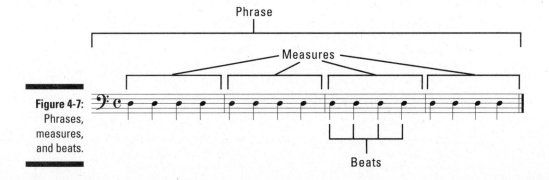

Figure 4-7: Phrases, measures, and beats.

To subdivide the phrases into smaller units, you need an understanding of rhythm and its notation. Figure 4-8 shows all the rhythmic notes discussed in this section and how they relate to each other. You may want to refer to this figure as you read through the section.

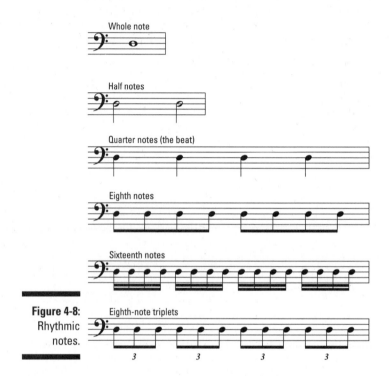

Figure 4-8: Rhythmic notes.

On Track 10, you can hear the different duration of each note in comparison to the beat. Whole notes are at 0:00; half notes at 0:11; quarter notes at 0:23; eighth notes at 0:35; sixteenth notes at 0:48; and eighth-note triplets at 1:00.

The quarter note

Each of the four beats (metronome clicks) in a measure (or bar) equals a *quarter note*. These four beats make up the *1-2-3-4* of the musical count. Imagine that you're marching on the street. You're walking at a steady, even speed, and your feet are going in a regular rhythm: Left, right, left, right, and so on. This steady marching is what your quarter-note rhythm feels like — a regular pulse: *1-2-3-4, 1-2-3-4,* and so on and on and on. . . .

Each of the four beats can in turn be divided into equal parts. To come up with interesting grooves and bass parts (like the ones I describe in Chapter 6), you want to be able to divide a beat in several different ways.

The eighth note

The *eighth note* is twice as fast as the quarter note. Imagine that you're still marching — left, right, left, right. As you continue, tap your hand twice on your thigh, at regular intervals, for each step you take. Instead of counting *1-2-3-4,* subdivide the beat by adding an *and* at the end of each number, making it *1 and 2 and 3 and 4 and,* evenly spaced. If you do this correctly, you're still moving at exactly the same speed as before.

Playing eighth notes on the bass works the same way as marching and tapping. Play two evenly spaced notes on your bass to each click of the metronome. Concentrate on keeping the notes evenly spaced — one note on the click and the other note halfway between the clicks.

The sixteenth note

The *sixteenth note* is twice as fast as the eighth note, and four times as fast as the quarter note. Imagine that you're still marching (by this time you're probably tired and miles from home) and counting *1 and 2 and 3 and 4 and.* Without changing your pace, tap your hand twice as fast as before. You're now tapping four times for each step. This is the sixteenth-note rhythm. Take your count of *1 and 2 and 3 and 4 and,* and add an *e* (pronounced "ee") after the number and an *a* (pronounced "uh") after the *and.* Keeping the count even, count *1 e and a 2 e and a 3 e and a 4 e and a.* Your pace is unchanged, and you're still marching at the same speed, but the subdivision of the beats gives you much more to "talk" about.

You may want to try this exercise with your metronome. Keep the tempo reasonable (between 60 and 80) until you get used to it. First try marching your feet to the clicks of the metronome and tapping out the subdivisions for the eighth and then the sixteenth notes with your hand. When you're comfortable with this exercise, try playing the subdivisions on your bass.

The half note

The *half note* is half as fast as the quarter note. In other words, two quarter notes fill the space of one half note. If you're still marching (by now you're probably halfway across the continent), tap your hand once for every two steps you take. You're still moving at the same speed, but your rhythm is now only half as fast.

The whole note

The *whole note* is half as fast as the half note, and four times slower than the quarter note. If you're still marching (and you haven't come to a large body of water yet), tap your hand *once* for every four steps you take. As always, your speed doesn't change; the rhythm of your hand is the only thing that changes.

The triplet

All the subdivisions of the notes I describe in the previous sections are either double or half and can be divided by two. In many tunes, however, the beats are subdivided into three parts, which brings me to the triplet.

A *triplet rhythm* subdivides the beat into three even rhythmic intervals. As you continue to march your way across the globe, tap your hand three times evenly for each step you take. Your step still represents the quarter note, but your hand is now tapping three notes for each quarter note. You call these *eighth-note triplets*.

The dot

The *dot* is a notational device that allows you to extend the *value* (duration) of a note by half of its original value. The quarter note, for example, has a value of two eighth notes. When you add a dot to a quarter note, you add one extra eighth note to its value, and you end up with a note that has a value of three eighth notes. Figure 4-9 shows you the most common dotted notes.

Figure 4-9:
The most common dotted notes.

1/4 + 1/8

1/8 + 1/16

The tie

The *tie* combines two notes. For example, if you tie a quarter note to another quarter note, you increase the length of the original quarter note by another quarter note. However, you don't restrike the second note. The tie simply adds the two notes together. You can combine any two notes with a tie. Figure 4-10 shows common ties between notes.

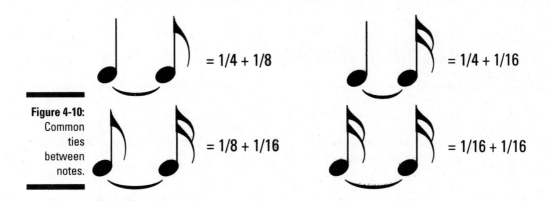

Figure 4-10: Common ties between notes.

The rest

You don't have to play a note on every single beat. Many beats are silent. The *rest* tells you when to be silent and avoid playing. It works exactly like the other rhythmic notations (including the dot) except that you don't make a sound.

Figure 4-11 shows you the rest that's equivalent to each note (a quarter-note rest takes the same amount of time as a quarter note, an eighth-note rest takes the same amount of time as an eighth note, and so on).

Figure 4-11: The values of notes and rests and their typical application.

On Track 11, you can hear the notes in Figure 4-11. In place of each rest, the word "rest" is spoken. (No, you don't have to say "rest" when you encounter one in your own playing; just give it a rest.)

Discovering How to Read Music

As you read this sentence, notice that you're not reading letter by letter; you're reading words. You read music the same way. Music notation is recognizable in chunks of notes (or musical words). Certain chunks tend to be repeated again and again, and you can train your eyes to recognize these patterns. When you get used to seeing and hearing music in chunks, you can get a good idea of what the music on the page sounds (and feels) like merely by scanning the page.

Rhythmic chunks

Reading music in chunks makes playing much easier. The chunks may be a group of four sixteenth notes or perhaps two eighth notes. Become familiar with the way these notes look when grouped together for faster recognition (see Figure 4-12), and practice playing and singing them to the click of your metronome. (For more on metronomes, check out the earlier section "Using the Metronome: You Know, That Tick-Tock Thing.")

(a)   (b)   (c)   (d)   (e)   (f)   (g)

Figure 4-12:
Seeing
beats as
chunks of
notes.

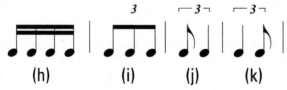

(h)   (i)   (j)   (k)

You can hear the notes from Figure 4-12 on Track 12. Memorize what each of the "chunks" of notes looks and sounds like.

You can substitute any of the notes with a rest of equal value and still have the same rhythmic chunk; the only difference is that now you have a "silent" note (the rest) in place of the note. The rhythmic value of the beat is still the same.

Figure 4-13 shows what the beats look like if you substitute a rest for any of the notes. These are still the same rhythmic combinations but with rests inserted. The top line of the figure shows the original beat with all the notes played. The bottom line shows the same rhythmic figure with a rest replacing one note at a time.

Beats and Rests as Chunks

Figure 4-13:
Beats and
rests as
chunks of
notes.

Listen to Track 13 to hear how the rests take the space of a note in Figure 4-13.

Interval chunks

You can read the notes of intervals in groups, much like you can read chunks of rhythm. Being able to recognize the intervals in chunks visually helps you read more fluidly. You can see the shapes of chunks rather than having to analyze each individual pitch. The relationship of the notes to each other gives you a hint at which interval you're facing.

For example, when your first note is on a line of the musical staff and the next note is in the space directly above that line, you have an interval of a *second* (2nd). You can see the two notes as a chunk. If your first note is on a line and your next note is on the line directly above, it's a *third* (3rd). (For intervals and how to play them, take a detailed look at Chapter 2.) You won't know right away whether it's a major or a minor interval, but you're already in the ball-park. With a bit of practice, you can see the intervals in an instant, much like recognizing words, and you can position your hand to be ready to play them.

The same holds true if your first note is in a space. Each line and each space represent a step and thus an interval. At first, you need to count from space to line to space and so on to recognize the interval. Eventually, your eyes get used to the distance between the notes, and you can see the intervals as chunks in an instant.

Take a look at Figure 4-14. Note that there's no bass clef, or clef of any kind. This is a conceptual approach. All you need are the lines and spaces to see how the notes form the intervals.

When you want to know what interval two notes form, just count the lines and spaces between them, starting with the line or space of the first note. For example, if the first note is on the lowest line of the staff and the next note is two lines and three spaces in the space above it, the interval is a *sixth* (6th). Note the line, space, line, space, line, space — six steps in all. It forms a picture that you can become familiar with.

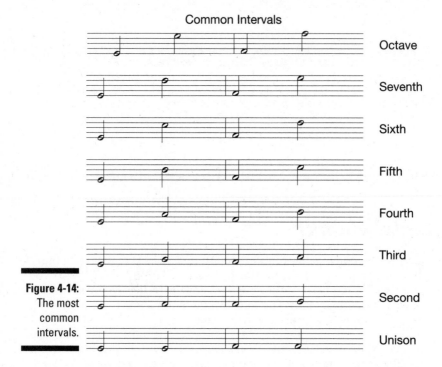

Figure 4-14:
The most common intervals.

What comes up must come down

A perfect example of the visual impact of music notation is Figure 4-15, a collection of all 12 major scales. Each scale is played with the exact same fingering, only moving that same hand position on the fingerboard to accommodate the new root. All the major scales move from line to space or from space to line, step by step. The sharps and flats adjust the intervals into the proper half and whole steps to create each major scale. When you see music notation like Figure 4-15, you can easily see that each chunk is a scale, and you can set up your hand accordingly.

Major Scales Notated

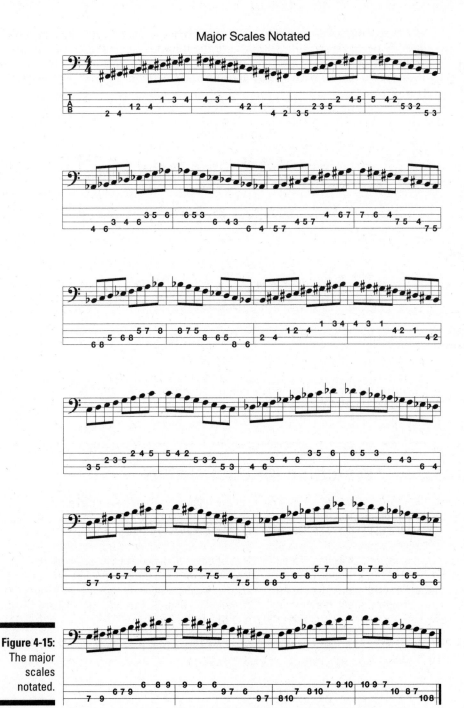

Figure 4-15:
The major scales notated.

No chapter on reading would be complete without taking a look at the chromatic scale. In Figure 4-16, you can see the notation of every note in the practical range of the bass guitar. Follow along as you play each note and see how the notes go up when the music goes up and the notes go down as the music goes down.

Chromatic Scale

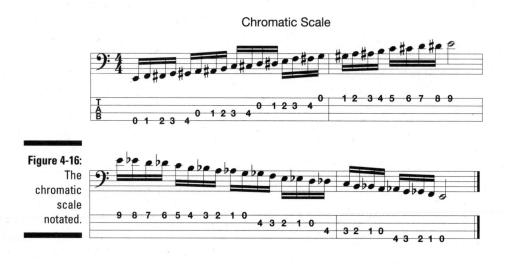

Figure 4-16: The chromatic scale notated.

The intricacies of reading music can fill an entire book, but this bit gets you started on the right track.

Watching for accidentals

Many times, the sharps or flats of a piece of music are stated at the beginning of the first line of a tune, next to the clef symbol, and are then in effect throughout the song. This notation is called a *key signature*. For example, if an F sharp is indicated in the key signature, then all the Fs in the piece are played as F sharps unless a *natural sign* (♮) precedes the note. Occasionally, a songwriter decides to use an F natural right in the middle of a piece that has an F sharp in the key signature. In this special case, a natural sign precedes the particular F note to indicate it has no sharp, and the natural is in effect until the end of the measure. Then the rest of the Fs in the piece revert back to F sharps. A natural sign can also be used to neutralize a flat. Sharps, flats, and naturals are all referred to as *accidentals*.

Playing Your First Song While Reading Music

It's about time to apply all the theoretical stuff in this chapter and play some music, wouldn't you say? With sheet music, you usually get one or two different notational devices to work with, such as notes and tablature, or a chord chart and a vocal chart. Behold, I have a special treat for you.

In this section, you get to read and play "Two Too Tight Shoes Blues," using all four notational systems in the same song. The first part is written as regular music notation with tablature underneath so you can play the intended bass part. I also include the vocal chart with the chords written above the words. Finally, you get to play with the chord chart, which shows you the chords for each measure. (Refer to the earlier section "Reading Notation: No Pain, Much Gain" if you need more information on notation.)

Listen to Track 14 to familiarize yourself with "Two Too Tight Shoes Blues." Then look at the notation in Figure 4-17 to see what the sound looks like. When you're ready, pick up your bass and play along with the song on the audio track. Make sure to keep your eyes glued to the page; this exercise is about reading and playing at the same time. When you're comfortable with the song, pan the bass out of the mix and play the song with the track on your own.

A word of advice: If you intend to make reading and playing music your new bedtime-reading activity, make sure you don't crank the amp and keep your entire household up until 2 a.m.

Notation for "Two Too Tight Shoes Blues"

Figure 4-17:
Notation for
"Two Too
Tight Shoes
Blues"
using four
notational
systems.

C
I've got the blues in my shoes

F   **C**
I've got the blues in my shoes

G   **F**   **C**
They're too tight, two tight shoes

Chapter 5

Understanding Major and Minor Structures

In This Chapter

▶ Playing scales

▶ Structuring chords, from bottom to top and top to bottom

▶ Discovering the seven main modes

▶ Using chromatic notes

▶ Building a groove with dead notes

▶ Playing around with accompaniments

▶ Access the audio tracks and video clips at www.dummies.com/go/bassguitar

Sing a note, any note. Go ahead. "Lah!" Now use this note to sing the first line of "Twinkle, Twinkle, Little Star." You have just established a tonal center. The tonal center is the most important note of a tune. The tonal center often begins the tune (as is the case when you sing "Twinkle, Twinkle, Little Star"), but not always. ("Happy Birthday," for example, doesn't start on the tonal center.) Almost all tunes, however, end on the tonal center. Just sing both tunes all the way through, and you end on the tonal center of each.

All the other notes in the tune relate to the tonal center and sound as though they're gravitating toward it. They gravitate toward the center in two basic ways: via a major scale, or via a minor scale. These two *tonalities* (sounds) rule the world of music. The major scale has a happy, bright sound, and the minor scale sounds dark and brooding. Without the contrast between major and minor tonalities, music would be about as interesting as a picture of white clouds on a white background.

Subtle variations exist within the major and minor tonalities, but the basics remain the same. In the first part of this chapter, I explain some technical stuff, such as scales (also called modes) and chords. Don't worry, I promise not to bore you to tears. You'll use all the information in this chapter again and again when you're playing bass. In the latter part of the chapter, you get to apply scales and chords the way they're used in music.

Building Major and Minor Scales

A *scale* is a series of notes (usually seven different notes) starting with a tonal center (the root) and ending on the eighth note, the octave (also the root). As an example, you can play a scale from C to the octave above or below it, the next C. Check out Figure 5-1 for an example of a scale.

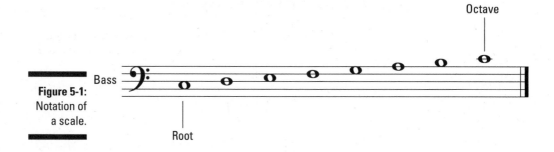

Figure 5-1:
Notation of
a scale.

Octave

Bass

Root

Musicians also refer to the entire group of notes, including the root and its octave, as an *octave.* Unfortunately, the same term is used for both, just to keep musical discussions lively.

An *interval* is the distance between any two notes you play. The two notes of any interval — and an octave is one example of an interval — are always positioned the same way on the fingerboard. You can finger an octave the same way, no matter where the first note occurs. Take a look at Chapter 2 for a list of intervals and their positions.

A half-step interval is the distance from one fret to the next on the same string. A whole-step interval skips one fret; for example, a whole step goes from the 3rd fret to the 5th fret (see Chapter 1 for more on frets). One octave equals 12 half steps.

Most scales are made up of sequences of notes in half-step and whole-step intervals. As is the case with intervals, the shapes of the scales remain constant in any position on the fingerboard of the bass guitar. If you know a scale in one position, you know it in all positions. Here's a little hint: Don't tell any of the other musicians that you don't have to think about each individual scale; they'll be jealous, and they may decide to pay you less.

Major scales

The major scale has seven different notes plus the high root. It begins on the root and is arranged in whole- and half-step intervals within one octave (the octave is the eighth note, or the new root).

✔ The starting note is the *root* (the tonal center).

✔ All the notes (*scale tones*) from the root to the octave are numbered in sequence. So the major scale consists of the root (or 1), 2, 3, 4, 5, 6, and 7.

✔ The note after the 7 is the *octave*. The octave is the same note as the 1 but higher. You can use this octave as the last note of the scale or as a new 1 (root) for repeating the first scale an octave higher.

When you describe the notes of the major scale, you call them the root, 2nd, 3rd, 4th, 5th, 6th, 7th, and octave.

Here's the structure of the major scale. I label the whole steps with "W" and the half steps with "H" to show you the distance from one note to the next in the major scale.

Root <W> 2nd <W> 3rd <H> 4th <W> 5th <W> 6th <W> 7th <H> octave

Figure 5-2 gives the structure of the major scale on a grid. (See Chapter 2 for a description of the grid.) The open circle represents the root, and the solid dots represent the other *scale tones* (notes).

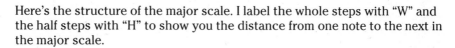

Figure 5-2:
The structure of the major scale on a grid.

Left Hand:
1 = index finger
2 = middle finger
3 = ring finger
4 = pinkie (little finger)

You can play the major scale anywhere on the fingerboard, without shifting, as long as you have three strings and four frets at your disposal. When you're going up, start the scale with the middle finger of your left hand to complete it without shifting. (For more on shifting, see the later section "Chromatic tones outside the box.") Going down, start the scale with your pinkie.

The major scale structure forms the basis for all your other scales and their intervals. All the other scales derive from the major scale intervals. When a note deviates from the notes in the major scale, it's specially marked with a ♭ or a ♯. Here are the guidelines:

✔ When you lower any note by a half step, the note is *flatted* (shown with the symbol ♭ next to the note or number).

✔ When you raise any note by a half step, the note is *sharped* (shown with the symbol ♯ next to the note or number).

Minor scales

Like the major scale, minor scales have seven different notes within an octave, but the whole and half steps are arranged in a different order. The *natural minor scale* is the basis of all other minor scales. Here's the sequence of the notes in a natural minor scale:

> Root, 2, ♭3, 4, 5, ♭6, ♭7, and octave

Notice that the 3rd, 6th, and 7th notes in the natural minor scale are each a half step lower than the 3rd, 6th, and 7th notes in the major scale. The ♭3 (flat 3) is the fundamental note in a minor scale. It defines the scale as minor instead of major; this note is often referred to in music theory as a minor 3rd.

Here's the structure of the natural minor scale:

> Root <W> 2nd <H> ♭3rd <W> 4th <W> 5th <H> ♭6th <W> ♭7th <W> octave

Start playing this scale with your index finger. You can play the natural minor scale without having to shift your left hand. Figure 5-3 shows you the structure of the natural minor scale.

Figures 5-2 and 5-3 are on Track 15. The major scale starts at 0:00, and the natural minor scale is at 0:11. Listen for the differences between the major and minor scales. Play along with the track and listen to each scale until you can tell them apart by ear.

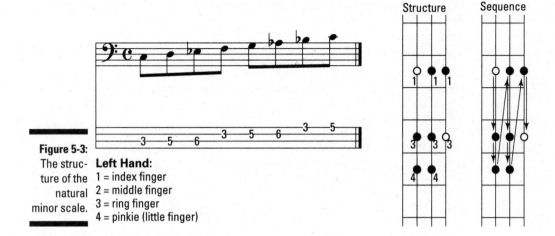

Figure 5-3:
The struc-
ture of the
natural
minor scale.

Left Hand:
1 = index finger
2 = middle finger
3 = ring finger
4 = pinkie (little finger)

Building Chords: One Note at a Time, Please

A *chord* is a combination of three or more notes taken from its related scale. Piano players and guitarists often play several notes of a chord simultaneously. For example, a guitarist may play a three-note chord on the first beat of a measure and let the complex chord-sound (or harmony) ring out for the rest of the measure. But bassists usually take a different approach when playing the notes of a chord. When playing bass, you generally execute chords by playing the notes one at a time. You can play the notes in any sequence and using any number of rhythmic patterns. (See Chapter 4 for different rhythmic patterns.)

When you play the notes of a chord in sequence (from the lowest note to the highest), it's called an *arpeggio*.

Triads: The three most important notes of a chord

The *triad* is the basic chord form, consisting of the three most important notes of any scale: the root, 3rd, and 5th. This structure is called a triad because it has three notes. You can find the notes for the triad by playing any scale up to the 5th note, skipping every other note. In other words, you play the root, skip the 2nd note, play the 3rd, skip the 4th, and play the 5th.

You can tell whether a scale is major or minor merely by listening to its triad. A major triad has a regular 3 (1, 3, 5) and produces a happy sound. A minor triad has a ♭3 (1, ♭3, 5) and produces a sad sound.

Musicians sometimes refer to triads as *chords*. For example, a major triad may be referred to as a major chord.

Major triads

The *major triad* is the chord that's related to the major scale. Just play the root, 3rd, and 5th notes of the major scale to get a major triad. You can easily play it with no shifts in your left hand. Make sure you start the major triad with your middle finger.

To see the form of the major triad, check out Figure 5-4. The open circle represents the root, and the solid dots represent the other chord notes. You may include the octave root (as in this example) if you like the sound. It's the same note (an octave higher) as the root and won't change your triad one bit.

Take a look at Figure 5-5 for some examples of major triad *accompaniments* (bass lines you play to support soloists). The simple structure of the major triad gives you enough notes to choose from to play some hip accompaniments.

You can hear the major triad and its subsequent accompaniments on Track 16 (Figures 5-4 and 5-5). The major triad is at 0:00; accompaniment (a) is at 0:11; accompaniment (b) is at 0:35; and accompaniment (c) is at 1:00. You can also see me playing triads in Video 6. Triads are a simple yet effective method to accompany a tune.

Minor triads

The *minor triad* comes from the minor scale. You construct the minor triad by playing the root, 3rd, and 5th notes of the minor scale, which translates into the root, ♭3, and 5. You can play any minor triad with no shifting of the left hand, and you start it with your index finger. Check out Figure 5-6 for the form of the minor triad.

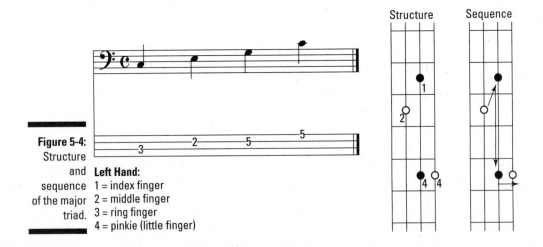

Figure 5-4:
Structure and sequence of the major triad.

Left Hand:
1 = index finger
2 = middle finger
3 = ring finger
4 = pinkie (little finger)

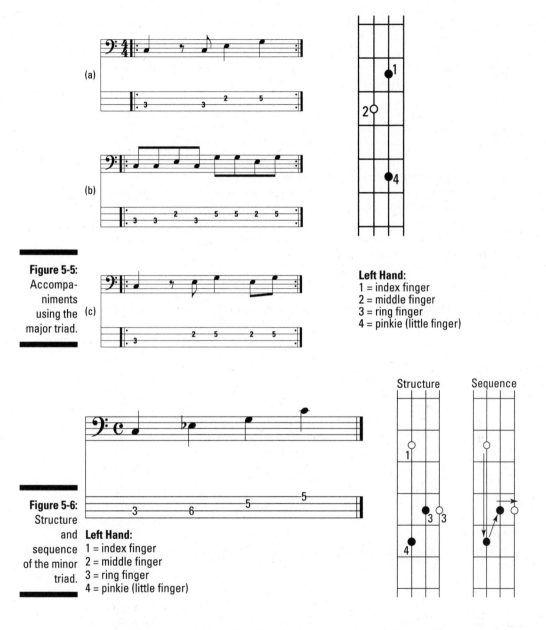

Figure 5-5:
Accompa-
niments
using the
major triad.

Left Hand:
1 = index finger
2 = middle finger
3 = ring finger
4 = pinkie (little finger)

Figure 5-6:
Structure
and
sequence
of the minor
triad.

Left Hand:
1 = index finger
2 = middle finger
3 = ring finger
4 = pinkie (little finger)

Like the major triad, the minor triad gives you plenty of notes to choose from for some cool accompaniments over minor tonalities. See Figure 5-7 for some examples.

You can play any of the notes in the grooves from Figures 5-5 and 5-7 in any key (not just in C), without changing the *shape* of the grooves (the pattern of the notes in relation to each other). For example, try starting on a different note, such as D (using the D as the root of the triad), when you play the note patterns shown on the grids in these figures.

You can hear the minor triad and accompaniments on Track 17 (Figures 5-6 and 5-7). The minor triad is at 0:00; accompaniment (a) is at 0:10; accompaniment (b) is at 0:34; and accompaniment (c) is at 0:59.

Applying the triad to a song

You may think the triad is a simple, unsophisticated device and certainly not the stuff of the big leagues. Well, think again. Just listen to Bruce Springsteen's song "Jersey Girl" or The Drifters' "Under The Boardwalk" or a number of other megahits, and you quickly realize that this seemingly unassuming device packs quite a punch.

Figure 5-7:
Accompa-
niments
using the
minor triad.

Left Hand:
1 = index finger
2 = middle finger
3 = ring finger
4 = pinkie (little finger)

On Track 18, you hear a song that has the bass laying down the triads as the perfect accompaniment. As you listen, follow along in Figure 5-8 (be sure to repeat the first line). All you have to do is get your fretting hand in position to play a major triad (starting with the middle finger on the root) or a minor triad (starting with the index finger on the root) as I've described earlier in this chapter. When you're comfortable with this, play the triads along with the song. Eventually, when you're familiar with the bass part, pan the music so you don't hear the bass and play the part along with the track. After that, it's only a matter of time before you can hang your own gold record on your wall.

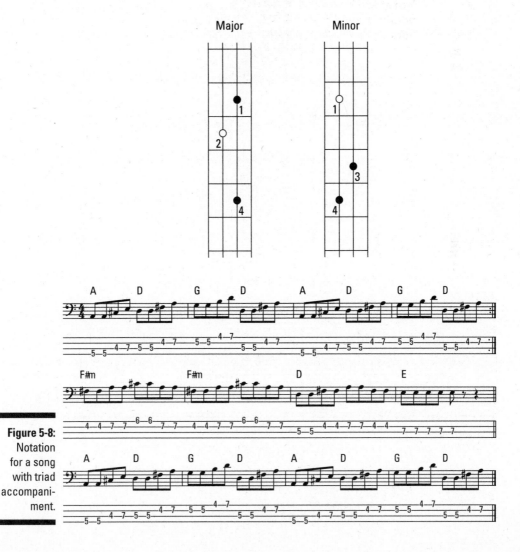

Figure 5-8: Notation for a song with triad accompaniment.

Augmented, diminished, and suspended chords

The most common chords by far are major and minor, and you're getting a good handle on them in this chapter, but every now and then you may run into one of three other kinds of triads: an *augmented chord* (marked with a plus sign next to the letter of the chord), a *diminished chord* (marked with a circle next to the letter of the chord), or a *suspended chord* (marked with a "sus" next to the letter of the chord). When you see one of these symbols, all you have to do is change one note in your triad and you're good to go. An augmented chord raises the 5th by

a half step and makes it an augmented 5th. A diminished chord lowers the 5th by a half step, making it a diminished 5th. A suspended chord, also called a *sus chord*, "suspends" the 3rd and you play the 4th instead.

The following figure gives you the shapes of all three chords. Just a piece of advice: Don't try to talk your way out of a mistake by claiming to be experimenting with "augminished chords." It won't work — I've tried.

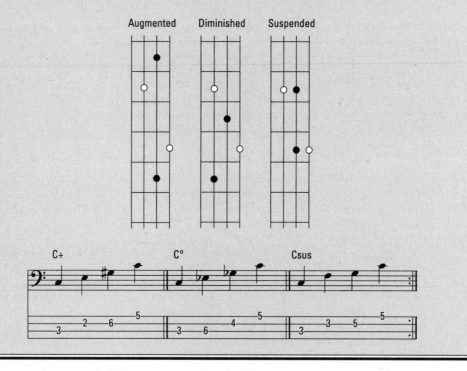

7th chords: Filling out the triad

The 7th chord has one more note than the triad: You guessed it, the 7. The sound of the 7th chord is a little more complex than the sound of a triad.

Contemporary music makes extensive use of the 7, and you frequently play the 7th chord in your accompaniments. As with triads, the 7th chord is based on a scale (usually the major or minor scale). You find the notes of any 7th chord by skipping every other note in the scale: You play the root, you skip the 2nd note, you play the 3rd, you skip the 4th, you play the 5th, you skip the 6th, and you play the 7th. The notes in any chord are called *chord tones*.

The four most commonly used 7th chords are the major, minor, dominant, and half-diminished chords. Table 5-1 gives you the structures of these four main 7th chords.

Table 5-1	The Main 7th Chord Structures
Chord Name	*Chord Tones*
Major	Root - 3 - 5 - 7
Dominant	Root - 3 - 5 - ♭7
Minor	Root - ♭3 - 5 - ♭7
Half-Diminished	Root - ♭3 - ♭5 - ♭7

In contemporary popular music, the term *dominant* refers to the tonality of the chord and not just to the function of that chord. A dominant chord is simply a major triad plus a flatted 7.

In Table 5-1, you see that the root, 3, and 5 follow either the basic major or basic minor structure. The *flatted 7* is what differentiates the dominant chord from the major chord. The *flatted 5* differentiates the half-diminished chord from the minor chord. Figure 5-9 shows the chords with their related scales.

Listen to Track 19 to hear what each chord with its appropriate scale sounds like. The notes of each chord overlap with the notes of the proper scale, as you see in Figure 5-9. The major 7th chord and Ionian mode is at 0:00; the minor 7th chord and Aeolian mode is at 0:11; the dominant chord and Mixolydian mode is at 0:24; the half-diminished chord and Locrian mode is at 0:35. Video 7 shows me playing 7th chords.

The word *scale* is interchangeable with the word *mode;* they both mean exactly the same thing.

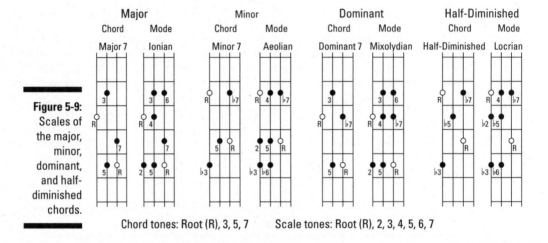

Figure 5-9: Scales of the major, minor, dominant, and half-diminished chords.

Chord tones: Root (R), 3, 5, 7   Scale tones: Root (R), 2, 3, 4, 5, 6, 7

Getting your kicks with boogie licks

So many notes, so little time. What can all these 7th chords and scales (modes) do for you? A lot! In this section, I show you a boogie bass line that's a great demonstration of how you can combine the chords and scales to create memorable sounds. This little ditty ought to be very familiar to you. Just listen to a tune like "In the Mood" and you recognize it right away.

You play the 7th chord, but in addition you add one note, the 6th of the scale. The bass line is root-3-5-6-♭7-6-5-3 in a dominant formation. (Look for the "Dominant" chord/mode combination in Figure 5-9.) You see? Just one little added note from the mode and your plain-old 7th chord is transformed into one of the most recognized bass lines on the planet.

Figure 5-10 gives you the structure of the bass line. You can get this boogie sound anywhere on your fingerboard without changing the structure (fingering).

Get your boogie boots on for Track 20. Here, you get to work out with a real honest-to-goodness boogie song. Start the pattern on the root that corresponds to the chart in Figure 5-10. First, listen closely to Track 20, and when you're ready, simply play along with the recording. Eventually, pan the bass out of the mix and be the *soul* provider — of the bass line, that is.

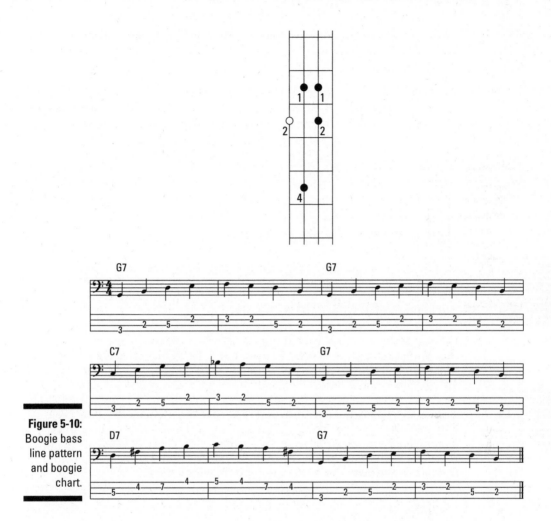

Figure 5-10: Boogie bass line pattern and boogie chart.

Inversions: Down Is Up, and Up Is Down

Sometimes you may want to begin playing a chord, such as a triad, on the 3rd or 5th, not the root. To do this, you need to be able to *invert* — to switch around the note order of your basic major and minor chords.

For example, to invert the C triad (C-E-G), instead of playing C-E-G, you can play the E first, the G second, and the C (the root) last, making it E-G-C. Or you can start on G, play C, and then play E, making it G-C-E. These switches are called *inversions*. You can play any of the inversions in this section without shifting your left hand.

Both the major chord inversions and the minor chord inversions appear on Track 21 in the order presented in the following two sections. And you can see me play the inversions in Video 8.

You use inversions rather than the regular chord to soften the impact of a chord change, making the chord progression smoother. Check out the advantages of inversions in Chapter 14 when you play with The Beatles' styles.

Never, ever lose track of your root. Everything you do as a bassist is based on the root. If you know where the root of a chord is, you can locate all the other notes related to it.

Major chord inversions

Here, I walk you through playing the inversions for the C major chord. You can use these same patterns for any major chord inversion. In these examples, I add the octave to the C major triad, so you play four notes — root, 3, 5, and octave (C-E-G-C) — rather than three.

Figure 5-11 shows you the major chord with C as the root, called the *root position*. In this chord, C is also in the *bass*. Here, the term *bass* refers to the note that sounds the lowest in any chord. Start with the C on the 8th fret of the E string, using your middle finger, and play the C major chord.

To play the 1st inversion chord, find the 3rd of the C major chord (it's the E on the 7th fret of the A string). Take a look at Figure 5-12, and play the C major chord starting with the 3rd in the bass. The chord is now E-G-C-E, with E being in the bass. C is still the root. Be sure to keep your hand in position by starting the inversion with your index finger on the E.

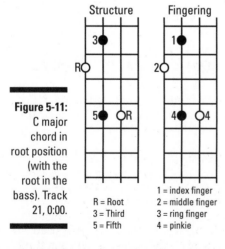

Figure 5-11: C major chord in root position (with the root in the bass). Track 21, 0:00.

R = Root
3 = Third
5 = Fifth

1 = index finger
2 = middle finger
3 = ring finger
4 = pinkie

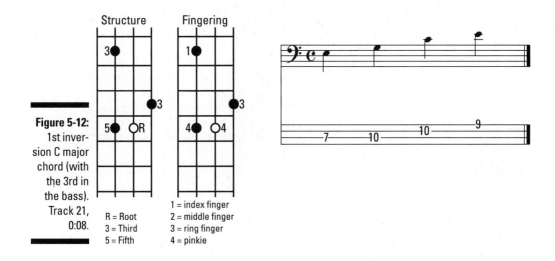

Figure 5-12: 1st inversion C major chord (with the 3rd in the bass). Track 21, 0:08.

Structure Fingering

R = Root
3 = Third
5 = Fifth

1 = index finger
2 = middle finger
3 = ring finger
4 = pinkie

For the 2nd inversion, find the 5th of C, which is G. You find the G on the 10th fret of the A string. G is now your starting note, but C is still the root of the chord you're playing. Follow the grid in Figure 5-13, and keep your hand in position, starting with your middle finger. The chord is now G-C-E-G.

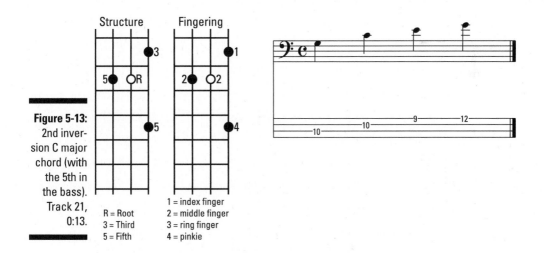

Figure 5-13: 2nd inversion C major chord (with the 5th in the bass). Track 21, 0:13.

Structure Fingering

R = Root
3 = Third
5 = Fifth

1 = index finger
2 = middle finger
3 = ring finger
4 = pinkie

Minor chord inversions

Minor chord inversions work on the same premise as the major chord inversions (see previous section). Here, I walk you through playing the inversions for the C minor chord. You can use these same patterns for any minor chord inversion. In these examples, I add the octave to the C minor triad, so you play four notes — root, ♭3, 5, and octave (C-E♭-G-C) — rather than three.

Figure 5-14 shows you the C minor chord with the root C in the bass, or root position. This chord is spelled C-E♭-G-C. Begin with the C on the 8th fret of the E string, and be sure to keep your hand in position.

To play the 1st inversion, find the 3rd of the C minor chord, the E♭. Position your middle finger on the E♭, which is on the 6th fret of the A string. Follow the grid in Figure 5-15, and play the C minor chord starting with the 3rd in the bass. The chord is now E♭-G-C-E♭. E♭ is in the bass, but C is still the root of the chord. No matter where you are or what chord you play, don't lose sight of your root.

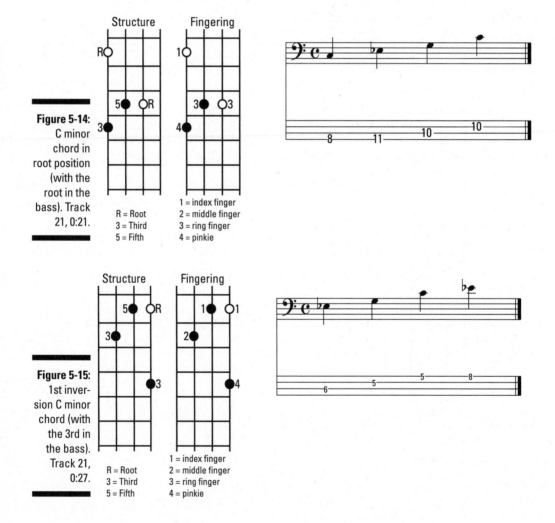

Figure 5-14: C minor chord in root position (with the root in the bass). Track 21, 0:21.

Figure 5-15: 1st inversion C minor chord (with the 3rd in the bass). Track 21, 0:27.

For the 2nd inversion, find the 5th of the C minor chord, the G. The G is on the 10th fret of the A string. Follow the grid in Figure 5-16, and keep your hand in position. Your chord is now G-C-Eb-G. G is in the bass, but C is still the root of the chord.

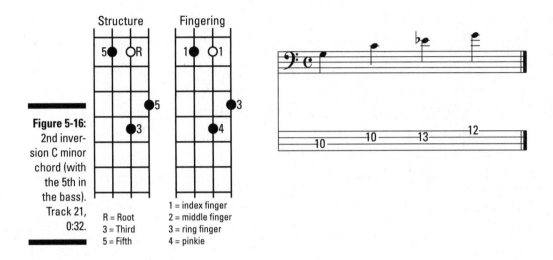

Figure 5-16: 2nd inversion C minor chord (with the 5th in the bass). Track 21, 0:32.

R = Root
3 = Third
5 = Fifth

1 = index finger
2 = middle finger
3 = ring finger
4 = pinkie

Spicing Up Your Sound: The Seven Main Modes (Scales)

More scales?! Don't panic. Four of them are from the previous section — the major, dominant, minor, and half-diminished scales — so playing three more is a piece of apple pie with ice cream. These new scales are closely related to the previous ones, and with all these scales at your fingertips, you get more choices in terms of flavor, or *color* (like different shades of blue, for example). Or you can think of it as starting with the same basic cooking recipe but adding different flavors (different sounds) to change it slightly.

In almost every song, one mode predominates. (*Mode* is simply a fancy word for scale.) When you play with other musicians, the first song may be primarily dominant, the next minor, and the next major. Know the mode you're in, and you'll be well on your way to providing great bass lines for any song.

Figure 5-17 shows the seven main modes and how they relate to the four main chords (major, minor, dominant, and half-diminished).

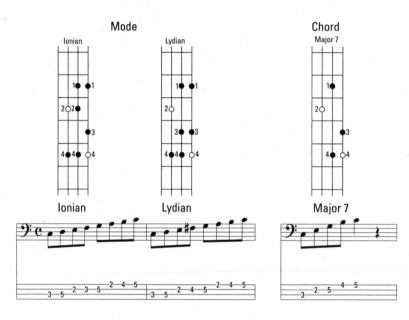

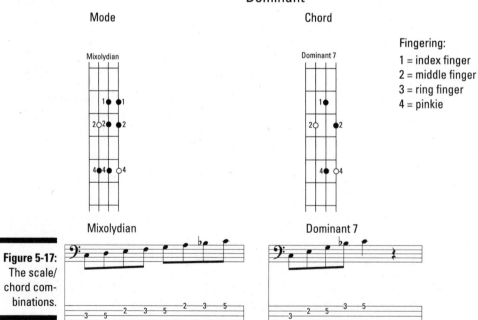

Figure 5-17:
The scale/
chord com-
binations.

Minor

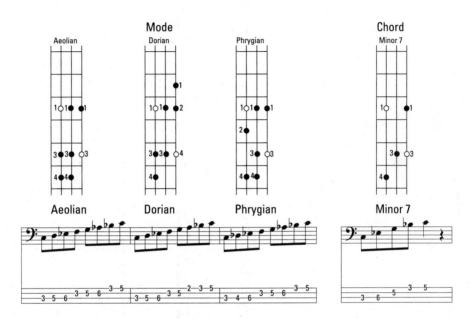

Half-Diminished

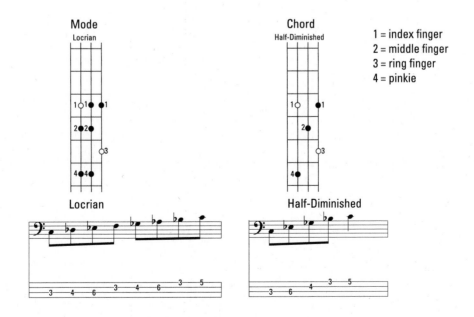

1 = index finger
2 = middle finger
3 = ring finger
4 = pinkie

On Track 22, you can hear all seven main scales in Figure 5-17 and also the chord they relate to. And you can see me play the scales in Video 9. Notice how the major and minor chords each have more than one possible matching scale.

You can see how the modes are related when you compare them to either the major or minor scale. Table 5-2 shows you how to adjust the major or minor scale to create each of the modes on the fingerboard. (See the nearby sidebar "The alpha and omega of the modes" for a detailed description of each of these modes.)

Table 5-2	The Mode Families
Mode	*Relation to Major or Minor Scale*
Ionian (major)	Major scale
Lydian	Major scale with sharp 4th
Mixolydian (dominant)	Major scale with flat 7th
Aeolian (natural minor)	Minor scale
Dorian	Minor scale with regular 6th
Phrygian	Minor scale with flat 2nd
Locrian (half-diminished)	Minor scale with flat 2nd and flat 5th

You can play each mode and its chord without shifting the left hand (in one position), with the exception of the Dorian mode. (In the case of the Dorian mode, you need to make a small, one-fret shift with your left hand to execute the mode.)

I refer to this position — playing without shifting the left hand — as the *box* because the notes fit into a boxlike pattern on the fingerboard (or look like a box on the grid). When you play a groove (see Chapter 6 for more on creating grooves), you want to keep the pattern within the box as much as possible so your playing is smooth and efficient. Practice each of these seven modes (scales) on your bass and listen carefully for the unique sound that each one produces.

The alpha and omega of the modes

The modes are easy to understand when you know their origin.

The C major scale (C, D, E, F, G, A, B, and C), which is also known as *C Ionian,* starts and ends on the 1 of the scale — the C. If you play the exact same C scale but start on its 2nd note (D), you end up with the *D Dorian mode* (D, E, F, G, A, B, C, and D). Even though D Dorian has the same notes as C Ionian, it sounds different — somewhat sad. A tune based on D Dorian also will sound sad.

If you start and end on the 3rd note of the C major scale (E), you end up with the *E Phrygian mode* (E, F, G, A, B, C, D, and E). You hear a sound that's different from the Ionian and Dorian modes, even though the notes are the same. It sounds somewhat exotic.

If you start and end on the 4th note of the C major scale (F), you get the *F Lydian mode* (F, G, A, B, C, D, E, and F). This mode produces a sound that's somewhat similar to the sound made by the Ionian mode — major and happy.

If you start and end on the 5th note of the C major scale (G), you get the *G Mixolydian mode*

(G, A, B, C, D, E, F, and G). This mode is the dominant scale.

If you start and end on the 6th note of the C major scale (A), you get the *A Aeolian mode* (A, B, C, D, E, F, G, and A), which also is your natural minor scale.

If you start and end on the 7th note of the C major scale (B), you get the *B Locrian mode* (B, C, D, E, F, G, A, and B), which produces a somewhat harsh sound.

As you can see, each mode starts on a different note of the C scale but uses the same notes. Also notice that each of these modes has its own triad and 7th chord — the 1, 3, 5, and also the 7 — and each chord sounds uniquely like the mode it's related to. For example, the 1, 3, 5, and 7 of C Ionian are C, E, G, and B — a major 7th chord. The 1, 3, 5, and 7 of D Dorian are D, F, A, and C — a minor 7th chord.

The common order of these modes is Ionian, Dorian, Phrygian, Lydian, Mixolydian, Aeolian, and Locrian. Sounds Greek to you, you say? Well, it actually is!

Most bass lines (the notes you use in accompanying a tune) are made up primarily of notes from the scales and chords in this section. Keep referring to Tables 5-1 and 5-2 and to Figure 5-17, because being familiar with the scale/chord combinations allows you to create great bass lines. See Part III for info on how to apply the scale/chord combinations when you're playing music.

Melodic and harmonic minor scales

The melodic and harmonic minor scales are special cases in the scale business. Both scales are a sort of hybrid of the minor and major tonalities. The *melodic minor scale* is a natural minor scale with a regular 7 instead of a ♭7 and a regular 6 instead of a ♭6 (see related figure). The *harmonic minor scale* is a natural minor scale with a regular 7 instead of a ♭7 (see related figure). You occasionally use the melodic and harmonic minor scales when playing melodies in a minor tonality. Both scales appear on Track 23. The melodic minor scale is at 0:00; the harmonic minor scale is at 0:09.

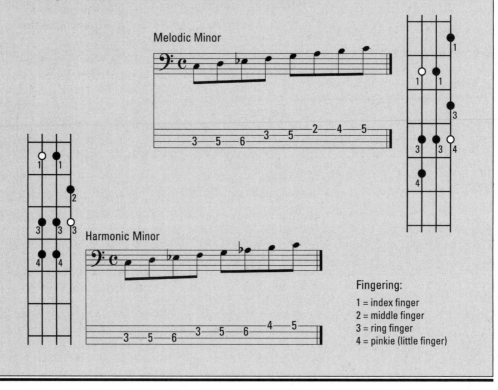

Fingering:

1 = index finger
2 = middle finger
3 = ring finger
4 = pinkie (little finger)

Using Chromatic Tones: All the Other Notes

When you play a bass line, you're not limited to the notes in the main modes; you can supplement them with notes outside the mode. The extra notes that fall within the box — the *chromatic tones* — are the most convenient notes for supplementing your modes.

Chromatic tones normally refer to any sequence of notes moving in half steps, either up or down, one fret at a time. For bass lines, however, chromatic tones refer to the notes outside the regular mode. These notes are a half step away from a scale tone. You play chromatic tones in passing to the stronger scale tones.

Chromatic tones within the box

Figure 5-18 shows a bass line in a major tonality using a chromatic tone. You don't need to shift your left hand to reach these chromatic notes, because they're in the box. You can use these notes as quick links to one of the chord tones (root, 3, 5, 7).

Figure 5-19 shows you a bass line in a minor tonality using a chromatic tone.

The chromatic tones in Figures 5-18 and 5-19 add a little tension to the bass lines — tension that's promptly released on the next note.

PLAY THIS!

You can check out and play along to both of these bass lines on Tracks 24 and 25. And see me play them in Video 10.

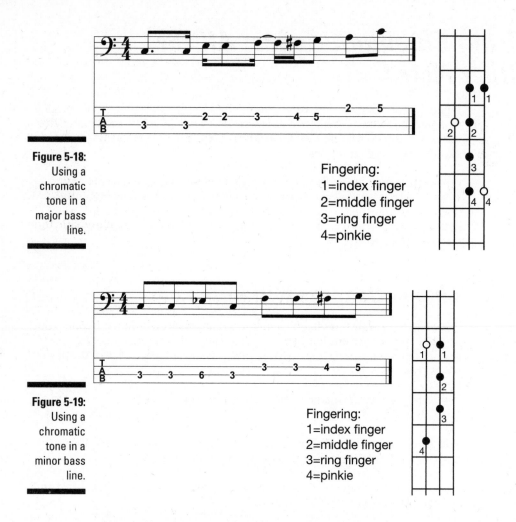

Figure 5-18:
Using a chromatic tone in a major bass line.

Fingering:
1=index finger
2=middle finger
3=ring finger
4=pinkie

Figure 5-19:
Using a chromatic tone in a minor bass line.

Fingering:
1=index finger
2=middle finger
3=ring finger
4=pinkie

Chromatic tones outside the box

Most songs, have a *shape,* or form. In other words, they have a certain way the melody moves up and down and repeats ideas, or phrases.

Tunes are arranged into measures and phrases; in the vast majority of cases, four measures equal a phrase (see Chapter 4 for details about how music is arranged). Just as horn players and singers pause at regular intervals to breathe, a tune also generally pauses between musical phrases. As the bassist, you're responsible for indicating the form of a tune to the other players. The notes you play tend to *set up* (lead to) the beginning of each new phrase, and you often can use chromatic tones to accomplish this.

You usually use chromatic tones that are inside the box to lead from one strong scale tone to the next, but you also may want to use chromatic tones that fall outside the box (which means you have to shift your left hand to reach them). Use them to lead to the chord tones (root, 3, 5, 7), which identify the tonality.

As you experiment with chromatic tones, make sure your overall tonality doesn't get obscured. You still want your sound to be recognizable as major or minor.

Figure 5-20 shows a bass line in a major tonality using a chromatic tone outside the box to lead to a strong chord tone (in this case, the 3 of the chord).

Figure 5-21 shows a bass line in a minor tonality that uses a chromatic tone outside the box.

Check out Tracks 26 and 27 to hear how the overall tonality in Figures 5-20 and 5-21 is preserved, despite the addition of chromatic tones outside the box. The chromatic tones serve to make the groove more interesting. You reach outside the scale temporarily to give the music tension, but then you resolve it (lead to a chord tone).

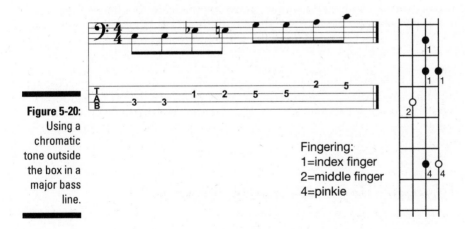

Figure 5-20:
Using a chromatic tone outside the box in a major bass line.

Fingering:
1=index finger
2=middle finger
4=pinkie

Figure 5-21:
Using a
chromatic
tone outside
the box in a
minor bass
line.

Fingering:
1=index finger
2=middle finger
3=ring finger
4=pinkie

Bringing a Groove to Life with Dead Notes (Weird but True)

You may need to enhance a simple groove rhythmically, but none of the notes, chromatic or modal (from the mode), seem to be quite right. You may feel that the bass line needs something more to really bring the music to life. Enter the dead note.

A *dead note* is a note that's heard as a thud without any pitch. It gives the rhythm some attitude. Dead notes are favorites among many contemporary bassists. Playing a dead note is a cool way to boost a rhythmic groove without getting into trouble by adding notes that may harmonically clash with the melody.

Playing dead — notes, that is

To play a dead note, rest two or more fingers from your left hand on a string. (Be sure not to press the string to the fingerboard, though.) Then strike that string with your right-hand index or middle finger. The result is a non-pitched thud. Figure 5-22 shows an example of a groove using dead notes, indicated by an "X." Notice how the second measure just keeps the rhythm going.

As you listen to the groove in Figure 5-22 on Track 28, be aware of the thud of the dead notes. Dead notes are completely devoid of pitch, but they sound as if they belong to the tonality. I demonstrate some dead note exercises in Video 11.

Figure 5-22:
Using dead notes in a groove.

Fingering:
1 = index finger
2 = middle finger
3 = ring finger
4 = pinkie (little finger)

Raking dead notes

Raking across the strings of your bass is a great, natural way to incorporate dead notes into your playing. *Raking* means striking a string with your right-hand index or middle finger and then striking the next lower (thicker) string with the same finger. You can rake across several strings with the same finger in one rake.

Here's how to play the dead note rake properly:

1. **Play the low note (the root) with your right-hand index finger.**

2. **Play the high note (the octave) with your right-hand middle finger.**

3. **Rake your right-hand middle finger across the string between the two notes (the root and the octave).**

   Mute the string you're crossing over by touching it lightly with at least two fingers of your left hand. (For more on muting, see Chapter 3.)

4. **Play the low note (the root) with your right-hand middle finger by raking across the low string.**

   You're now back at the beginning of the groove.

5. **Play the high note (the octave) with your right-hand index finger.**

6. **Rake your right-hand index finger across the string between the two notes (the root and the octave).**

   Mute the string you're crossing.

7. **Play the low note (the root) with your right-hand index finger.**

   You're once again at the beginning of the groove.

Figure 5-23 shows a groove, which doubles as an exercise, to help you use the dead note in conjunction with the rake.

On Track 29, listen to how smoothly the dead note connects the sounded notes in Figure 5-23. The groove sounds much busier than it really is. It's sort of like talkin' loud and sayin' nothin'. Listen to whether your groove matches the one on the recording.

This groove is a useful and cool one for your own groove repertoire. (For more on grooves, see Chapter 6.) As you practice, notice that your hand works only about a third as fast as your groove sounds. That's because you're using right-hand string crossing and dead notes. (I discuss proper string-crossing technique in Chapter 3.) Pretty powerful stuff, eh?

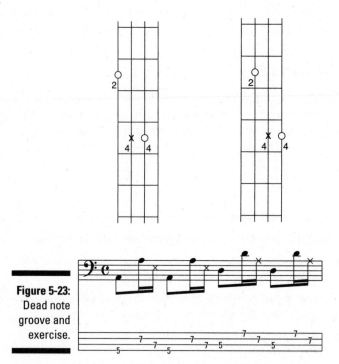

Figure 5-23:
Dead note
groove and
exercise.

Sampling Accompaniments

If you've read through the previous sections of this chapter, you may be feeling eager to put some of your newfound knowledge to good use. So strap on your bass and let me guide you through a few bass grooves.

The word *groove* is used in two ways in the bass world: It can refer to a *bass line,* which is the overall accompaniment to a tune, or it can refer to a *phrase* (usually one, two, or four measures long) that a bassist repeats throughout a tune to establish the rhythm and the harmony.

The following grooves are based on a chord tonality that is dominant (root, 3, 5, ♭7) and thus are related to the Mixolydian mode (root, 2, 3, 4, 5, 6, ♭7). The tonal center (or root) is the same for all these grooves, so you can compare one groove with the next. In each of the following examples, the basic groove uses the same chord.

When you embellish a simple groove with other chord and scale tones, chromatic tones, and dead notes, it develops into a much more interesting and intricate bass line.

Figure 5-24 shows a groove based solely on a chord — a triad (root, 3, 5). This groove isn't very interesting, but it does the job of outlining the harmony with some rhythm.

Figure 5-25 shows the groove with the 7 added to the triad. The ♭7 defines the groove as a definite dominant chord (1, 3, 5, ♭7).

Figure 5-26 shows the groove with the mode used in its entirety (root, 2, 3, 4, 5, 6, ♭7). The mode fills out the harmonic content of the groove. You're now solidly entrenched in the Mixolydian mode, and you have a solid box. Notice that in the box, your left hand doesn't have to shift.

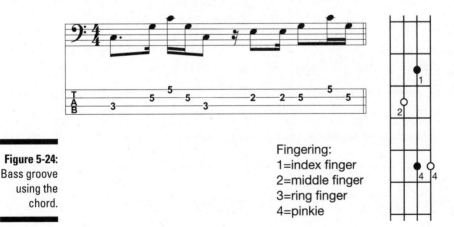

Figure 5-24:
Bass groove
using the
chord.

Fingering:
1=index finger
2=middle finger
3=ring finger
4=pinkie

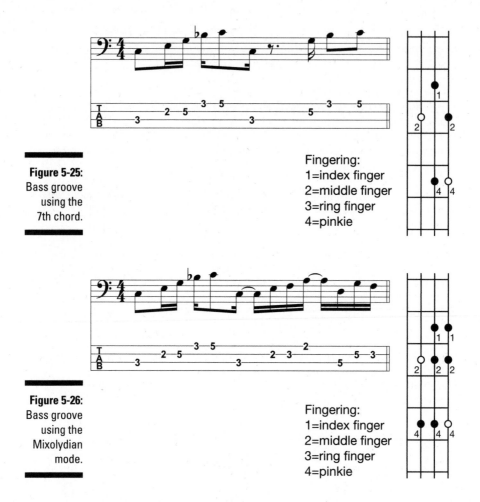

Figure 5-25:
Bass groove
using the
7th chord.

Fingering:
1=index finger
2=middle finger
3=ring finger
4=pinkie

Figure 5-26:
Bass groove
using the
Mixolydian
mode.

Fingering:
1=index finger
2=middle finger
3=ring finger
4=pinkie

Figure 5-27 shows the groove with some chromatic tones added, both inside and outside the box. This groove is definitely developing some flavor and attitude now. At the same time, the groove is getting a bit more difficult to play. Your left hand has to shift to play a chromatic tone outside the box.

Figure 5-28 shows the groove with dead notes added as a finishing touch. You get to play some dead notes to fill the space and solidify the rhythm. Compare this groove with the previous ones, and retrace the steps of adding each device.

Figure 5-27:
Bass groove using chromatic tones.

Fingering:
1=index finger
2=middle finger
3=ring finger
4=pinkie

Figure 5-28:
Bass groove using dead notes.

Fingering:
1=index finger
2=middle finger
3=ring finger
4=pinkie

You don't want to use all these devices in every groove, but you do want to have them close at hand so you can beef up a groove whenever you feel the urge to do so.

Check out Tracks 30–34 to hear all the grooves in Figures 5-24 through 5-28. And see me playing them in Video 12. Listen to how each groove gets a little bit more complex as you add more devices yet essentially retains its basic character in terms of tonality and rhythm.

Using your accompaniments in a tune

You can see how the grooves earlier in this section get more and more complex as you add scale tones, chromatic tones, and even dead notes to the basic chord tones. These souped-up grooves can be useful when you're jamming on a "one-chord wonder" with your band. If you're playing the same chord for a while and you feel like taking the groove to another level, try these devices to give the music some interesting variety while playing the same one-chord jam, thus keeping it interesting for the listeners as well as for the players.

A one-chord tune is pretty common when you're playing a jam with other musicians. But whatever you do, don't underestimate the power of the single-chord groove — just listen to how well James Brown does it.

On Track 35, you can hear a song based on a single chord, C7 in this case. Find a C on your fingerboard (the 3rd fret on the A string would be a great choice), and then get your hands comfortable with the scale for C7, or C Mixolydian. (You can read more about which scales go with which chords earlier in this chapter.) Unless you're jamming with a bunch of A-type personalities, you're not very likely to get sheet music for a one-chord jam. Usually, the bandleader just says, "Let's jam in C."

The deal with Dorian

In traditional music, the most common minor scale (or mode) is the Aeolian mode, also known as the *natural minor*. With the advent of funk and groove contemporary music, the Aeolian mode has been gradually replaced with the edgier Dorian mode. These days, when a groove is called for and the harmony is minor, the mode of choice is Dorian rather than Aeolian.

As you're playing along with Track 35, play any of the grooves in Figures 5-24 through 5-28. You can either stick with the same groove for the entire song or you can try building the complexity of your groove by playing one of the grooves for a while (Figure 5-24, for example), switching to another (perhaps Figure 5-27), and so on.

On the audio track, you hear the bass play each groove for two or four bars and then move on to the next groove in succession. Listen to how the same chord takes on a whole new character with each new groove.

Keeping your groove gloriously ambiguous

What happens if your bandleader calls for a jam in C, but you're not entirely sure what *kind* of C is expected? (After all, you have an arsenal of chords and modes to choose from.) This is a great opportunity to get into *harmonic ambiguity*. Harmonic ambiguity means that you choose to play notes in your groove that don't define a chord type. These ambiguous notes are shared by almost all modes, and you can use any of them no matter what tonality you play in, especially in a one-chord groove jam.

As a general rule, your one-chord groove is almost always based on either a dominant (Mixolydian mode) or a minor (Dorian mode) tonality. Out of seven different notes of the modes, these two tonalities share — ready for some serious ambiguity? — six! Whew! Who'd have thought? This is great! In order to play all kinds of different grooves and keep them ambiguous, all you have to do is avoid one note — the 3, both minor and major. (For a look at the 3, check out the intervals in Chapter 2.) Everything else matches just fine and funky.

Take a look at Figure 5-29 for a comparison of the Mixolydian and the Dorian modes. The 3 (which is the third note) of each mode is marked with an "X" rather than a dot so you remember not to play it.

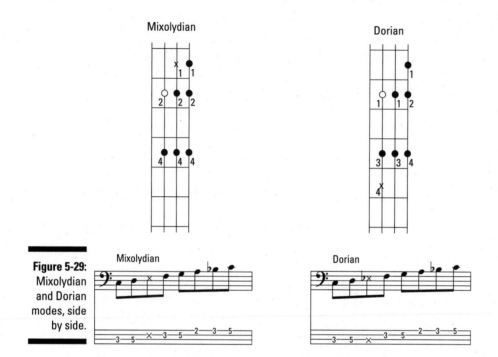

Figure 5-29:
Mixolydian
and Dorian
modes, side
by side.

Figure 5-30 shows some possible *harmonically ambiguous* grooves.
(What a mouthful! I'd *love* to see the face of your guitar player the first time
you use *that* term in rehearsal.) Familiarize yourself with these grooves, and
try coming up with some of your own, using the same structure.

Play your grooves along with Track 36, in which the harmony shifts between
dominant and minor over the same root, a C in this case. Listen to how the bass
part fits really well over both harmonies. It's almost like a comfortable sweat
suit — one size, er, harmony fits all. On this track, (a) is at 0:00, (b) is at 0:10,
(c) is at 0:23, (d) is at 0:35, and (e) is at 0:50.

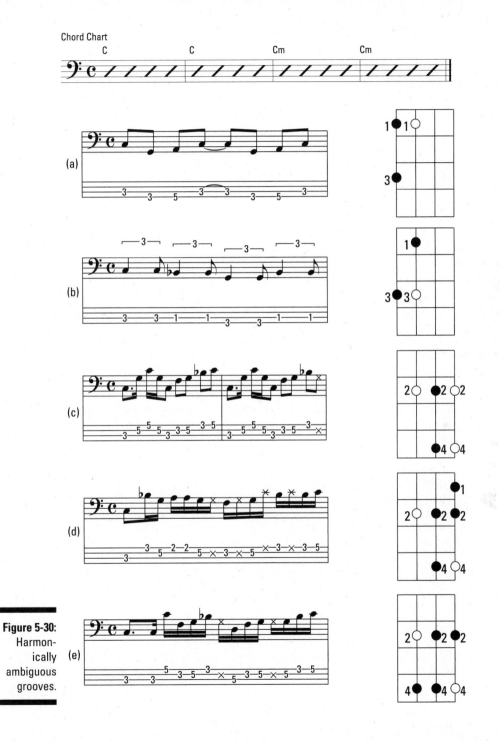

Figure 5-30: Harmonically ambiguous grooves.

Part III
Making the Moves, Creating the Grooves

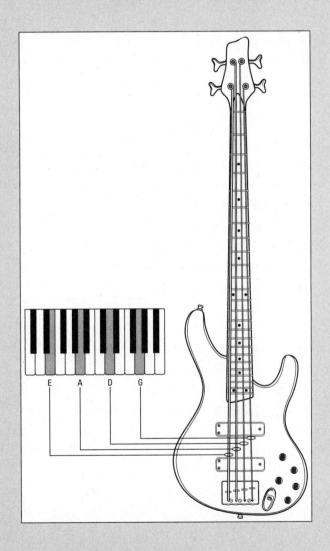

Visit www.dummies.com/extras/bassguitar for an article on bass grooves.

In this part...

- Dissect and assemble all the elements of a great bass groove.
- Create your very own bass groove.
- Tap into your creativity while playing bass.
- Gather the tools for soloing.
- Discover all about creating fabulous fills.

Chapter 6

Creating the Groove

● ●

In This Chapter

▶ Analyzing the elements of a groove

▶ Creating a groove of your very own

▶ Building grooves with a drummer

▶ Grooving with other musicians

▶ Changing up existing grooves

▶ Access the audio tracks and video clips at www.dummies.com/go/bassguitar

● ●

*W*hat do rock, funk, blues, reggae, and all the other musical styles have in common? Each one has its own distinctive groove. A *groove* is a short musical phrase made up of notes from chords and scales that a bassist plays repeatedly throughout a tune. Grooves establish the rhythm and harmony for the band and the listener. Knowing how to create grooves in different styles is absolutely essential for a bass player — and it's a lot of fun.

This chapter introduces you to the wonderful world of grooves. To get the most out of the chapter, you need to have a handle on two vital concepts. Hmmm, if the groove establishes rhythm and harmony, could those two vital concepts be . . . rhythm . . . and harmony? Yes! Rhythm gets the audience snapping their fingers, and harmony sends them home singing. (You can find out more about rhythm in Chapter 4 and harmony in Chapter 5.) Are you ready? Then get into the groove!

Anatomy of a Groove: Putting Together the Necessary Elements

A good groove can make you tap your feet, bob your head, and snap your fingers. You can move the same groove from chord to chord in a tune without changing the basic phrase. Sounds wimpy, you say? Actually, grooves are anything but wimpy. One of my teachers (a long, long time ago) told me something I'll never forget: "With the right groove, a good bassist alone can move a whole roomful of people." A groove is constructed of several elements, and you can use these different elements to create your own earth-shaking grooves. To get started, check out the guidelines in this section.

Getting your groove skeleton out of the closet

The first two notes of any groove are what I refer to as the *groove skeleton*. A groove can contain other notes besides the groove skeleton, but these first two notes are the most important because they establish the root of the chord, the pulse or tempo for the tune, and the feel of the rhythm:

- **The root of the chord:** You usually play the root as the first note of your groove. The root of any chord (or scale) is the most important note in that chord — it's the note your ear gravitates toward (the most satisfying note). The second note, or the other half of the groove skeleton, is usually a chord tone (root, 3, 5, or 7) that further defines the chord. With these two notes, you give the listener a good idea of the harmony in a tune. Check out the chord tones for each *tonality* (sound) in Chapter 5.

- **The pulse (tempo) of the tune:** Music has a certain pulse. The *pulse* is the speed at which you count the beats in a measure (1-2-3-4) — the speed at which you tap your feet in time with a tune. The pulse can be fast, slow, or something in between. The time that elapses between the first and second notes of the groove skeleton establishes the pulse for the groove and for the song. It tells the listener how fast the music is.

- **The feel of the rhythm:** You can divide a beat only so many ways: into quarters, eighths, sixteenths, or triplets. No, I'm not referring to babies. *Triplets* divide a beat into three equal parts. (See Chapter 4 for more on rhythm.) When you choose the division of the beat for your groove skeleton, you signal the feel of the groove and song to the listener, whether it's funk, Latin, or rock. The feel has nothing to do with tempo (see the previous bullet). For example, a Latin song can go at a fast tempo or at a leisurely pace. On the other hand, different feels can be applied to the same tempo. A *feel* can give the listener a sense of urgency or a sense of laziness in a tune, all without changing the overall tempo of the music. Figure 6-1 shows how the groove skeleton creates different feels.

(a)

(b)

(c)

(d)

(e)

(f)

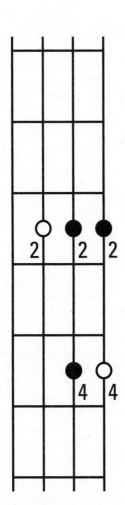

Fingering:
1 = index finger
2 = middle finger
3 = ring finger
4 = pinkie

Figure 6-1:
Six grooves
with differ-
ent groove
skeletons.

As you listen to the grooves from Figure 6-1 on Track 37 (also Video 13), tap your feet in tempo. At the beginning of the audio track, you can hear the count-off, which establishes the tempo. Groove (a) is at 0:00, (b) is at 0:15, (c) is at 0:30, (d) is at 0:33, (e) is at 1:00, and (f) is at 1:15. Notice how the tempo for all six of these grooves remains the same. Also notice that all six grooves use exactly the same notes. Even so, as you listen to them, pay special attention to how very different they are from one other. Each groove has its own unique characteristics, created simply by slight changes in the rhythm of the two notes in the groove skeleton. This variation shows the power of the groove skeleton: If you change the groove skeleton and leave everything else exactly the same, you still end up with a completely new groove. In this audio track, the groove skeleton is the only thing that changes from groove to groove.

Playing a song using only the groove skeleton

How important is the groove skeleton? It's so important that you can accompany an entire song on your bass using solely (or is it "soul-ly"?) the groove skeleton. Doing so isn't just an arbitrary exercise, either. It's a perfectly legitimate and successful method of playing bass on a song.

Need proof? Just listen to the hit "Stand by Me," one of the top rock 'n' roll hits of all time. And plenty of modern dance hits operate on the same premise of using just the groove skeleton alone on the bass with little else.

When you're learning a new tune, starting with just the groove skeleton is a great way to get to know its harmonic structure — the movement of the roots of the chords — without having to worry about playing a complex groove on each one of those chords. You can always add notes to the groove later as you become more familiar with it.

On Track 38, you can hear a song that's accompanied by only the groove skeleton. Figure 6-2 shows the harmony of the song. To play it with the audio track, all you need to do is find the roots of the chords on your bass neck and play the groove skeleton for each root. Are you comfortable playing along with the bass on the audio track? If so, pan it out and be the only bass.

Player beware! Space is the most difficult thing to play, and if you're playing only the two notes of the groove skeleton, you have plenty of space to contend with for the remainder of the measure. (For more on measures, also called *bars*, see Chapter 4.)

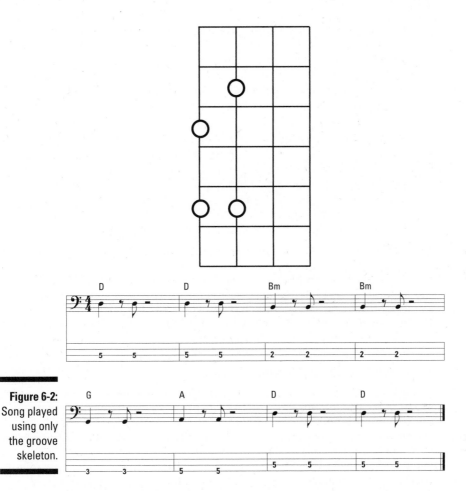

Choosing the right notes for a groove

Playing grooves is an elusive art form. I remember when I came out of school
I could only copy other people's grooves. I didn't have a clue about how to
create my own. Finally, after years of research and analysis, I discovered what
makes a groove . . . *groove*. Yes, there's a method to the madness, and a science to the art.

A few basic guidelines

The following list gives you a few basic guidelines to remember when you're
creating any groove:

✔ **Choose notes from the appropriate scale for the chord.** Almost every tune has its own unique set of chords that accompany the music. The notes you choose when playing it need to come from the scales and chords particular to that tune. If your groove doesn't match harmonically with what's going on in the music, it's no longer music; it's noise. You can check out Chapter 5 to see which scales go with which chords.

✔ **Settle on a finger position.** Try to choose notes for your groove that fit into a *box* (a pattern of notes on your fingerboard that requires no, or very little, shifting with your left hand; see Chapter 5 for more info). The less you shift your left hand, the easier it is to play the groove. You may think that sliding all over your fingerboard looks cool, but the best bassists tend to hold one position for as long as possible. Your hand gets used to a certain sequence, and you don't even have to think about playing the groove (after you've practiced it enough, of course).

✔ **Make your groove mobile.** Some tunes consist of only one underlying tonality throughout, so you don't have to move your groove around (just listen to some James Brown tunes). In most tunes, however, the chords change as the tune proceeds, which means you have to move your groove to match the chord changes within the tune. With this type of tune, you need to make sure you pick a group of notes that are simple to execute when you move from chord to chord.

Ranking the best and leaving the rest

The list in the preceding section gives you a general idea of what to consider when creating a groove. Now, I want to give you some guidelines in choosing the best notes to incorporate into your groove. The three most commonly used scales in a groove are the major, minor, and dominant scales. Chords are made up of the root, the 3, the 5, and sometimes the 7 of the scale they're related to. Check out Figure 6-3 for the structure of the major (Ionian), minor (Dorian), and dominant (Mixolydian) scales. Take a look at Chapter 5 for more on these scales.

Not all notes are created equal. Certain notes in a scale sound better in a groove than others. The following notes are the prime choices for your grooves (listed in order of importance):

✔ **Root:** There's no question about it; you have to know the root of each chord in the tune. The root identifies the sound of the chord for your band and for the listener. For example, a D minor chord has D as the root; an E dominant chord has E as the root. The root is the most important note in a chord. Your band counts on you to define the sound of each chord for them. That's why bassists play the root as the first note almost every time the chord changes; so be sure to play that root with authority.

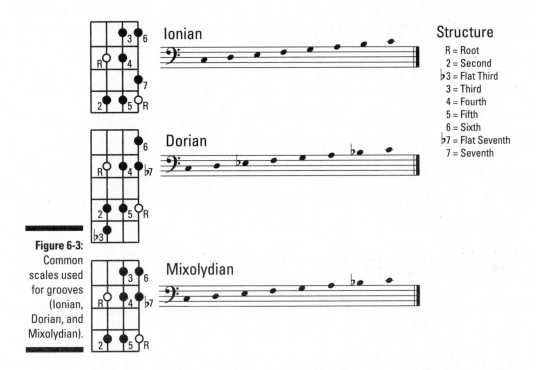

Ionian

Dorian

Mixolydian

Structure

R = Root
2 = Second
♭3 = Flat Third
3 = Third
4 = Fourth
5 = Fifth
6 = Sixth
♭7 = Flat Seventh
7 = Seventh

Figure 6-3:
Common scales used for grooves (Ionian, Dorian, and Mixolydian).

✔ **5th:** The 5 reinforces the root, and it's fairly neutral (it fits over any major, minor, or dominant chord). The interval (distance) between the root and the 5 is the same for major, minor, and dominant chords. If you have a lot of chord changes between major, minor, and dominant in a tune, the root and 5 combination is the perfect choice for your groove notes.

✔ **3rd:** The 3 identifies the chord as either major or minor. Choosing the 3 also forces you to settle on a hand position. If the chord is major and therefore requires a major 3, start your groove with your middle finger on the root to reach all the notes in the scale for that chord without shifting. If the chord is minor and therefore requires a minor 3 (♭3), start the groove with your index finger on the root. (Check out the fingering of the scales in Chapter 5 for more info.)

✔ **7th:** The 7 is another excellent choice for a groove, especially if the chord is minor or dominant. Both minor and dominant chords have a ♭7. If the chord is major, the 7 is commonly substituted with the 6 because it's just a more pleasant sound.

✔ **4th:** The 4 is a great note to play as a *passing note* (an unstressed note that you play on your way to the next important note). A passing note adds a little spice to the groove (it gives the groove an interesting sound). Just be careful not to emphasize a passing note, because doing so tends to obscure the chord. (However, keep in mind that an emphasized passing note makes a good choice if you intend to play an ambiguous groove, as I explain in Chapter 5).

✔ **6th:** The 6 is a good choice to play as a *neutral note*. In other words, no matter what your chord is, the 6 will generally fit. As with the 4, you don't want to emphasize it too strongly, though. Using the 6 as a passing note is ideal. Passing notes are used to smooth the passage from one strong note to the next.

✔ **2nd:** The 2 isn't exactly a terrific choice to include in your groove. It's too close to the root (only two frets away), so it clashes, and it doesn't give your bass line enough variety. However, the 2 can work as a passing note.

Creating Your Own Groove

With a little help from your friend (that's me!), you can create your own groove. The process that goes on in your head each time you create a groove for a tune is the same, no matter what kind of chord you're playing (major, minor, or dominant).

If you haven't already looked at the section "Choosing the right notes for a groove," earlier in this chapter, you may want to now to familiarize yourself with the important decisions you need to make *before* creating a groove.

Covering the "basses": Creating dominant, minor, and major grooves

The process in preparing to play any groove is the same, but you need to make a few adjustments to accommodate your groove to each kind of chord: dominant, minor, and major (see Chapter 5). Read on for some help in creating some unforgettable grooves.

The dominant groove

Imagine that you're getting together with a bunch of other musicians to play some music. The guy in charge says, "Let's jam in D7." (He's talking about playing in D dominant.) Don't panic. The following list gives you some guidelines for determining what notes to play during a D7 jam. Figure 6-4 shows you the process.

Root

(a)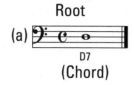

D7
(Chord)

Groove Skeleton Choices

(b)

Structure

(c)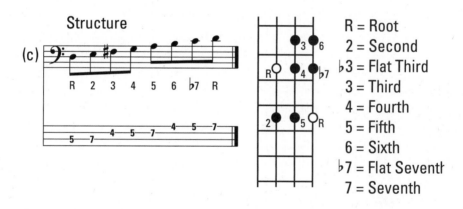

R = Root
2 = Second
♭3 = Flat Third
3 = Third
4 = Fourth
5 = Fifth
6 = Sixth
♭7 = Flat Seventh
7 = Seventh

Fingering

(d)

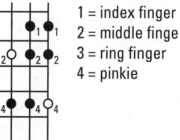

1 = index finger
2 = middle finge
3 = ring finger
4 = pinkie

Figure 6-4:
Creating
a groove
for D7 (D
dominant).

1. **Determine the root of the chord.**

   In this case, the chord is D7, so the root of the chord is D (see Figure 6-4a).

2. **Decide what kind of groove skeleton you want to play.**

   Figure 6-4b shows your basic choices. This groove example uses two eighth notes, but feel free to experiment with the other possibilities. In fact, let your ear decide which rhythm sounds best for the given situation. (For more on the groove skeleton, see "Getting your groove skeleton out of your closet," earlier in this chapter.)

3. **Choose the appropriate scale for the chord.**

   For the D7 chord groove in this example, the proper scale is D Mixolydian (see Figure 6-4c). Chapter 5 can help you find which scale goes with which chord.

   To play the D Mixolydian scale, start the scale on the 5th fret of the A string and end on the 7th fret of the G string. Choose the notes for your groove from this scale. You can pick the choice notes (see "Ranking the best and leaving the rest," earlier in this chapter, for details) from the intervals marked in Figure 6-4c. My choices are the root, 5, and ♭7 for the simple groove, and the root, 3, 4, 5, and ♭7 for the complex groove (see Figure 6-5).

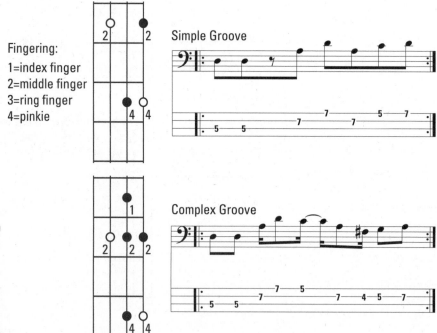

Fingering:
1=index finger
2=middle finger
3=ring finger
4=pinkie

Figure 6-5:
A simple groove and a complex groove for D7.

4. **Position your left hand.**

   You want to play the groove with the least amount of effort, so you need to avoid any unnecessary shifting with your left hand. Start the D Mixolydian scale with the middle finger of your left hand on the root D (5th fret of the A string). You can reach all the notes of the scale from this position without moving your left hand. Refer to Figure 6-4d for the fingering for this scale.

5. **Determine how mobile your groove needs to be.**

   If the tune has different chords (if the roots change), your groove has to be *mobile,* moveable from chord to chord. In this case, you need to make your groove simple. Choose only a few notes and make them easy to play.

   However, if you stay on one chord for a while (which is the likely scenario if someone wants to jam in D7), you can make your groove a bit more complex to keep it interesting. Refer to Figure 6-5 for both a simple and a complex version of the same groove.

6. **Enjoy playing your groove.**

   You read correctly. Have fun! Whatever groove you come up with, make it meaningful. Jamming isn't work — it's play!

On Track 39, you can listen to the steps necessary when creating a dominant groove. And you can see me play the grooves in Video 14. First, you hear the D7 chord played on the keyboard, with the bass playing just the root. Then you hear the bass playing different groove skeletons on the root of the D7 chord. Next is the sound of the Mixolydian mode, the correct scale for D7. Finally, you hear a simple groove in D7, followed by a complex groove in D7. As you listen, follow the process in Figures 6-4 and 6-5.

The minor groove

You're playing with the band, jamming on a dominant groove . . . but wait . . . what if the guy in charge yells, very enthusiastically, "Let's jam in D *minor!*" Uh, oh . . . a minor adjustment is in order. Relax. Figure 6-6 shows you the process.

Root

(a)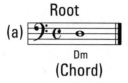

Dm
(Chord)

Groove Skeleton Choices

(b)

Structure

(c)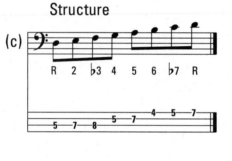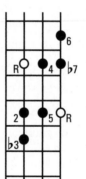

R = Root
2 = Second
♭3 = Flat Third
3 = Third
4 = Fourth
5 = Fifth
6 = Sixth
♭7 = Flat Seventh
7 = Seventh

Fingering

(d)

1 = index finger
2 = middle finger
3 = ring finger
4 = pinkie

Figure 6-6:
Creating a
groove for D
minor.

1. **Determine the root of the chord.**

   In this case, the chord is D minor (Dm or Dm7), so the root of the chord is D (see Figure 6-6a).

2. **Decide what kind of groove skeleton you want to play.**

   I show you the basic choices in Figure 6-6b. My choice is the dotted eighth and sixteenth notes as the groove skeleton, but you can experiment with the other possibilities.

3. **Choose the appropriate scale for the chord.**

   For the D minor chord in this example, the proper scale is D Dorian (see Figure 6-6c). For more info about the D Dorian scale, see Chapter 5.

   To play the D Dorian scale, start the scale on the 5th fret of the A string and end it on the 7th fret of the G string. Choose the notes for your groove from this scale. You can pick the choice notes from the intervals marked in Figure 6-6c. My choices are the root, 5, and ♭7 for the simple groove, and the root, ♭3, 4, 5, and ♭7 for the complex groove (see Figure 6-7).

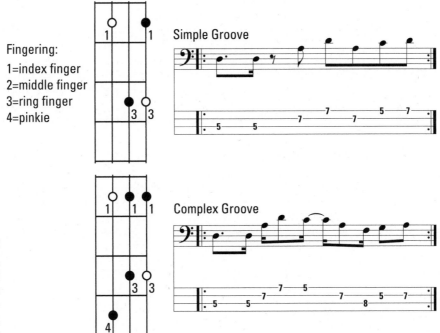

Fingering:
1=index finger
2=middle finger
3=ring finger
4=pinkie

Simple Groove

Complex Groove

Figure 6-7: A simple and a complex groove for D minor.

4. **Position your left hand.**

You want to avoid any unnecessary shifts with your left hand. The D Dorian scale requires one (itty, bitty) shift, however, so it's best to begin the D Dorian scale with the index finger of your left hand on the root D (5th fret of the A string). You can reach all the notes of the scale from this position until you get to the G string. At that point, you need to shift your hand toward the nut by one fret to reach the remaining three notes. Check out Figure 6-6d on how to finger this scale.

5. **Determine how mobile your groove needs to be.**

Your groove has to be mobile if the tune has different chords. In this case, be sure to create a groove that's simple. Choose only a few notes that are easy to play. Even though the D Dorian scale requires you to shift your hand, you don't have to play every single note in that scale. You may decide to choose only the notes of the scale that you can reach from one position (without shifting).

If you stay on one chord for a while (which is the likely scenario if someone wants to jam in D minor), you can make your groove a bit more complex to keep it interesting. Figure 6-7 shows both a simple and a complex version of the same groove. Notice that neither of the two grooves requires any shifting with the left hand.

On Track 40, check out the steps necessary when creating a minor groove. First, the D minor chord is played on the keyboard, with the bass adding the root. Next, different groove skeletons are played on the root of the chord. Then you can hear the sound of the Dorian mode, the correct scale for D minor. Finally, you can listen to a simple groove in D minor, followed by a complex groove in D minor. Follow this process along in Figures 6-6 and 6-7.

The major groove

Say you're jamming away with the band on a minor groove when all of a sudden the guy in charge yells (with uninhibited enthusiasm), "Let's jam in D major!" Hmmm, does he really mean *major?* Here's the way to respond to that enthusiasm. Figure 6-8 shows you the process.

Root

(a)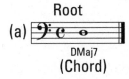

DMaj7
(Chord)

Groove Skeleton Choices

(b)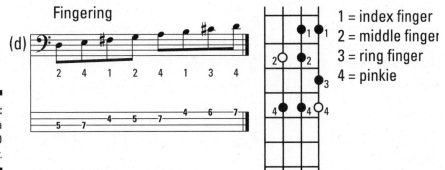

Structure

(c)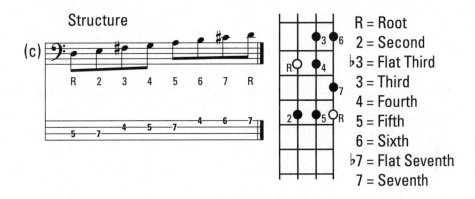

R = Root
2 = Second
♭3 = Flat Third
3 = Third
4 = Fourth
5 = Fifth
6 = Sixth
♭7 = Flat Seventh
7 = Seventh

Fingering

(d)

1 = index finger
2 = middle finger
3 = ring finger
4 = pinkie

Figure 6-8:
Creating a
groove for D
major.

1. **Determine the root of the chord.**

   In this case, the chord is D major (DMaj or DMaj7), so the root of the chord is D (see Figure 6-8a).

2. **Decide what kind of groove skeleton you want to play.**

   Figure 6-8b shows the basic choices. I chose the two sixteenth notes as the groove skeleton, but you can experiment with the other possibilities as well.

3. **Choose the appropriate scale for the chord.**

   For the D major chord in this example, the proper scale is D Ionian (see Figure 6-8c). You can find more info on the Ionian scale in Chapter 5.

   To play the D Ionian scale, you start the scale on the 5th fret of the A string and end it on the 7th fret of the G string. Choose the notes for your groove from this scale. You can pick the choice notes from the intervals marked in Figure 6-8c. My choice is the root, 5, and 6 for the simple groove, and the root, 3, 4, 5, and 6 for the complex groove (see Figure 6-9).

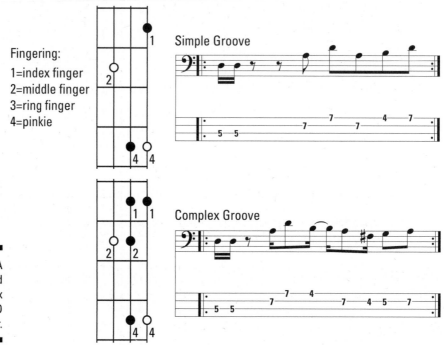

Fingering:
1=index finger
2=middle finger
3=ring finger
4=pinkie

Simple Groove

Complex Groove

Figure 6-9: A simple and a complex groove for D major.

4. **Position your left hand.**

   You want to avoid any unnecessary shifting with your left hand. So start the D Ionian scale with the middle finger of your left hand on the D (5th fret of the A string), which is the root. You can reach all the notes of the scale from this position without moving your left hand. You can refer to Figure 6-8d for the fingering for this scale.

5. **Decide how mobile your groove needs to be.**

   If the tune has different chords — if the roots change — your groove has to be mobile (moveable from chord to chord), so the groove you create needs to be a simple one. Use only a few notes and make them easy to play.

   If you stay on one chord for a while, you can make your groove a bit more complex to keep it interesting. You can see both a simple and a complex version of the same groove in Figure 6-9.

In the case of the major chord, you have to consider one more thing when choosing the notes for the groove: The 7 of the Ionian scale doesn't sound all that great in a groove format, so avoid it if you can. Choose the 6 instead; the 6 is usually a great choice, but let your own ears decide what's right.

On Track 41, check out the steps necessary for creating a major groove. First, the D major chord is played on the keyboard, with the bass adding the root. Next, different groove skeletons are played on the root of the chord. Then you hear the sound of the Ionian mode, the correct scale for D major. Finally, listen to a simple groove in D major, followed by a complex groove in D major. Notice how the 6 of the mode is played in the groove rather than the 7. Follow this process in Figures 6-8 and 6-9.

Waggin' the groove tail

You can find a tail at the end — the end of a puppy, the end of a horse, and the end of a groove. Alerting your fellow band members that the next groove is coming up with a *groove tail,* or the back end of a groove, is essential to keeping everyone harmonically and rhythmically aligned.

The *groove tail* occurs in the last beat or two before the end of the groove, and its sole purpose is to lead to the next groove, whether it's a repeat of the current one or a brand new one. A groove tail is a bit of a free radical; it doesn't have to be part of either the old or the new groove's harmony, and it can use notes that aren't part of the scale of either groove. This causes momentary tension, but tension and release are the name of the game. The groove tail leads into the next groove pattern, which releases the tension built up by the groove tail.

No hard and fast rules exist for how to use the groove tail. You kind of put your own stamp on your style of playing, depending on how you use it. Be creative and remember to keep the first part of the groove consistent.

Check out some examples of the groove tail in Figure 6-10. Listen to Track 42 or see Video 15 to appreciate how the groove is consistent in the first part and then different in the second part. It still sounds like the same groove, but it has a bit of an unexpected element in it now, which keeps things interesting. However, despite the different groove tails, there's never a doubt where the groove starts — and that's the point. Oh, and by the way, playing nothing at the end of the groove can be a very cool groove tail as well. Never underestimate the power of silence.

Figure 6-10:
Creating a
groove tail.

Movin' and groovin' from chord to chord

Imagine that you're jamming on D7, D minor, and D major (all three are covered in the previous section), and the grooves are just cascading off your fingers. The whole room is positively rocking. In fact, things are going so well that the leader of this musical extravaganza decides to surprise you by handing out *chord charts* (pages of musical notation) of a tune he or she wrote the previous week.

The chords of the tune move all over the place and change between major, minor, and dominant more frequently than your lead-footed cousin Jimmy changes lanes on a four-lane highway. Should you tremble? Absolutely not. Just take a look at the chord chart in Figure 6-11 and find out where the roots are located. Using the concepts from the previous sections, you can come up with a simple groove that you can move easily from chord to chord. All you have to do is set up your groove skeleton, embellish it by adding the proper notes, and then create a groove tail that helps you move the groove from one chord to the next.

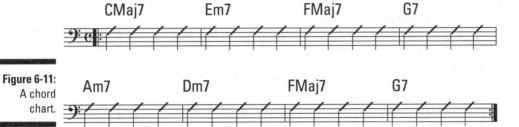

Figure 6-11: A chord chart.

Using constant structure

Using constant structure is one way to move a groove easily between chords with different tonalities (major, minor, and dominant). *Constant structure* refers to a group of notes in a groove that can be moved from chord to chord, regardless of whether the chords are major, minor, or dominant tonalities (for more on tonality, check out Chapter 5). The root and 5 of a scale are one of the most common constant structures for grooves and can be easily moved between chords. Grooves using the root and 5 are simple but powerful. In fact, most songs incorporate root-5 grooves. The following steps, along with Figure 6-12, show you how to create a mobile groove:

1. **Create a groove.**

   To create a groove, take a look at the section earlier in this chapter, "Covering the 'basses': Creating dominant, minor, and major grooves." Keep the groove simple, because you need to move it to several different chords. My choice is a groove that doesn't require any shifting of your hand to reach all the notes (see Figure 6-12a).

   To play this groove, you need access to two strings above your root, so choose the root on either the E or the A string. You won't have enough strings to play this groove if you start on either the D or G string.

2. **Find the roots of the chords.**

   Look at your chord chart (simulated in Figure 6-11) and find the root of each chord on the fingerboard of your bass. Remember that all your roots have to be on the E or A string to play this groove. Figure 6-12b shows you where the roots for the chords on the chord chart are located on your bass.

3. **Practice moving the groove smoothly from one chord to the next.**

   You have to make these moves without any hesitation. Figure 6-12c shows the movement of the chords on your fingerboard. Use the *groove tail* to lead from one chord to the next. Keep in mind that the groove tail isn't necessarily part of the harmony; it just has to lead to the next chord or groove.

The groove you hear on Track 43 can be moved anywhere without your having to change the fingering. You do, of course, have to shift your hand into position for each new chord, however. Follow the chart in Figure 6-12.

Using chord tones

Another way to move a groove between chords with different tonalities is to use chord tones. *Chord tones* are the notes in any chord (root, 3, 5, and 7) that identify the chord type.

When you play a song that includes several tonalities, such as major, minor, and dominant, you need to make slight adjustments in your groove to play the different chord tones. Your fingering changes as you move from one kind of chord to the next. Keep the groove simple, because you have your hands full (pun intended) just changing the groove from chord to chord.

The following steps and Figure 6-13 help you create a mobile groove that uses chord tones:

1. **Create a groove.**

   Make your groove simple enough to handle. My choice is a groove that includes the root, 3, and 5 of a chord. You can see the different patterns for major, minor, and dominant in Figure 6-13a. (For the sake of comparison, all the patterns start on C.) Practice this groove, starting on one note to get comfortable with it. This groove covers three strings: the string you play the root on, and the two above it. You can start the groove on the E or A string.

2. **Find the roots of the chords.**

   Using the chord chart (refer to Figure 6-11), find the roots of the chords on your fingerboard. Your roots can start on the E or A string. Refer to Figure 6-12b for the locations of the roots for this particular chord chart.

3. **Practice moving the groove smoothly from one chord to the next.**

   You have to change your fingering from chord to chord. Practice until you can transfer this fingering without hesitation. Figure 6-13b shows the configuration of the groove for different chords. Use a *groove tail* to get from chord to chord. If you like, you may try using different notes than shown for your groove tail; just be sure it gets you to the next chord.

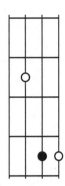

(a)

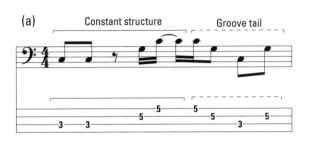

(b)

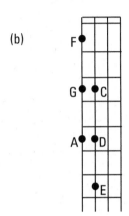

(c)

Figure 6-12: Mobile groove using constant structure.

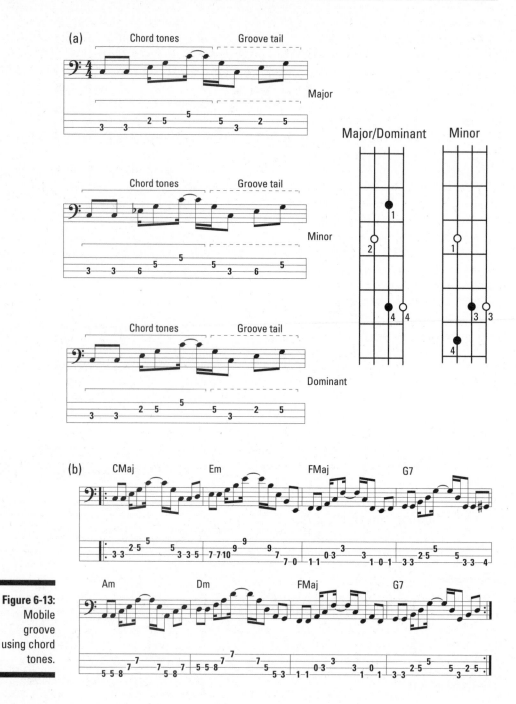

Figure 6-13:
Mobile
groove
using chord
tones.

The groove on Track 44 changes shape with each new chord tonality, which means you need to adjust your fingering with each chord (in addition to shifting your hand into position). Keep an eye on Figure 6-13 to get a handle on this concept.

Finding the perfect fit: The designer groove

Every now and then you hear a bass groove that simply knocks your socks off — a groove that seems to fit the song like a glove. I call these grooves *designer grooves;* the musician literally designs the groove to fit perfectly with everything that's going on harmonically and rhythmically in a particular tune. Just listen to Michael Jackson's "Shake Your Body (Down to the Ground)." In addition to having the groove skeleton (for details, see "Getting your groove skeleton out of the closet," earlier in the chapter), designer grooves also have a *groove apex,* which I discuss in the following sections.

The groove apex

An *apex* refers to the highlight of something, and in this case, the *groove apex* is the note that's the highlight of a groove. Every groove has an apex. The groove apex is usually either the highest or the lowest note of the groove. Either way, it's often the note farthest from the root of your groove.

Determining which note is the groove apex is open to interpretation. If you hear one note in a bass groove that really sticks out for you, that note is the groove apex.

Accenting the groove apex helps your groove fit better with the music. For example, you can accent a hit by your drummer or a special rhythm by your singer — whatever you think deserves more attention.

The upper groove apex

An *upper groove apex* is the highest note of a groove. Figure 6-14 shows a groove with a clear upper groove apex. Notice how the groove skeleton sets up the groove.

Figure 6-14:
Groove
with upper
groove
apex.

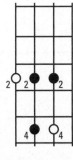

To practice playing an upper groove apex, check out the exercise in Figure 6-15. This exercise focuses on the upper groove apex alone, and practicing it can greatly improve your ability to execute the groove apex on any note.

Figure 6-15: Upper groove apex exercise.

Track 45 includes an example of a groove with an upper groove apex, followed by an exercise to practice playing it accurately, as shown in Figures 6-14 and 6-15.

The lower groove apex

The *lower groove apex* is the lowest note of a groove. Figure 6-16 shows a groove that has a lower groove apex. Notice how the groove skeleton establishes the groove.

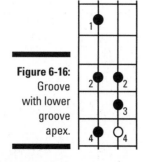

Figure 6-16: Groove with lower groove apex.

To get comfortable playing the lower groove apex, check out the exercise in Figure 6-17. This exercise shows you how to place the lower groove apex on any part of the beat.

Figure 6-17:
Lower groove apex exercise.

On Track 46, you hear an example of a lower groove apex. You can see it in Figures 6-16 and 6-17. In Video 16, I play both the upper and lower groove apex.

In both the upper groove and lower groove apex exercises (wow, that's a mouthful), the groove apex follows right behind the groove skeleton (the first two notes). These exercises are a great way to get comfortable playing not only grooves but also rhythms.

After you're comfortable playing along with the audio tracks, try playing these exercises without them. For even more of a challenge, try setting your metronome at varying speeds (refer to Chapter 4 for more on setting a metronome).

Grooving with a Drummer

No instrument is more important to your well-being as a bass player than the drums. (By the way, the bass is just as important to the well-being of a drummer.) Bassists and drummers work hand in hand to create grooves. If you want to build great grooves (and great relationships) with drummers, you need to know what all the different drums on a drum set sound like and what they're generally used for. This section gives you a quick overview of the different types of drums. If you want to read more, you can always check out *Drums For Dummies,* by Jeff Strong (Wiley).

The bass drum

The bass drum produces the lowest sound on the drum set. This drum is very closely aligned with your part as a bass player. Generally speaking, drummers play the bass drum on the first beat of a measure to start the groove and then play it at least once more within that measure. If you play notes that match the rhythm of the bass drum, you'll fit right in. Figure 6-18 shows you how to match the rhythm of the bass drum.

Fingering:

1 = index finger
2 = middle finger
3 = ring finger
4 = pinkie

Figure 6-18: Grooving with the bass drum.

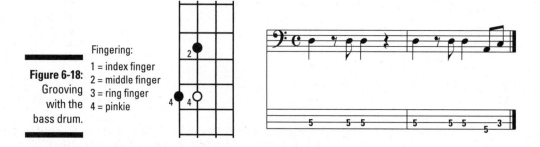

You can listen to Track 47 for a demonstration of how the bass drum sounds, followed by a bass groove that enhances the bass drum (at the 0:04 mark of the track).

The snare drum

The snare drum is the loudest drum on the drum set. This drum is usually played on the *backbeat* (beats 2 and 4) of each measure. You can match up one of your notes with the snare drum, or you can create some *sonic space* (where you don't play at that moment) so the snare drum sounds alone. Hmmm, now there's an interesting concept: Instead of looking confused when you're lost, just give the band leader your most serious look and say you're experimenting with sonic space.

Listen to Track 47 for the sound of the snare drum (playing along with the bass drum), and then take a look at Figure 6-19 to find out how you can join in with the snare and bass drums. On the track, the snare drum is at 0:16, followed by the groove at 0:21.

Figure 6-19: Bass grooving with the snare drum and the bass drum.

Fingering:
1 = index finger
2 = middle finger
3 = ring finger
4 = pinkie

The hi-hat

No, the hi-hat isn't a tall cap you wear on your head. The *hi-hat* (the two interconnected circular brass plates that snap together when played) is your real-life metronome. The drummer uses the hi-hat to mark the subdivisions of the beat (usually eighth notes or sixteenth notes) and keeps the hi-hat snapping right through a groove.

Sometimes, instead of using the hi-hat, the drummer uses one of the *cymbals* (the big, circular brass plates on the drum set) to keep the rhythm. You may have trouble hearing the hi-hat at first, but after you get used to listening for its constant sound, you'll be able to play your notes easily, because the rhythm of most of the notes you play on the bass coincide rhythmically with the hi-hat.

Listen to Track 47 for the sound of the hi-hat playing along with the snare and bass drums, and check out Figure 6-20 for a groove you can play with the three instruments. On the track, the hi-hat is at 0:34, followed by the groove at 0:42.

Figure 6-20:
Grooving
with the
hi-hat, the
snare drum,
and the
bass drum.

Jammin' with Other Musicians

Jammin' is the all-important yet elusive activity that musicians do to get to know one another and create some memorable music in the process. Sometimes the jam participants agree on a chord or even on a set of chords (see Chapter 5 for more information) ahead of time, but in its purest form a jam starts by someone playing and the rest of the band joining in. As you can imagine, jam sessions can get pretty chaotic — sort of like a bunch of people riding their bicycles crisscross in a deserted parking lot at full tilt at night in total darkness. Yeah, it can be painful.

So how do you join in a jam session if you don't know what anybody else is playing? Well, of course, you can be the one who starts playing first, and then the other jammers have to figure out what to do, but I have a feeling this works only occasionally. Most of the time, you have to use your ears and figure out what sounds best.

You're jamming! You aren't playing a composition or somebody else's idea of a song. You're part of a creative collaboration for making music. Jamming lets you shed any fears of making mistakes. In its truest form, there are no mistakes — only choices that sound better than others. So take this as your chance to experiment. Just remember that jamming is a truly democratic process. Everybody's input is of equal importance, so go forth and create!

In the following sections, you get a clear, step-by-step guide on what to do in a jam session.

Preparing your ear

First things first: You can't just step into the ring (even the musical ring) to spar with your bandmates without proper preparation. Jamming is ear-based, thus you have to prepare your ear. The best way to hear is to sing! That's right, to hear you have to be able to locate the notes by singing them. Harmony is based on scales; therefore, singing the different steps in a scale is a great way to acquire an ear for jamming.

Play a root on your bass, just one note. Now sing the major scale (for more about the major scale and a host of others, check out Chapter 5). Then try singing the root, followed by one of the other scale tones (2, 3, 4, 5, 6, 7, or the octave). In other words, play the root (such as C), sing the note, and then sing the 3 of that major scale (in this case, E). You can also sing the root and any of the other notes; just make sure you can relate back to the root, which is what helps you center the harmony.

Eventually, you want to try doing this exercise with all seven basic modes (see Chapter 5). This exercise helps you find your way around the harmony without having to rely entirely on your bass. In essence, you're training your ear.

Listening for "the note"

In a jam session, somebody (it may not even be the person who begins the jam) comes up with a musical *phrase,* a sequence of notes that's repeated several times. Be alert for this phrase and treat it as a melody. Here's what you do to get in on the action and contribute mightily to a jam session. The first part is the "ear" part, where you have to listen.

1. **Listen for one note that sounds like it's at the center of the phrase.**

   Hum the note until you have it solidly established in your head (don't do anything else until you have a firm grasp of the note). Try to find it on your bass. See the sidebar "A trick to finding a note that's in your head (or in your ear)" for the process of finding a note on your bass. You are looking to form a chord.

2. **Listen for a second note that seems important to the phrase.**

   Go ahead and find that note on your bass as well.

3. **See how the two notes relate to each other.**

   You need to figure out whether the two notes you've found can form a chord. I guarantee you they can; just look at Figure 6-21 for guidance.

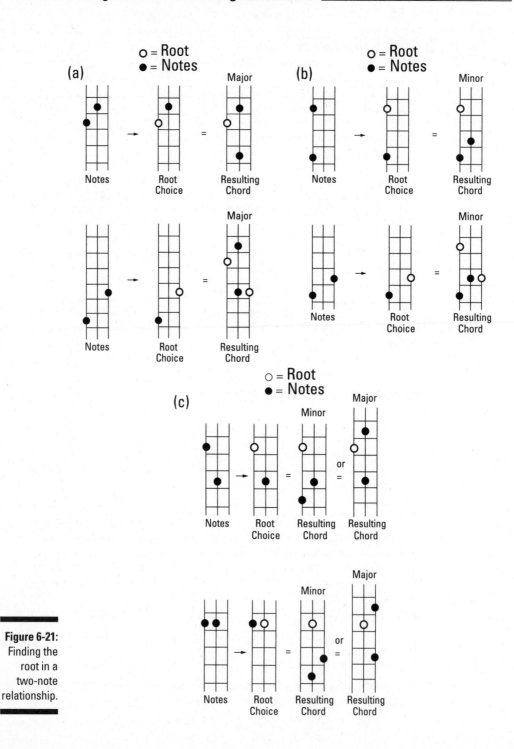

Figure 6-21:
Finding the
root in a
two-note
relationship.

4. **Name your two notes.**

   Knowing the names of your notes isn't absolutely essential, but it does make your life a lot easier if you know what they're called.

5. **Locate the two notes within three strings and four frets of each other on your bass.**

   Locating these notes in this way enables you to see what *interval* they form and generally where you're going to place your hand. (For more on intervals, flip to Chapter 2.)

6. **Choose your root.**

   One of the two notes you've already picked is the root. Use the diagram in Figure 6-21 to identify which one it is. At that point, you know where to place your fingers: index finger on the root if it sounds minor or middle finger if it's major or dominant.

The final part of the process is the "play" part, where you get to . . . well, play:

1. **Fill in your chord and mode according to the root you've picked using Figure 6-21.**

   Chapter 5 provides more information on filling in your chord and mode.

2. **Settle on a groove.**

   See the earlier section "Creating Your Own Groove" to find out how to develop a groove.

3. **Jam!**

   Go ahead and find out how your groove can influence what your band-mates are playing, and then play to your heart's content; this is the fun part. Don't worry about so-called "wrong" notes — just try to make the music sound good. The more you jam, the better you get.

Seems pretty complicated, doesn't it? Don't worry; if you're with the right group of musicians, jamming is really a blast! Just keep listening. Jamming is like a conversation. You have to hear what the others are saying to be able to join in with relevant ideas of your own. As with everything else, the more you do it, the better you get. After you establish the prevailing harmony in a jam, the other players usually rally around you. Jamming is very much a team sport, so don't fret it. (Well, actually *do* fret the notes, but don't fret anything else.)

Pivoting the note

Imagine that you're jamming away with a group of musicians. Things are positively hot, and your groove is simply smokin'. In fact, the music is sounding so good that you want to take it to another level and add another chord or two instead of staying on the same chord throughout the jam. In this case, it's time to pivot the note!

Pivoting the note that's at the center of your jam harmony allows you to create new chords that relate to it and to each other. The new chords then give the music a fresh direction by adding variety and making it more interesting. After all, no matter how smokin' hot a groove is, how interesting can you make a song if it stays on the same chord for three hours?

The trick to pivoting a note is to treat the central note (the root) of the chord you're playing as if it's not the root at all but a supporting note to the *new* central note (root) in a new chord. You're using the old note to pivot to a new chord.

For example, if you're tired of jamming in E, you can treat the E (the 1 of the chord) as if it's the 3 of another chord by finding and playing a second note that's three steps lower in the scale — which happens to be C. (E is the 3 of the C major chord.) Now you can continue playing, using C as the new 1, and E as the new 3. E has pivoted from a 1 of one chord to a 3 in another. The E is still an important part of the harmony, but it's not quite so central anymore. How can you get away with simply changing the root in the harmony? You're the bassist and roots are *your* business!

The root is the bassist's business, whether *you're* choosing it or you're hearing it from another player, especially from the soloist (or whoever's playing the melody). Always listen to the other players, because one of them may initiate a new chord sound, in which case you follow the guidelines in the previous section for finding two central notes. The diagram in Figure 6-22 shows you the best choices for pivoting the central note.

When you create new chords in a jam, keep in mind that it's easier to move around from chord to chord if you're playing a simple groove rather than a complex one. (Check out the earlier section "Covering the 'basses': Creating dominant, minor, and major grooves" for more information on simple and complex grooves.) The rule of thumb is this: The more chords you have and the faster they change, the simpler you want your groove to be. Often, the best initial move is to just lay down a pumping eighth-note rhythm on the root. (Head to Chapter 8 for the eighth-note rhythm on the root.)

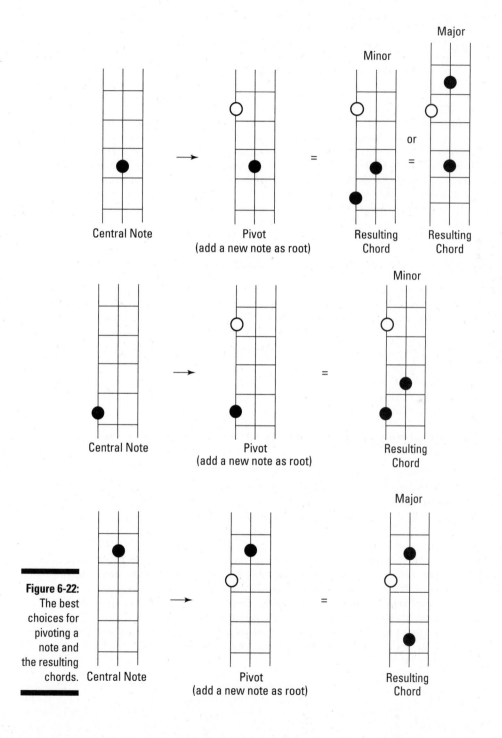

Figure 6-22:
The best choices for pivoting a note and the resulting chords.

A trick to finding a note that's in your head (or in your ear)

When you're looking for a specific note, whether it's one you're hearing in your mind or one you're hearing someone else play or sing, use this *one-string chromatic* approach to make finding it more efficient: Play only on your G string and play only one fret at a time, step by step in sequence, from the open G string to the octave G at the double dot of your fingerboard. One of these notes is a match to the one you're hearing and a couple of others simply sound good with it. By playing the 12 notes in that range, you're covering all the notes in the chromatic system, leaving none out. Staying on one string allows you to keep track of which notes you've played and eliminated; otherwise, you may be jumping around the fingerboard without a plan, wasting time and energy on notes you've already tried. The G string is the highest pitched string on your bass and the notes are easiest to hear, so take a ride on that G string. (Oh, and keep it clean in the G-string joke department.)

Let your own ear be the final judge of whether a choice you make sounds good, and give it a little time to ferment, especially in a jam session. To let a groove ferment, you have to keep your choice of chords consistent and repeat them over and over again to give the other players a chance to get familiar with the duration and sequence of your chords (also called a *chord progression*) and to respond with musical phrases that enhance the new progression.

Getting Creative with Existing Grooves

Music is a creative art, and being creative is something every musician must be comfortable with. Just as is the case with technique and repertoire, creativity is something you can practice. Without using the creative juices, every bass player in the world would sound exactly the same, and that's certainly not the case. So how *do* you put your own personal stamp on your music?

You can get really creative with your bass playing by using the elements of a groove from earlier in this chapter. Just pick a groove — either yours or someone else's — and start making little changes: a different *groove tail* perhaps, or displacing the *groove apex*, or how about changing the feel pretty drastically by using a different rhythm in the *groove skeleton*? You'd be surprised by how a little change can affect the music in a big way. It keeps the song fresh, and it makes it unique — uniquely *yours*.

Altering a (famous) groove

An absolutely fabulous way to practice your creativity is to take a famous groove and to change it in a way that keeps the basic structure of the groove in place (making it recognizable) but gives it enough of a variation to make it a new groove, your own. For example, take Paul McCartney's bass line on The Beatles' song "Come Together," one of the most recognizable bass grooves in music.

First, check out the original groove by listening to "Come Together" by The Beatles. It's beyond obvious; the bass groove is central to the song and comes in right at the beginning. You can hear the first two notes (the *groove skeleton*) establishing the rock feel. Then there's a little transition before the bass soars to the high note and lets it ring (the *groove apex;* this one really sticks out). Then the last part of the groove leads back to the beginning of the next groove by way of an array of different notes, sometimes just one, sometimes several (typical of a *groove tail*).

You can alter this groove mildly, by adding some dead notes or some notes in the groove tail that don't bear a lot of weight. You can also alter the groove drastically by changing the rhythm of the groove skeleton or by moving the groove apex onto different parts of the beat. You can also gradually change the groove as you play through the song, which is especially effective if your song goes on for several minutes and the groove never changes.

Figure 6-23 shows you a few variations on the theme of "Come Together," which by no means exhaust the possibilities. So experiment with these variations and then come up with your own. You can hear these variations on Track 48.

Figure 6-23a (at the start of the track) is a variation of the "Come Together" groove, using a few dead notes (see Chapter 5). The dead notes have a very light impact on the original groove and really change it only mildly.

Figure 6-23b (at 0:29) shows a denser version of the same groove. The groove apex is played on a lower octave (for more on octaves, see Chapter 4), making it less dramatic, and the groove tail varies from one measure to the next, giving the groove variety.

In Figure 6-23c (at 1:02), you can see a change in the groove skeleton, which is always a consequential change, because it alters the feel and possibly even the genre of the groove. In this case, it makes it more of a funk groove. The groove apex is still in the same place as the original groove.

Figure 6-23: Different variations of "Come Together."

Things get really interesting in Figure 6-23d (at 1:32). The groove skeleton has a funky sixteenth note feel, and the groove apex is now rhythmically displaced; it occurs later in the measure than the original.

Finally, in Figure 6-23e (at 2:01), you can see the whole shape of the groove inverted. Instead of a groove apex soaring up, it now goes down (and actually becomes part of the groove skeleton, because it's now the second note in the groove).

Listen to all these variations of the "Come Together" groove on Track 48 and play along with them. In fact, play them with the original recording and see how you like them. Try equalizing the bass down so you can hear your own versions more clearly.

Simplifying a groove

At times, you may want to simplify a groove, giving it more space by eliminating some of the notes. This task seems easy at first glance, but it's actually a real challenge. After all, you need to choose the notes that keep the integrity of the original groove intact. Take out the wrong ones, and the groove becomes unrecognizable.

Figure 6-24 and Track 49 give you several examples of how to proceed. Make sure you refresh your ear by listening to the original bass groove of "Come Together" (The Beatles' version). Then go ahead and experiment with Figure 6-24a (at the start of the track), which is a pared down version of the same groove. It consists of only the groove skeleton, the groove apex, and the one-note groove tail of the original groove. The transitional notes between the groove skeleton and the groove apex are gone, and the groove tail is in its simplest version.

Figure 6-24b (at 0:30) changes the groove skeleton, making it funky, and also displaces the groove apex harmonically and rhythmically to give it variety. In the second measure of this groove, you play only the groove skeleton. This turns a one-measure groove into a two-measure groove by making the sequence twice as long before repeating it.

In Figure 6-24c (0:57), the paring down process is taken to an extreme by eliminating the groove apex. You can hear that the groove still functions, but it now has lost some of its distinctive character. This works well when you're building a groove and plan to really launch into it at a later point in the tune, making it more climactic.

Figure 6-24:
Different
pared down
variations
of "Come
Together."

Check out Video 17 and play these variations along with the original recording of "Come Together" and see how they work for you. You can also try playing some of the variations of Figures 6-23 and 6-24 and build from one to the next, getting a whole lot of dynamic range in your groove.

Chapter 7

Going Solo: Playing Solos and Fills

In This Chapter

▶ Choosing solo scales based on your chord tonality

▶ Playing fills to make your groove dazzle

▶ Access the audio tracks and video clips at www.dummies.com/go/bassguitar

*I*magine that you're playing with a great bunch of musicians and you're holding down a monster groove so solidly that the music takes on a life of its own (see Chapter 6 for more on creating a groove). In fact, things are sounding so good that the other musicians decide to reward you with a solo — a chance to show off your bass chops (bass-speak for "skills"). Looks like you need to prepare for your moment in the sun, because when the time comes for your solo, you want to burn (bass-speak for "showing off your chops").

This chapter presents three surefire scales you can use to create a solo or a fill (a mini-solo) that will make you and everyone else *smoke* (bass-speak for "dazzle").

Soloing: Your Moment to Shine

A *solo* is the music (musical and rhythmic line) you create when you're the featured player in a band. Solos usually are reserved for the traditional melody instruments, such as the guitar, saxophone, and trumpet, but bassists also are asked to perform a solo on occasion.

Making a solo sound good is a bit more challenging for the bassist, because the sound of the instrument is very deep and you don't have a groove backing you. (You can't play a groove and a solo at the same time.) Despite these challenges, bass solos can be very effective in the hands of a good player.

The following sections introduce some common scales that are sure to help you create a killer solo for your moment in the spotlight.

Playing with the blues scale: A favorite solo spice

The *six-note blues scale* is one of the most commonly used scales in soloing — and with good reason: It's comfortable to play, it's easy to move from chord to chord, and it sounds great. The blues scale is a one-size-fits-all scale, no matter what the chord tonality (major, minor, or dominant). However, as with those one-size-fits-all pieces of clothing, the blues scale doesn't always give you a perfect fit; you may have to move a note or two by a fret.

When you create a solo with the blues scale, it of course will sound bluesy. Let your ears be the judge of which notes you can linger on and which notes you should use as *passing tones* (unaccented notes that connect two strong notes). It's just like salt for the soup: When you add the right amount, it's delicious; when you use too much, you spoil the broth.

You need three strings to complete the blues scale for one octave, so start on either the E or A string on the root of the chord you're playing (see Chapter 5 for more about chords). However, when you're playing a bass solo, it sounds really nice if you extend into the next octave and use all four strings of your bass for the blues scale licks (musical themes). The following steps explain how to play a blues scale, and Figure 7-1 shows you its structure.

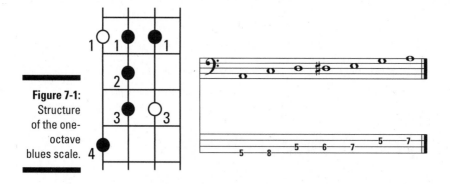

Figure 7-1:
Structure of the one-octave blues scale.

1. **Press the index finger of your left hand down on the root of the chord (on the E or A string) and play the note.**

2. **Press your pinkie down on the same string and play the note.**

   This note is ♭3 (flat 3); it's one of the *blue* (slightly dissonant) notes.

3. **Press your index finger down on the next higher (thinner) string and play the note.**

   This note is a 4; it sounds fairly neutral.

4. **Press your middle finger down on the same string and play the note.**

   This note is a ♯4 (sharp 4); it's another blue note.

5. **Press your ring finger down on the same string and play the note.**

   This note is a 5; it's present in almost all chords.

6. **Press your index finger down on the next higher (thinner) string and play the note.**

   This note is a ♭7 (flat 7); it's usually a cool choice.

7. **Press your ring finger down on the same string and play the note.**

   This note is your octave; you've arrived at the root again.

Three strings. No shifts. The blues scale couldn't be easier.

You can use the notes of the blues scale in any order — not just straight up and down. You also can use the blues scale over any chord: major, minor, or dominant. Use the blues scale tastefully and sparingly; don't overdo it. Pay attention to which notes sound good for any of the chords. For example, don't hang on the ♭7 when you're soloing over a major chord; instead, just pass through it and land on the root (that's just one option).

Figure 7-2 shows you some useful blues-scale licks. A lick, in this case, doesn't refer to how your dog welcomes you home. A *lick* is a short melodic phrase you play in a solo — a solo is a succession of licks. You can collect a repertoire of licks from your favorite musicians, and you also can create some of your own.

On Track 50, you hear what a blues scale (in A) sounds like, followed by three distinctive blues-scale licks (each preceded by a groove). To view the fingering for each, look at Figures 7-1 and 7-2. Figure 7-2 uses an extended four-string pattern to increase the range of your blues scale and to make the lick more lickety-slick. If you start the extended-range blues scale on the E string, you won't have to shift. You can see me playing the scales in Video 18.

Jamming with the minor pentatonic scale: No wrong notes

The structure of the *minor pentatonic scale* is very similar to the blues scale (which I cover in the previous section). However, the minor pentatonic scale has only five different notes: one fewer than the six-note blues scale.

You use the minor pentatonic scale when the tonality of the chord you're playing is minor. (For more on chord tonality, see Chapter 5.) You need to make sure you have three strings available to complete the scale in one octave, so find your root on the E or A string. The following steps explain how to play the minor pentatonic scale, and Figure 7-3 shows the pattern of the scale.

Groove

Solo Lick 1

Solo Lick 2

Solo Lick 3

Figure 7-2:
Blues-scale
licks.

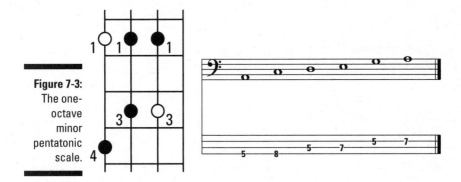

Figure 7-3:
The one-octave
minor
pentatonic
scale.

1. **Press the index finger of your left hand down on the root of the chord (on the E or A string) and play the note.**

2. **Press your pinkie down on the same string and play the note.**

   This note is a ♭3 (flat 3); it's one of the main ingredients of the minor chord.

3. **Press your index finger down on the next higher (thinner) string and play the note.**

   This note is a 4; it's part of the minor scale.

4. **Press your ring finger down on the same string and play the note.**

   This note is a 5; it's another main ingredient of the minor chord.

5. **Press your index finger down on the next higher (thinner) string and play the note.**

   This note is a ♭7 (flat 7); it's yet another main ingredient of the minor chord.

6. **Press your ring finger down on the same string and play the note.**

   This note is your octave; you've arrived at the root again.

Voilà! Three strings. No shifts. No problem.

As with the blues scale, you can use the notes of the minor pentatonic scale in any order when playing your solo — not just straight up and down. Use this scale over any minor chord. All the notes sound good played over a minor chord, so you can land on any of them. If you find that your solo needs spice, use the blues scale. (Flip to the section "Playing with the blues scale: A favorite solo spice," for more information.)

Figure 7-4 shows some useful licks you can play, using the minor pentatonic scale. These licks use the extended four-string version so your solo gets more of a range and sounds more interesting. To extend the range, start the scale on the E string. The minor pentatonic scale comes in handy in every solo, so add it to your repertoire.

Groove

Solo Lick 1

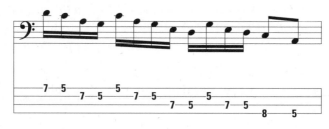

Solo Lick 2

Solo Lick 3

Figure 7-4:
Minor
pentatonic
scale licks.

You hear the minor pentatonic scale and three minor pentatonic licks (each lick is played four times) on Track 51. Follow along with Figures 7-3 and 7-4 and Video 18.

Using the major pentatonic scale: Smooth as can be

You can use the *major pentatonic scale* for two different chord tonalities: the major chord and the dominant chord. Think of this scale as a two-for-one deal. (For more on major and dominant chords, see Chapter 5.)

You need only three strings to complete one octave of the major pentatonic scale, so start it on the E or A string. The following steps explain how to play the major pentatonic scale, and Figure 7-5 shows its structure.

Figure 7-5:
One octave of the major pentatonic scale.

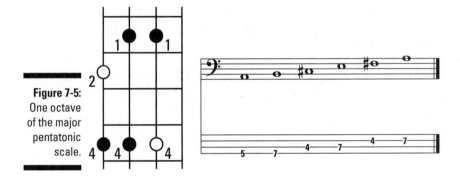

1. **Press the middle finger of your left hand down on the root of the chord (on the E or A string) and play the note.**

2. **Press your pinkie down on the same string and play the note.**

   This note is a 2; it's a fairly neutral note that's part of the scales of both the major and dominant chords.

3. **Press your index finger down on the next higher (thinner) string and play the note.**

   This note is a 3; it's one of the main ingredients of both the major and dominant chords.

   4. **Press your pinkie down on the same string and play the note.**

      This note is a 5; it's another main ingredient of the major and dominant chords.

   5. **Press your index finger down on the next higher (thinner) string and play the note.**

      This note is a 6; it's another neutral note that's part of the scales used for both the major and dominant chords.

   6. **Press your pinkie down on the same string and play the note.**

      This note is your octave; you've arrived at the root again.

   Three strings. No shifts. Okay, you're ready for the limelight.

   You can use the notes of the major pentatonic scale in any order — not just straight up and down. Play this scale for any major or dominant chord. All the notes of the major pentatonic scale sound good with a major or dominant chord, so you're perfectly safe landing on any of them. If you find that things start to sound bland, you can add some spice in the form of the blues scale. (See "Playing with the blues scale: A favorite solo spice" earlier in this chapter for more information.)

   Figure 7-6 shows some specific licks you can play using the major pentatonic scale. You can play these licks throughout your solo. To make it even more effective, use the extended four-string version and start it on the E string.

   You can hear the major pentatonic scale on Track 52 and Video 18, followed by three distinct major pentatonic licks (each lick is played four times) as shown in Figures 7-5 and 7-6.

Moving from chord to chord

If your band is playing a tune and all of a sudden your solo comes up, don't worry. The blues, minor pentatonic, and major pentatonic scales (see the three previous sections) give you plenty of ammunition for playing a cool solo.

Groove

Solo Lick 1

Solo Lick 2

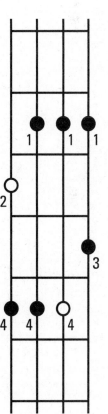

Solo Lick 3

Figure 7-6:
Major
pentatonic
scale licks.

When performing a solo, you use the minor pentatonic scale for a minor chord, the major pentatonic scale for a major or dominant chord, and the blues scale for any chord to add a little twist to the harmony. The following steps give you some guidelines to follow when soloing for a tune that has all three of the common chords (minor, major, and dominant). These steps tell you how to approach each individual chord:

1. **Find the root of the chord.**

   You need to make sure you have enough strings to cover the entire scale, so stick with the E and A strings, preferably the E string to give you the extended range option.

2. **Determine whether the chord is minor, major, or dominant.**

   • **If the chord is minor, place your index finger on the root of the chord.** You're now in position to execute the minor pentatonic scale for this chord.

   • **If the chord is either major or dominant, place your middle finger on the root of the chord.** You're now in position to execute the major pentatonic scale for this chord.

3. **Add some spice to your solo by occasionally placing your index finger on the root of any chord and playing a blues-scale lick.**

   Check out "Playing with the blues scale: A favorite solo spice" earlier in the chapter to find out more.

Figure 7-7 shows you a chord chart for a tune. Listen to Track 53 for samples of soloing over these chords, and then try coming up with your own solo.

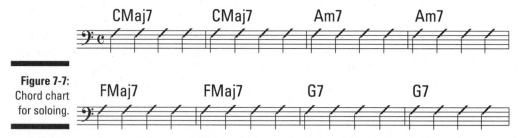

Figure 7-7: Chord chart for soloing.

Creating Fills without Any Help from Your Dentist

Fills are mini-solos that give grooves a little flash every now and then. (Check out Chapter 6 if you aren't sure what a groove is.) The purpose of the fill is to

 ✔ Lead you back to the beginning of the groove

 ✔ Give your *line* (the bass part you're playing) some variety

 ✔ Fill a little space when the rest of the band is quiet

A fill works the same way as a solo: You use the minor pentatonic scale as a fill when playing a minor chord, the major pentatonic scale as a fill when playing a major or dominant chord, and the blues scale as a fill when playing any chord. (Refer to the section "Soloing: Your Moment to Shine," earlier in this chapter, for more details on how to use these scales as solos.)

A fill is usually short (only about two to four beats long), so you need to fit the notes of the fill within the allotted beats and blend them smoothly with the other notes.

A match made in heaven: Connecting your fill to the groove

You can take more liberties in terms of rhythm with a solo than you can with a fill. When fills are a part of the groove, the rhythm for the fill has to relate closely to the rhythm of the groove.

When you put a fill into a groove, you need to be acutely aware of the number of beats you have to fill before returning to the beginning of the groove. You can't miss the beginning of a groove — not even for the greatest of fills.

Timing a fill

Most of the time a fill within a groove lasts for about two beats — the *last* two beats of a measure. In other words, you play beats 1 and 2 (the first two beats of the measure) as a regular groove, and then you replace beats 3 and 4 (the last part of your groove) with a fill.

Don't play a fill every time you play a groove, because it will obscure the groove, which is the sound the band depends on to guide them in rhythm and harmony. A fill is usually only played every fourth measure or every eighth measure.

Figure 7-8 shows examples of fills for major, minor, and dominant chords using eighth notes, triplets, and sixteenth notes. The following list guides you step by step through the process of creating a fill.

1. **Establish a groove.**

   See Chapter 6 to find out how to establish a groove.

2. **Determine where the third beat starts in your groove.**

   Because you'll be substituting your fill for beats 3 and 4, play the groove up to the third beat.

3. **Determine how many notes you can hit in the two beats (beats 3 and 4).**

   The two beats for the fill have a total of four eighth notes, six triplets, or eight sixteenth notes. (See Chapter 4 for more about rhythms.) A lot depends on the tempo of the groove and on how accurately you can fit the notes into the two beats of the fill before the first note of the next groove. You can fit more notes into a fill at slower tempos.

4. **Work out a fill, paying attention to the number of notes you can play and using the appropriate pentatonic or blues scale for the chord of the groove.**

   For details on how the different scales relate to the different chords, see "Soloing: Your Moment to Shine," earlier in this chapter.

5. **Practice going back and forth between the groove and the fill until your transitions are seamless.**

   To create a successful fill, your groove must flow without hesitation, leading into the next groove seamlessly and on time.

6. **Play your fill no more than every four or eight bars so that each fill sounds special.**

   If you play your fill more often than every four or eight bars, it will just sound like another groove.

On Tracks 54, 55, and 56, listen to examples of two-beat fills. And watch me play them in Video 19. All the fills have different subdivisions: The first group (Figure 7-8a, Track 54) subdivides the beat into eighth notes, the next (Figure 7-8b, Track 55) subdivides the beat into triplets, and the last (Figure 7-8c, Track 56) subdivides the beat into sixteenth notes. Each group includes first the blues scale for the fill, then the minor pentatonic, and last but not least the major pentatonic. To make the exercise more realistic, it begins with a groove and then immediately is followed by the fill in the last two beats, just the way you would play it in a song.

When you feel comfortable playing the fills from Figure 7-8, incorporate them into some of your more complex grooves. (The grooves in Figure 7-8 consist of simply three roots and a dead note in the first two beats so you can concentrate on getting the fills at the end right.) You also can create a collection of your own favorite fills and incorporate them into your playing.

Blues-Scale Fills

Minor Pentatonic Fills

Major Pentatonic Fills

Extended Range
Blues Scale

Extended Range
Minor Pentatonic

Extended Range
Major Pentatonic

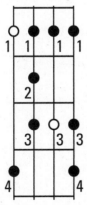

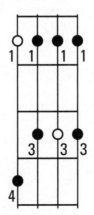

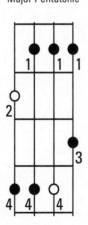

Figure 7-8a:
Groove
with an
eighth-note
fill.

Blues-Scale Fills

Minor Pentatonic Fills

Major Pentatonic Fills

Extended Range
Blues Scale

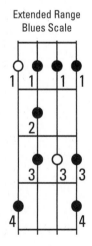

Extended Range
Minor Pentatonic

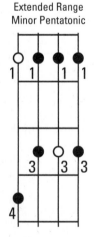

Extended Range
Major Pentatonic

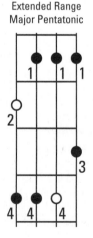

Figure 7-8b:
Groove with
a triplet fill.

Blues-Scale Fills

Minor Pentatonic Fills

Major Pentatonic Fills

Extended Range
Blues Scale

Extended Range
Minor Pentatonic

Extended Range
Major Pentatonic

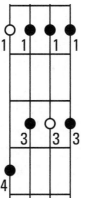

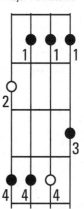

Figure 7-8c:
Groove
with a
sixteenth-
note
fill.

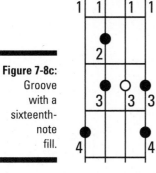

Part IV

Using the Correct Accompaniment for Each Genre

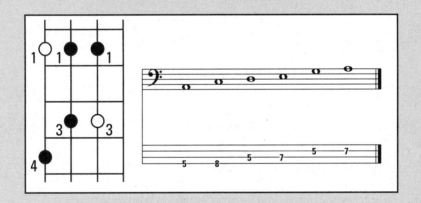

In this part...

✔ Play grooves in the most popular styles and genres.

✔ Expand your playing into odd meters.

✔ Take control of the genre of a tune.

✔ Discover the Beatles' solution.

Chapter 8

Rock On! Getting Down with the Rock Styles

***

In This Chapter

▶ Playing rock 'n' roll

▶ Chipping away at hard rock and prog rock

▶ Uncorking pop rock

▶ Rocking the blues

▶ Saddling up with country rock

▶ Exploring a universal groove

▶ Access the audio tracks and video clips at www.dummies.com/go/bassguitar

***

The term *rock* encompasses a number of different styles, ranging from country rock to hard rock, all of which have certain traits in common. All rock styles use rhythms dominated by driving eighth notes. (For more on rhythm, see Chapter 4.) The bassist locks in tightly with the drums and plays grooves that stress the root, the first note of any scale. (You can find out about grooves in Chapter 6.) The main difference between each rock style lies in the rhythmic and melodic feel of the bass lines.

In this chapter, I show you how to rock out with attitude, even if you don't have a single stitch of black clothing in your wardrobe. Strap on your bass and rock the joint. You have enough material in this chapter to keep jammin' for quite a while.

You can play any of the grooves featured in this chapter in any key (starting with any root) by using the grids in the figures. Just make sure you have enough frets and strings at your disposal — usually four or five frets and three strings.

Rock 'n' Roll: It's The Attitude!

Rock 'n' roll refers to the style of rock that originated in the 1950s and '60s (think Elvis Presley or Buddy Holly). The bassist maintains a quarter-note or eighth-note rhythm and a distinctive melodic bass line that spells out the harmony for the band and the listener. Check out Figure 8-1 for an example of a rock 'n' roll accompaniment. The example uses one note — the root — with an eighth-note rhythm. (The open circle on the grid represents the root.)

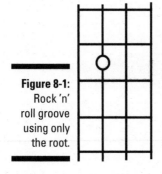

Figure 8-1:
Rock 'n' roll groove using only the root.

As you listen to Track 57 or watch Video 20, notice how the rhythm of the notes in Figure 8-1 (at the start of the track) is evenly divided and how the bass locks in with the drums.

You can start the groove in Figure 8-1 with any finger, because only one note is used — the root. You also don't have to worry about the chord tonality. (Chapter 5 discusses tonality.)

In Figure 8-2 (at 0:11 on Track 57), you add the 3 and 5 (the third and fifth notes of the major scale) to the groove to form the chord. (Check out Chapter 5 for some general info on chords.) In the grid, the root is the open circle, and the solid black dots are the other chord tones (the notes in the chord). Figure 8-2 has to be played with your middle finger on the root to avoid shifting during the groove.

Notice how the eighth notes are driving the rhythm in the grooves from Figures 8-2 through 8-4. The bass and drums are tightly locked in with each other. The choice of the bass notes indicates to the band members the tonality of the chords: major, minor, or dominant.

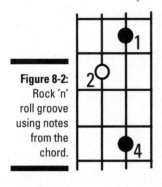

Figure 8-2: Rock 'n' roll groove using notes from the chord.

You can alter the examples in this chapter to fit any tonality. Simply lower the regular 3 to a ♭3 to change the tonality from major to minor, or raise the ♭3 to a regular 3 to change it from minor to major. This change isn't a major problem, just a minor adjustment.

The groove shown in Figure 8-3 (at 0:23 on Track 57) is the same as the one in Figure 8-2 with one exception: The groove in Figure 8-3 has a minor 3 (♭3) instead of a major 3 (or 3). The lowering of the major 3 to the ♭3 changes the entire chord into a minor chord. Start this groove with your index finger on the root to avoid any unnecessary shifting of your left hand.

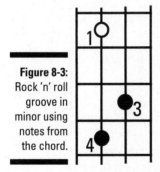

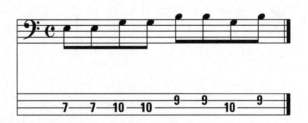

Figure 8-3: Rock 'n' roll groove in minor using notes from the chord.

Figure 8-4 shows an example of a more elaborate rock 'n' roll groove (at 0:34 on Track 57), using notes that come not only from the major chord but also from the Mixolydian mode (scale), making it dominant. (See Chapter 5 for a discussion of modes, including the Mixolydian.) Start this groove with your middle finger on the root.

Figure 8-4:
Rock 'n'
roll groove
using notes
from the
chord and
mode.

The groove in Figure 8-4 fits nicely over a dominant chord, which is a common chord in rock 'n' roll. The dominant chord consists of the root, 3, 5, and ♭7 of the Mixolydian mode. Figure 8-5 shows you the thought process behind the creation of this groove.

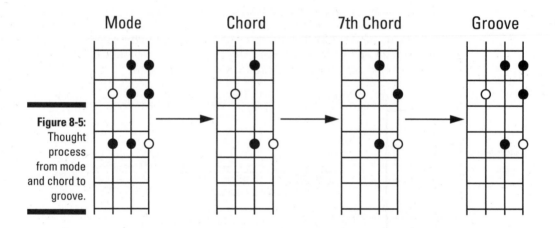

Figure 8-5:
Thought
process
from mode
and chord to
groove.

For a denser rock 'n' roll groove, check out Figure 8-6 (at 0:46 on Track 57), which includes not only notes from the chord and its related mode (Mixolydian in this case) but also *chromatic tones* — notes outside the regular mode that *lead* to the notes within the chord (see Chapter 5 for more on chromatic tones).

You can play all the notes of this groove in the same position, as long as you start with your middle finger. I call this a *box groove* because the positioning of the notes forms a *box;* your left hand is positioned so that your fingers can reach all the notes without shifting.

Figure 8-6:
Rock 'n' roll
box groove.

You can alter the groove in Figure 8-6 to play over a minor tonality by lowering the 3 to ♭3, which converts the dominant chord tonality into a minor tonality. Check out Figure 8-7 to see what this groove looks like in a minor tonality (at 0:58 on Track 57). To play the groove in Figure 8-7, start with your index finger on the root so you don't have to shift your left hand.

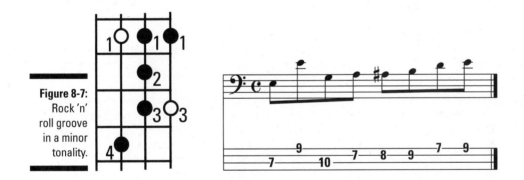

Figure 8-7:
Rock 'n'
roll groove
in a minor
tonality.

You also can convert this groove into a major 7th tonality (see Figure 8-8, which is at 1:10 on Track 57). To do so, raise the ♭7 of the original groove (refer to Figure 8-6) and then play the groove using a major 7th chord (root, 3, 5, and 7). Begin with your middle finger on the root. The major 7th tonality is rare in rock 'n' roll, but it's still useful to know how to play it.

When accompanying a rock tune that has a major 7th tonality, you may want to substitute the 6 of the major mode for the 7 in your groove. The 6 softens the sound and makes it more pleasant to the ear. The 7 is very rarely used in a groove. Take a look at Figure 8-9 for an example of the use of a 6 in a major 7th tonality. It's at 1:21 on Track 57.

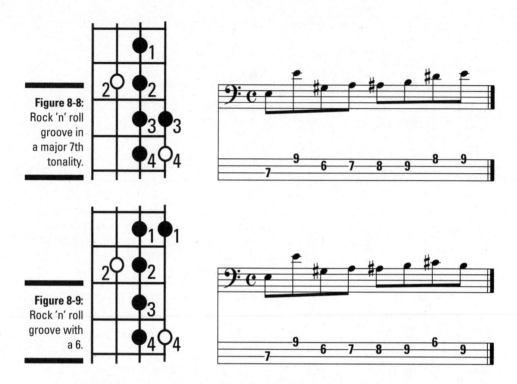

Figure 8-8:
Rock 'n' roll groove in a major 7th tonality.

Figure 8-9:
Rock 'n' roll groove with a 6.

With the 6 in place, in Figure 8-9, you can use the groove over a major 7th tonality as well as over a dominant tonality. The only difference between these two tonalities is the 7: The major 7th chord has a regular 7, and the dominant chord has a ♭7. A groove with a regular 7 clashes with a dominant chord; a groove with a ♭7 clashes with a major chord. In the groove shown in Figure 8-9, however, the 6 doesn't clash with either chord. (In fact, it sounds pretty good.) You can use this groove to give the other players of your band more leeway in their choice of notes. It doesn't lock them into having to choose between either a 7 or ♭7.

When you listen to the audio track corresponding to Figures 8-6 through 8-9, you can hear how one groove can be adapted to fit over different tonalities: the dominant (Figure 8-6), the minor (Figure 8-7), the major 7th (Figure 8-8), and a major tonality with a 6 rather than a 7 (Figure 8-9).

You can change the sound of a groove to a different tonality by changing the 3, the 7, or even the 5. Check out Chapter 5 for more on scale/chord compatibility.

A history of rock styles from the bassist's perspective

Rock had its beginnings in the 1950s when the rhythm section (bass, guitar, drums, and piano) began to take on a more prominent role in popular music. With the invention in 1951 of the Fender Precision bass (the first popular electric bass), the electric bass guitar slowly started displacing the acoustic (upright) bass.

With the improvement of recording and sound technology, the bass could now be heard clearly instead of just being felt, and by the 1960s, the electric bass was the instrument of choice in popular music. The bass guitar gained an ever-increasing role in rock music, and bassists developed lines that were more melodic and complex to accompany the music. In the 1970s, hard rock and progressive rock emerged, along with faster and even more complex bass lines — and steadily increasing volume. Bass lines of *driving sixteenth notes* (sixteenth notes played in a continuous, even stream, often on one pitch) were becoming more common in accompaniment. Rock didn't simply abandon one style in favor of the next; it absorbed each new musical trend, sharing its unique feel and attitude.

Check out the sounds of Adam Clayton of U2 or of the late John Entwistle of The Who if you want to hear some great rock bassists. And while you're at it, listen to John Myung of Dream Theatre and Geddy Lee of Rush for some excellent progressive rock bass playing.

Hard Rock: Going at It Fast and Furious

Hard rock, which includes progressive rock along with metal and its numerous offspring, is the fastest category of rock. The rhythm is hard and driving, and the tempo can be downright wicked (as in superfast). You may frequently encounter sixteenth notes (see Chapter 4) and odd meters (see Chapter 12) in this style. Hard rock bass lines often are based on minor pentatonic sounds (check out Chapter 7 for pentatonic scales).

When you and your band members play *unison riffs* (licks using the same notes in the same rhythm) in hard rock, you want to get your sixteenth notes up to speed so you can keep up with the others. (For an example of a typical unison riff, check out Figure 8-13.)

Listen to Tom Hamilton of Aerosmith or John Paul Jones of Led Zeppelin if you want to hear some excellent bassists who play the hard rock style.

Figure 8-10 (at the start of Track 58) shows a hard rock bass groove played on the root only, using a combination of eighth and sixteenth notes.

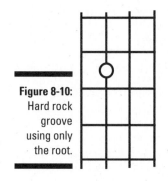

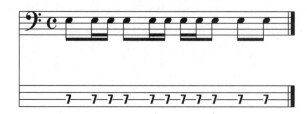

Figure 8-10:
Hard rock
groove
using only
the root.

Hard rock grooves often sound very aggressive. To hear this kind of groove, listen to Track 58 or watch Video 21. You can hear the grooves from Figures 8-10 through 8-13 all on the same track. Check out how they evolve as you add notes from the chord and mode.

The groove in Figure 8-11 (at 0:12 on Track 58) adds the ♭3 and 5 to the root (the ♭3 gives it a minor tonality). Minor is the most common chord choice in hard rock, but you may occasionally encounter major tonalities as well. Start this groove with your index finger on the root.

Figure 8-12 (at 0:26 on Track 58) shows a bass groove that includes notes from both the minor chord and the minor modes. You can really feel your fingers move when you play this groove. Make sure you start with your index finger on the root.

The hard rock groove in Figure 8-13 (at 0:39 on Track 58) uses a *chromatic tone* (a note outside the regular minor mode) to embellish the bass line. This example shows a typical box groove (no shifts with the left hand) that's played on the bass and guitar in unison (not by the same person, of course).

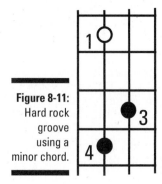

Figure 8-11:
Hard rock
groove
using a
minor chord.

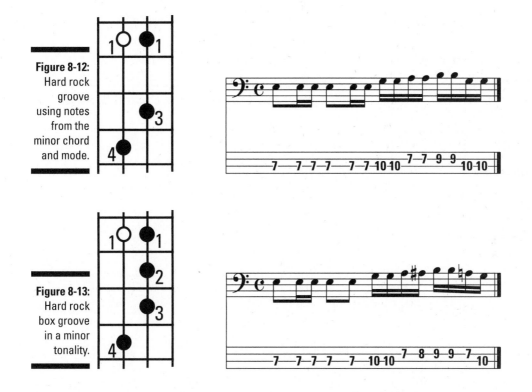

Figure 8-12: Hard rock groove using notes from the minor chord and mode.

Figure 8-13: Hard rock box groove in a minor tonality.

Pop Rock: Supporting the Vocals

The term *pop* is short for popular music, which refers to a style of rock that's popular with a wide range of the general population. Yes, I know this definition leaves the genre wide open, but I'm sure you know what I'm talking about.

For example, have you ever heard of a band called The Beatles (with Paul McCartney on bass)? How about Elton John? (Several bassists play with Sir Elton, but the great Pino Palladino and Dee Murray stand out.) In pop music, the song tells a story, so you don't want to overshadow the vocals with an outrageous bass line.

Figure 8-14 (at the start of Track 59) shows the quintessential singer-songwriter groove (using only the root) that you so often hear in pop. The beat is divided equally and often is set up (approached) by an eighth note. The eighth and quarter notes are the most frequent note choices for pop bass lines.

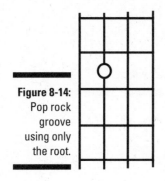

Figure 8-14:
Pop rock groove using only the root.

On Track 59 and Video 21, you can hear the sound of the pop grooves corresponding to Figures 8-14 through 8-17. Check out how the line starts out simply and then gets more complex as you add notes.

Figure 8-15 (at 0:11 on Track 59) shows a pop rock groove that uses a major tonality. When playing this groove, you add the 3 and 5 to fill out the chord (here, a major). Make sure you start this groove with your middle finger on the root.

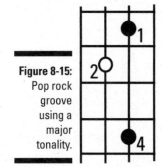

Figure 8-15:
Pop rock groove using a major tonality.

Figure 8-16 (at 0:23 on Track 59) shows a pop rock groove that uses notes in the dominant tonality. The first half of the measure sets up the feel for this groove. The second half of the measure is much busier; it prepares for the calm first half of the next repetition of the groove. The groove builds up tension and then releases to a satisfying resolution. (You can read about tension and release in Chapter 5.) You use notes from the Mixolydian mode for this groove. Start with your middle finger on the root to keep your left hand in position.

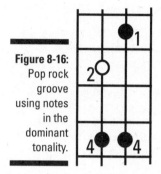

Figure 8-16:
Pop rock groove using notes in the dominant tonality.

Figure 8-17 (at 0:36 on Track 59) shows a box groove (no shifts) that uses the dominant chord, the mode (Mixolydian, in this case), and a chromatic tone outside the mode. Remember to start the groove with your middle finger on the root. Listen to the solid establishment of the groove in Figure 8-17 in the first half of the measure and the embellishment in the second half of the measure.

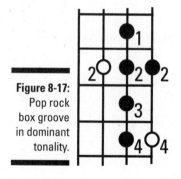

Figure 8-17:
Pop rock box groove in dominant tonality.

Blues Rock: Doin' What "Duck" Does and Playing a Countermelody

The bass lines in blues rock are very distinctive and repetitive. They form a little countermelody to accompany the real melody. When thinking of great blues rock bassists, the Allman Brothers's late bassist Berry Oakley comes to mind. Donald "Duck" Dunn, who played with the Blues Brothers and Booker T. & the MG's, also is a great example of a blues rock bassist.

In a blues style, the chords move in a specific sequence called the *blues progression* (a progression is the sequence of chords in a song). The official term for the standard blues progression is the *I-IV-V progression* (1-4-5 progression). The chords are either all dominant or all minor tonalities, except for the two measures of V, which almost always are dominant. Figuring out a blues progression is pretty straightforward. Here's what you do:

1. **Determine the root of your tune's starting chord (C, for example).**

   This chord is your I chord (or 1 chord).

2. **Using the scale of the I chord (C, in this case), find the 4 and 5 — the F and G (they're notes 4 and 5 of both the C dominant and C minor scales).**

   For a blues progression in C, F will be the root of the IV chord, and G will be the root for the V chord.

You now have the roots for your I-IV-V progression. The sequence used in the vast (and I mean *vast*) majority of blues tunes is

4 measures of I (C in the example from the previous list)

2 measures of IV (F)

2 measures of I (C)

2 measures of V (G)

2 measures of I (C)

Rinse and repeat — er, I mean you repeat this chord sequence throughout the song.

Because blues songs almost always move harmonically in a certain sequence, your groove needs to be easily moveable as well. Use notes that are easy to reach — within three strings and four frets.

Figure 8-18 (at the start of Track 60) shows a blues rock groove that uses only the root, albeit in two octaves. Start the groove with either your index or middle finger on the root. The beat, as with all the rock styles, is evenly divided.

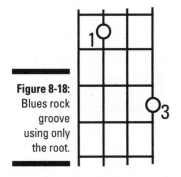

Figure 8-18: Blues rock groove using only the root.

The grooves in Figures 8-18 through 8-21, which you can hear on Track 60 or view in Video 21, sometimes use the octave for variety. As you add notes from the chord, mode, and box, the grooves get more and more dense … and interesting.

Figure 8-19 (at 0:10 on Track 60) shows a groove that adds the 3 and 5 to spell out the chord (a major chord here). You start the groove with your middle finger on the root so you don't have to make any shifts with your left hand. The groove uses only two strings, making it easy to move from chord to chord.

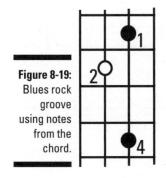

Figure 8-19: Blues rock groove using notes from the chord.

The groove in Figure 8-20 (at 0:21 on Track 60) adds notes from the mode (Mixolydian, in this case) to the 3 and 5 to really flesh out the dominant tonality. (Check out Chapter 5 for an explanation of modes, chords, and tonalities.) Start this groove with your middle finger on the root.

Figure 8-20: Blues rock groove using notes from the chord and mode.

The groove in Figure 8-21 (at 0:33 on Track 60) adds some chromatic tones to the scale tones and chord tones, making this groove particularly dense. You can play this groove in one position (which makes it a box groove). Start it with your middle finger on the root, and make sure you don't shift your left hand. In this particular case, you also may start with your index finger, because the groove uses only three frets.

Figure 8-21: Blues rock box groove.

Country Rock: Where Vocals Are King, and You Take a Back Seat

Like pop songs, country tunes tell a story — and the story needs to be heard (just think of Garth Brooks or Kenny Rogers). This means that you, as the bassist, take a back seat in country rock. (Don't worry. You get to shine in funk; see Chapter 10.) In the bass groove for country rock, the root and the 5 dominate.

Figure 8-22 (at the start of Track 61) shows a root-based groove for country rock. Even though it's a simple groove, it's one of the most popular grooves used in country music.

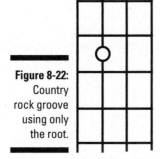 

Figure 8-22:
Country
rock groove
using only
the root.

On Track 61 and Video 21, you can listen to the simplicity of the bass grooves shown in Figures 8-22 through 8-25. Pay attention to how they lock in solidly with the drums, especially the bass drum. Notice how the grooves remain unobtrusive, despite added notes. You don't want anything to distract from the melody and lyrics of the song.

The country rock groove in Figure 8-23 (at 0:12 on Track 61) uses the root and the 5. I leave the 3 out of this example, because the 3 isn't used often in country rock. You can play this groove over both major and minor chords. The 3 differentiates the major from the minor, so, without the 3, the groove works over both chords.

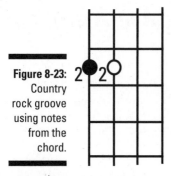

Figure 8-23:
Country
rock groove
using notes
from the
chord.

Notice that the 5 is played below the root in the groove shown in Figure 8-23. The 5 also can be played above the root.

Figure 8-24 (at 0:25 on Track 61) shows a country rock bass groove that uses the mode (the root and 5, plus one other note from the mode). In most country rock songs, you have to keep the bass line simple. Start the groove in Figure 8-24 with your pinkie on the root; your ring finger works, too.

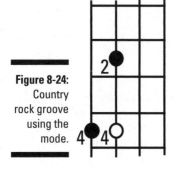

Figure 8-24:
Country
rock groove
using the
mode.

The box groove in Figure 8-25 (at 0:38 on Track 61) uses a chromatic tone outside the mode. This bass groove is simple and locked in with the drums. Grab your 10-gallon hat and play 'til the cows come home . . . and make sure your left hand is in position by starting with your pinkie on the root (though, you can also use your ring finger).

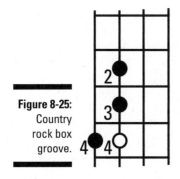

Figure 8-25:
Country
rock box
groove.

One Rock Fits All: Applying a Standard Rock Groove to Any Rock Song

What do you do when you're on the spot to play some of that great rock 'n' roll music? Wouldn't it be nice to have one standard groove you can pull out of your hat — or rather amp — that properly sums up the rock genre and is ambiguous enough to fit over just about any chord? Well, you're in luck. Here it is!

The groove in Figure 8-26 is just what you're looking for. It's a generic yet hip rock pattern that lets you move around the fingerboard with ease and speed. You can apply the groove in Figure 8-26 to the song on Track 62, which I play in Video 22.

If you're asked to perform a rock song and you're stumped with deciding what to play, this groove is a great starting point. You can always tweak your part later, after you're more familiar with the song, but this pattern usually does the trick and keeps you in the game.

The song in Figure 8-26 is a standard rock *chord progression* (a sequence of chords in a song). You're certain to encounter it — and similar ones — many times during the course of your bass-playing career.

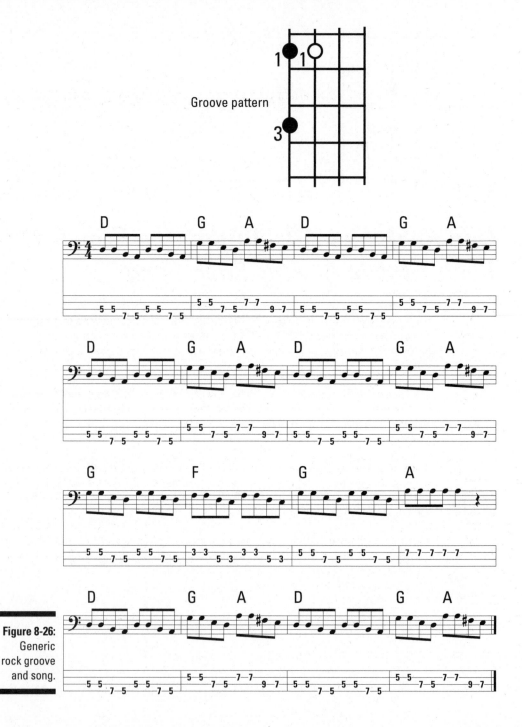

Figure 8-26: Generic rock groove and song.

Chapter 9

Swing It! Playing Styles That Rely on the Triplet Feel

....

In This Chapter

▶ Swinging in swing style

▶ Working the jazz walking bass line

▶ Shuffling through blues style

▶ Combining styles with the funk shuffle

▶ Access the audio tracks and video clips at www.dummies.com/go/bassguitar

....

*T*ri-pe-let, *tri*-pe-let, *tri*-pe-let . . . snap your fingers while you say it out loud, accenting the italicized syllables. Now take a wild guess at what kind of feel (rhythm) this chapter is about. That's right; it's the triplet feel, the feel that all the styles I feature in this chapter are based on. Triplet styles come in two flavors: swing and shuffle.

In music that has a triplet feel, each of the four beats in a measure is broken into three equal parts. Instead of counting "1, 2, 3, 4," you count "1-trip-let, 2-trip-let, 3-trip-let, 4-trip-let." You hear four triplets in each measure for a total of 12 hits (occurrences).

In this chapter, you can move all the grooves from chord to chord (check out Chapter 6 for more on moving grooves); be sure to practice moving the groove patterns in these grids from root to root. Consistent fingering is the key to success for moving these grooves smoothly.

Swing: Grooving Up-Tempo with Attitude

Swing style originated in the late 1920s and early '30s. The style of the Glenn Miller and Benny Goodman bands typifies the music of the early swing era. Bands like The Brian Setzer Orchestra bring swing to today's music scene. In swing style, the first note of the two eighth notes in each beat is *slightly longer* than the second — long, short, long, short — and it gives the feeling of . . . swinging, of course. Each of the four beats in a measure still has the three parts of a triplet, but you tend to play on only the first and third of each — on the "tri-" and on the "-let" of the "tri-pe-let."

The bass line in swing style is predictable but cool (it makes you want to snap your fingers). The vast majority of swing tunes are based on a major or a dominant tonality. (I cover tonality in Chapter 5.)

Figure 9-1 shows you a swing groove in a major tonality, using a major pentatonic scale. (See Chapter 7 for an explanation of pentatonic scales.) Start this groove with your middle finger to avoid shifting your left hand.

Figure 9-1: Swing groove using a major pentatonic scale.

As you listen to the groove from Figure 9-1 on Track 63 (Video 23), notice how the notes of the bass line are played on the beat and how the drums subdivide each of those beats into — that's right — triplets.

Figure 9-2 shows an example of a swing groove using a mode — in this case, the common Mixolydian mode. (Check out Chapter 5 for information about modes.)

Figure 9-2:
Swing
groove
using a
Mixolydian
mode.

Again, as you're listening to the groove from Figure 9-2 (on Track 63 at 0:18), notice how your bass line is concentrated on the beats, whereas the drums subdivide the beat into triplets.

Jazz: Going for a Walk

A *walking bass line* simply walks through the appropriate scale of each chord, one note per beat, hitting every beat of each measure. The walking bass line in the jazz style is a more creative form of bass playing than the other swing styles because you choose new notes each time you play the same song. The walking bass line was developed by upright bassists, such as Ray Brown, Milt Hinton, Paul Chambers, and Ron Carter, but these days it's played just as commonly by bass guitarists. The triplet is implied in each beat; just listen to how these master bass players embellish their walk with dead notes (see Chapters 5 and 6 for dead notes).

Creating a walking bass line is one of the more elusive art forms in the bass world, but this section takes you through it step by step (pun intended) so it doesn't seem so obscure. The formula for a successful walking bass line is simple:

1. **Beat 1: Determine the chord tonality (major, minor, dominant, or half-diminished) so you know which finger to start with, and play the root of that chord.**

   In some cases, you may want to use something other than the root of the chord to give the line more melodic variety. If so, you can play a strong chord tone (the 3rd or the 5th of that chord) on beat 1, instead of the root. (See Chapter 5 for more about chord tonalities.)

2. **Beat 2: Play any chord tone of the chord, or any note in the scale related to that chord.**

   If you're not sure which scale belongs to which chord, check out Chapter 5.

3. **Beat 3: Play any chord tone or scale tone of the chord.**

   Yep — same as Step 2, but pick a different note.

4. **Beat 4: Play a leading tone to the next root.**

   A *leading tone* leads from one chord to the next. The sound of the leading tone isn't related to the current chord; it's related to the chord you're approaching. In other words, the leading tone prepares the listener's ear for the sound of the new chord. The most important point to understand about a leading tone is that it aims for the *following* chord's root. For example, if you're going from a C chord to an F chord, your leading tone relates to the *F* (never mind the C).

   Leading tones come in three types:

   - Chromatic (half-step)

   - Diatonic (scale)

   - Dominant (the 5 of the new chord)

   Figure 9-3 shows the location of each type of leading tone. The root of the new chord is represented by the open circle; the leading tones are represented by the solid dots. The arrows show which way the leading tone moves to resolve to the root of the new chord.

   In a walking bass line, beat 4 of the measure is reserved for the leading tone.

Figure 9-3:
The locations of the chromatic, diatonic, and dominant leading tones.

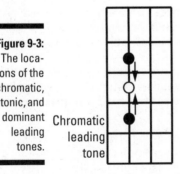
Chromatic leading tone

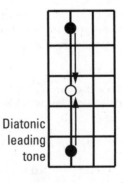
Diatonic leading tone

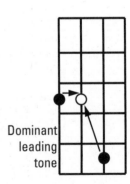
Dominant leading tone

Working the walk

Creating walking bass lines can be overwhelming at first because they don't seem to follow any predictable template the way regular grooves do (check out Chapter 6 for more on creating grooves). However, you can break down walking into three main concepts, and the whole thing becomes as clear as a 5th-fret harmonic on a brand new G string. Here are the three main concepts for walking bass lines:

- ✔ Walking using the root, the 5, and a leading tone
- ✔ Walking using chord tones and a leading tone
- ✔ Walking using scale tones and a leading tone

All three of these walking concepts have one element in common: The all-important leading tone on the last beat, the note that leads you — and your band — to the next chord. The leading tone is what makes or breaks your walking line. Be sure you're absolutely familiar with each of the three leading tone types in Figure 9-3.

Figure 9-4 shows a typical jazz *progression* (sequence of chords) that includes the main chord types: major, minor, dominant, and half-diminished.

Figure 9-4:
Jazz
progression
for walking
bass.

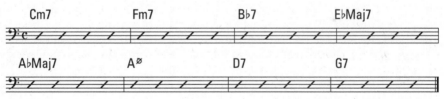

The root-5 concept

Figure 9-5 is an example of a walking bass line that uses only the root of a chord (including the octave), the 5, and the all-important leading tone that comes on the last beat of each measure (octaves and measures are explained in Chapters 5 and 4, respectively).

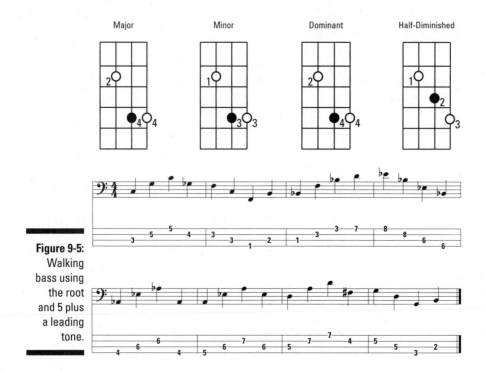

Figure 9-5:
Walking
bass using
the root
and 5 plus
a leading
tone.

The most important asset of this method is that you can use the same struc-ture on all the major, minor, and dominant chords in a song. You can move the pattern as a *constant structure* from chord to chord with ease (see Chapter 6 for information on constant structure). Only the half-diminished chord requires a slight alteration in the pattern — you lower the 5 by a half step (or one fret), making it a *diminished* 5, which is the defining note for a half-diminished chord.

Listen to Track 64 and watch Video 24 for guidance on how to play the root-5 concept in a song, and check out Chapter 5 for any help you may need with the chord types. After you're comfortable playing the line in Figure 9-5, note for note, pan out the bass and come up with your own line.

The chord-tone concept

You can bump your bass line to a new level of sophistication when you understand the chord-tone concept. Try playing the etude in Figure 9-6. (*Etude* is a fancy name for musical exercise.) In this case, you're using the *chord tones* of each chord, both ascending and descending, plus the crucial leading tone to walk your way from chord to chord through the harmony.

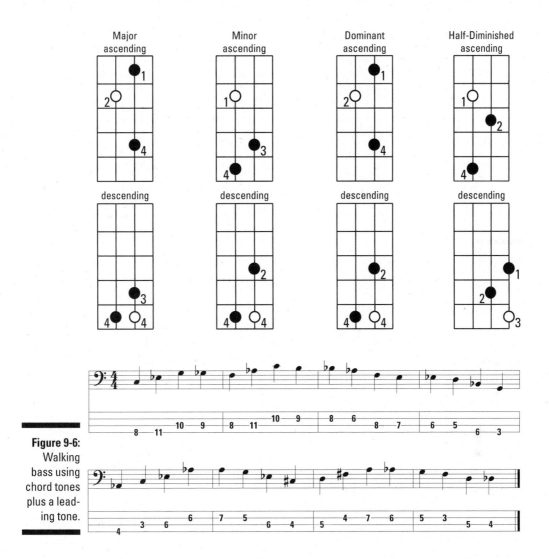

Figure 9-6:
Walking bass using chord tones plus a leading tone.

To start, get your fretting hand into the proper position for each chord. Just follow the grid pattern in Figure 9-6 so you can cover all the notes for each chord without shifting. In other words, shift your hand into position at the beginning of each new chord, and then stay there until you have to shift into position for the next chord.

Play the entire example in Figure 9-6, note for note, and get used to the sound of a well-constructed walking bass line by listening to Track 65 or watching Video 24. After you're comfortable with it, pan the bass out of the recording and come up with your own bass part, using the concept of chord tones plus leading tones.

The scale-tone concept

The smoothest and most *linear* (moving step by step in a scale) walking concept is the one that uses scale tones; you can find an example in Figure 9-7. Play the first three notes of the appropriate scale for each chord, either ascending or descending, and add the leading tone on the last beat of each measure to get smoothly to the next chord (for a thorough explanation of the chord-scale relationships, check out Chapter 5).

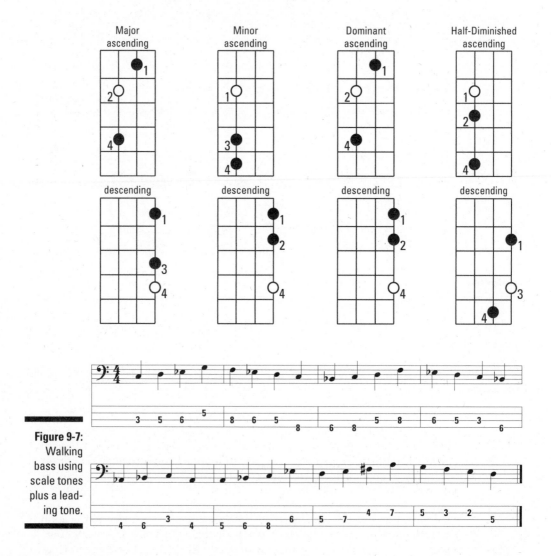

Figure 9-7: Walking bass using scale tones plus a leading tone.

You may want to practice your scales a bit before diving into the etude in Figure 9-7, especially your descending scales. When you're ready, play the bass part, note for note, with the recording. Eventually, you can get rid of the recorded bass by panning to one side and come up with your own bass line of scale tones plus a leading tone. Ah, and just in case I forgot to mention it, leading tones are crucial to a great walking bass line.

You can hear how easily this walking line moves from chord to chord on Track 66 and Video 24. Pay very close attention to the use of the leading tone at the end of each measure; it's what makes a walking line move smoothly to the next chord.

Which of the walking concepts in Figures 9-5 through 9-7 is right for you? Well, actually, all of them are great. If you have a good handle on all three concepts, you can switch among them while you're playing your bass part in a song. You'll sound cool, off-the-cuff, and unpredictable. And why not? Walking should be fun to play and interesting to listen to.

Applying a jazz blues walking pattern

You can walk through almost any jazz tune. To demonstrate the jazz walking style properly, I show you how to walk in a *jazz blues progression* (see Figures 9-8 and 9-9). In these figures, the chords are printed above each grid. The notes for each measure are clearly marked: Each open circle represents the root that begins the sequence; then you play the light gray circle, followed by the dark gray circle. The leading tone is the last note in each sequence (follow the arrows). You can start this progression on any root. Figure 9-8 is written in B♭; you start the pattern on the E string with your middle finger. The pattern in Figure 9-9 is in F, and you start it on the A string with your pinkie.

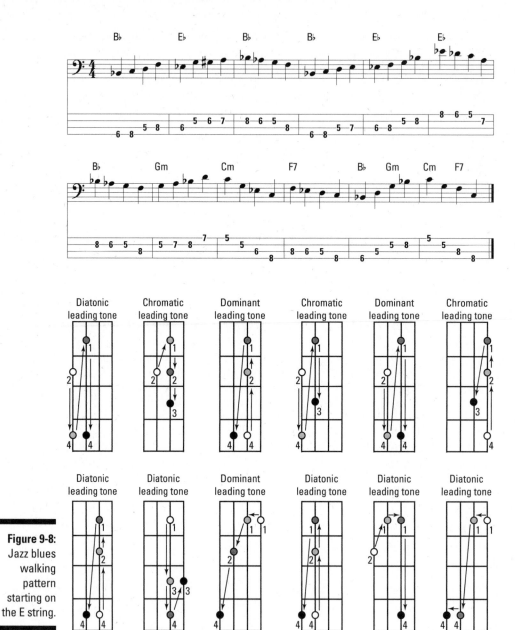

Figure 9-8:
Jazz blues walking pattern starting on the E string.

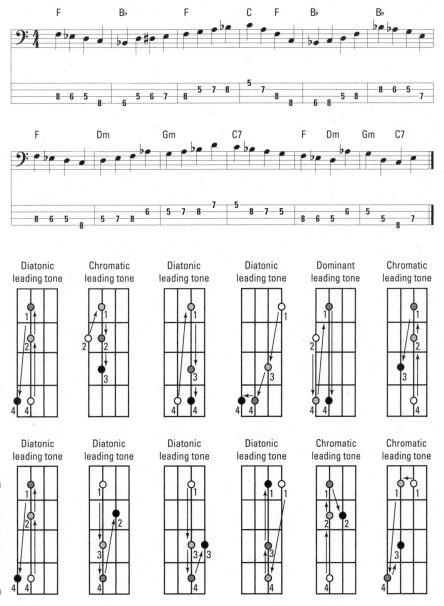

Figure 9-9:
Jazz blues walking pattern starting on the A string.

Which pattern is the right one for which key? Simple. Play the blues in keys G, G♯/A♭, A, A♯/B♭, B, and C, using the pattern that starts on the E string. Play the blues in keys C♯/D♭, D, D♯/E♭, E, F, and F♯/G♭, using the pattern that starts on the A string. In this way, your notes stay in the low register, making your walking bass line more authoritative — and who would argue with authority?

By the way, playing these patterns is easy (despite the complex sound) because you don't have to shift your left hand. Just make sure you begin the pattern with your middle finger if you're starting on the E string or your pinkie if you're starting on the A string.

As you listen to Tracks 67 and 68 or watch Video 24, notice how every kind of leading tone is used. The bass part is so intricate that you can even repeat it several times without changing a single note.

Take your time when starting to play a new tune; you need to figure out the scales for each chord before you play it. The more you play, the faster you become.

Blues Shuffle: Walking Like Donald Duck (Dunn, That Is)

The *blues shuffle* is one of the most recognizable triplet feels in music. The bass line is an organized walk — it's a walking bass line that's repeated throughout the tune. When you play the blues shuffle, you may feel as if you're playing a lopsided rhythm. The first note is long, the second is short, the third is long, and so on.

Tommy Shannon (bassist for Stevie Ray Vaughan), Roscoe Beck (bassist for Robben Ford), and the incomparable Donald "Duck" Dunn (of the Blues Brothers and Booker T. & the MG's) are three wonderful blues bassists who are superbly skilled at playing the blues shuffle.

Figure 9-10 (at the start of Track 69) demonstrates a blues shuffle groove that uses only one note: The root. You can use this groove for any chord.

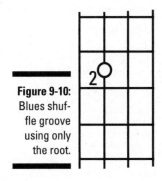

Figure 9-10:
Blues shuffle groove using only the root.

Figure 9-11 (at 0:11 on Track 69) shows another example of a blues shuffle groove. The 3 and 5 are added to this groove to form a major chord. Start the groove with your middle finger.

Figure 9-11:
Blues shuffle groove using a major chord.

In Figure 9-12, (at 0:39 on Track 69) notes from the Mixolydian mode (see Chapter 5 for more about modes) are added to the root, 3, and 5, filling out the chord to form a dominant tonality. Start this groove with your middle finger on the root.

Figure 9-12: Blues shuffle groove using a Mixolydian mode.

But what if the blues tune you're playing is on the sad side, in a minor tonality? (After all, sad tunes *are* a strong possibility when you're playing the blues.) If you want to play the groove in Figure 9-12 over a minor tonality, you need to make a minor adjustment: Simply change the tonality by flatting the 3 (making it a ♭3). Figure 9-13 (at 0:59 on Track 69) shows a blues shuffle that includes notes from the minor mode (the Aeolian or Dorian mode).

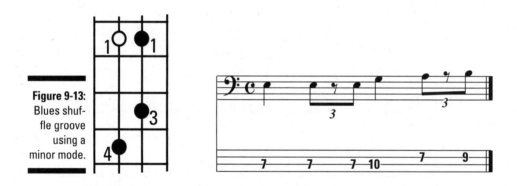

Figure 9-13: Blues shuffle groove using a minor mode.

The blues shuffle groove in Figure 9-14 (at 1:18 on Track 69) is more complex. It includes not only notes from the chord and its related modes (in this case, Mixolydian for the dominant chord) but also *chromatic tones* (notes moving in half steps; see Chapter 5 for more on chromatic tones).

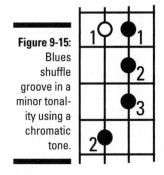

Figure 9-14:
Blues shuffle groove using a Mixolydian mode with a chromatic tone.

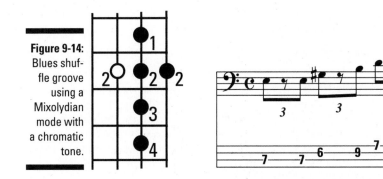

Finally, Figure 9-15 (at 1:38 on Track 69) shows a complex blues shuffle, using a chromatic tone, that you play over a minor tonality.

Figure 9-15:
Blues shuffle groove in a minor tonality using a chromatic tone.

Figures 9-10 through 9-15 show different variations on the shuffle groove patterns. You can hear them all on Track 69 or watch Video 25. Listen for the lopsided feel of the shuffle in each of the grooves — the long-short-long-short rhythm of the notes. While you're at it, notice the differences in tonalities and also how some sound busier than others.

The grooves in Figures 9-14 and 9-15 use a strong *triplet figure* (three notes per beat) on the last beat of the measure. This triplet figure helps establish the strong triplet feel for this style. Play around with these grooves and come up with some of your own. By the way, these grooves work well over a blues progression. (See Chapter 8 for the structure of the blues progression.)

Funk Shuffle: Combining Funk, Blues, and Jazz

Funk shuffle (also called *shuffle funk*) is a hybrid groove style, which means that it combines several elements of other styles — funk, blues, and jazz. When funk, which normally uses straight sixteenth notes, is combined with blues and jazz, which use triplets, the resulting combination is a lopsided sixteenth-note groove (a combination of long and short notes) — a very cool combination. This type of groove is pretty challenging to play, but some useful tricks of the trade can help make it a lot easier.

Check out Figure 9-16 (at the start of Track 70) for an example of a funk shuffle groove. This groove uses only the root (in two octaves) with an added *dead note* (a note that sounds like a thud; see Chapter 5 for a complete explanation). The drums are crucial in this style because they drive the rhythm along in tandem with the bass. You can start this groove with your index or middle finger on the low root (the starting note).

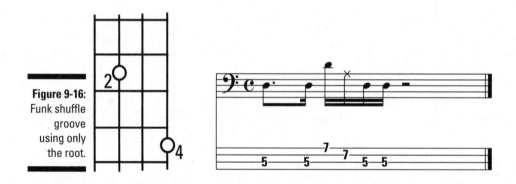

Figure 9-16: Funk shuffle groove using only the root.

Figure 9-17 (0:29 on Track 70) shows an example of a funk shuffle groove that uses notes common to both the Mixolydian (dominant) and Dorian (minor) modes. Whoa! The groove in Figure 9-17 fits over both dominant *and* minor? Yep! In fact, it's an *ambiguous groove* (see Chapter 5 for an explanation of ambiguous grooves). This groove isn't all that easy to master, but after you get comfortable with it, you can get lots (and lots) of use out of playing it over any dominant or minor chord. In the funk shuffle style, almost all chords are dominant or minor.

Figure 9-17: Funk shuffle groove for dominant and minor chords.

The funk shuffle in Figure 9-18 (0:58 on Track 70) includes more notes from both the Mixolydian and Dorian modes; notice the cool syncopation — the way a note anticipates the beat that it's normally expected to land on. (Chapter 10 covers syncopation.) The groove in Figure 9-18 can be used over most chords in shuffle funk tunes (that's right; it's an ambiguous groove). Most of the chords are either dominant (Mixolydian) or minor (Dorian). Start the groove with your index or middle finger to keep it in the box (so you don't have to shift your left hand).

Figure 9-18: Funk shuffle groove using notes from the dominant or minor modes.

You can hear Figures 9-16 through 9-18 on Track 70, or watch Video 25. As you listen to the funk shuffle grooves, your head should be boppin' with the beat. The funk shuffle has a much more . . . well . . . funky sound than the other shuffle styles. You still have the lopsided shuffle feel but with a lot more attitude.

When you're grooving on a funk shuffle, you can keep going for hours and hours without getting the least bit bored; because of its complexity, a funk shuffle is going to keep you busy. Keep the shuffle funky, "'cause it don't mean a thing if it ain't got that swing."

The quintessential generic shuffle/swing song is a good old-fashioned blues, like the one in Figure 9-19. (For more on the structure of a typical blues song, check out Chapter 8.)

Groove pattern

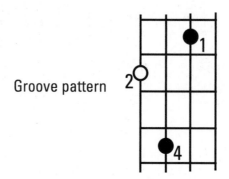

Figure 9-19: Generic shuffle song.

To really get yourself into the proper mood for the blues, get up on a rickety bar stool, pour yourself a blues-approved beverage (mixed drinks, peach-flavored diet iced tea, and sparkling water are *not* blues-approved drinks — black coffee and muddy water *are*), and start playing the blues along with Track 71.

Chapter 10

Making It Funky: Playing Hardcore Bass Grooves

In This Chapter

▶ Feelin' R & B

▶ Igniting the Motown engine

▶ Creating a fusion of styles

▶ Playing funk

▶ Hopping to hip-hop

▶ Bringing in da funky groove

▶ Access the audio tracks and video clips at www.dummies.com/go/bassguitar

*G*imme da funk! You gotta gimme da funk! When these words echo across the bandstand, they're directed at you (and your alter ego, the drummer). From Motown to hip-hop, the bass player takes a starring role in funk, and your skill and dexterity are put to the test. Funk is essentially party music, and your job is to keep every foot in the room moving to the beat.

Hardcore bass grooves give a real workout for any bass player. In funk, the sixteenth note is the rhythm of choice, and you play quite a few of them. In this chapter, I give you a selection of prime funk grooves that you can use when the words "Gimme da funk!" echo in your direction across the bandstand.

In addition to listening to the audio tracks mentioned in the chapter, you can watch me play many of the grooves in Video 26.

R & B: Movin' to Rhythm and Blues

R & B (rhythm and blues) originated in the late 1940s and is often referred to as "R & B/Soul." It's still one of today's most popular styles of music. R & B is dominated by *session players* — musicians who record with numerous artists.

Often, record producers hire the same rhythm section (session players) to accompany all their artists. So you have the same bassist, drummer, guitarist, and keyboardist playing together for years and years on countless sessions with different artists. It's a sure recipe for some serious rhythm section interplay; these cats *know* each other's playing style.

Tommy Cogbill (who played with such singers as Aretha Franklin, Dusty Springfield, and Wilson Pickett) and Chuck Rainey (who played with Aretha Franklin, Quincy Jones, and Steely Dan) are two great session players. Because of this tradition of using session players, you can hear excellent grooves behind some fabulous singers. These musicians are completely at ease with one another after having recorded a multitude of successful songs together over the years.

The bass groove in R & B consists of a fairly active bass part, locked in tight with the drums. Because R & B music often has such a busy bass line — the harmony includes both scale and chord tones — you need a lot of different notes to keep it interesting and not overly repetitive.

The use of *syncopation* — a tied note that anticipates a beat (for more on ties, check out Chapter 4) — makes the R & B groove funky. You create syncopation by striking a note when it's not expected and then failing to restrike the note where it *is* expected. When playing grooves with syncopation, you anticipate the beat by playing a note sooner than expected. This technique gives the music a kick, like a roller coaster that suddenly drops toward the ground when you least expect it.

Figure 10-1 (at the start of Track 72) shows an R & B groove in a major tonality. (If you need help creating grooves for different tonalities — major, minor, and dominant — check out Chapter 6.) Start this groove with your middle finger to avoid shifting your left hand.

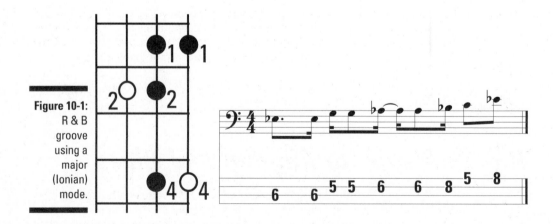

Figure 10-1: R & B groove using a major (Ionian) mode.

The groove in Figure 10-1 uses notes from the major chord and its related Ionian mode for a major tonality. (See Chapter 5 for information about mode and chord compatibility.) You can also play this groove as a dominant tonality by playing it as is or by using the ♭7 rather than the 6.

Figure 10-2 (at 0:27 on Track 72) shows an R & B groove in a dominant tonality using the Mixolydian mode. Start this groove with your middle finger to avoid shifting.

Figure 10-2: R & B groove using a dominant (Mixolydian) mode.

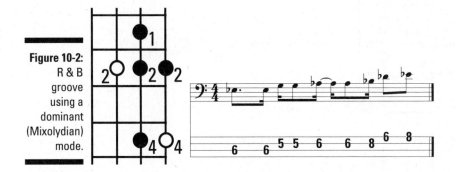

In Figure 10-3 (at 0:53 on Track 72), you can see what the groove from Figure 10-1 looks like in a minor tonality. This groove is based on a Dorian or Aeolian mode (either one will do in this case), and it fits perfectly over a minor chord. Start the groove with your index finger.

Figure 10-3: R & B groove using a minor (Dorian or Aeolian) mode.

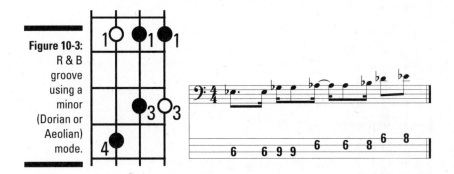

You have to listen carefully to hear the subtle difference between the major and dominant grooves shown in Figures 10-1 and 10-2; only one note (the second-to-last note) is different. Figure 10-3 changes the tonality from dominant to minor by changing one note from Figure 10-2. You can hear all three grooves on Track 72.

Dead notes and chromatic tones are frequently used in all funk styles, including R & B. (See Chapter 5 for an explanation of dead notes and chromatic tones.) Figure 10-4 shows you what the grooves in Figures 10-1, 10-2, and 10-3 look like with dead notes and chromatic tones added. The grooves in Figure 10-4 tend to sound fairly complex.

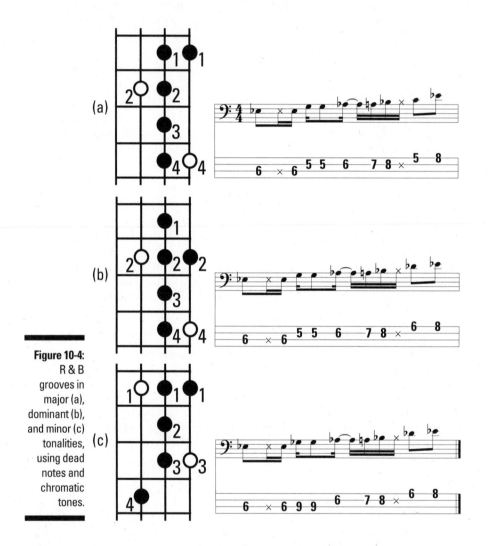

Figure 10-4: R & B grooves in major (a), dominant (b), and minor (c) tonalities, using dead notes and chromatic tones.

Figure 10-4 utilizes dead notes to make the groove sound busier. Listen to Track 72 starting at 1:20 for the very subtle thud of the dead notes in each groove.

To keep your R & B grooves interesting, you may want to start with simple rhythms and notes, and then you can add dead notes and chromatic tones as you get deeper into the tune.

The Motown Sound: Grooving with the Music of the Funk Brothers

Motown is the name of a record label that got its start in Detroit in the late 1950s. The *Motown style* is actually part of the R & B family, which you can read about in the preceding section. Numerous singers recorded for Motown, and the vast majority of them were fortunate enough to be able to use the Motown house band — the famous Funk Brothers (a group of top-notch session players) — for their recordings.

James Jamerson (also known as Funk Brother #1) not only defined the label's sound with his active, syncopated lines on hundreds of hits, but he also forged the template for modern electric bass playing. Marvin Gaye, The Temptations, Stevie Wonder, and a slew of other artists benefited from the outstanding groove-creating abilities of Jamerson and the Funk Brothers. Your bass skills also can benefit from the Jamerson/Motown-style grooves featured in this section.

Many of the Motown grooves use *constant structure*. Constant-structure grooves use notes that occur in more than one tonality. (The shared notes are called *common tones;* see Chapter 6 for more about constant-structure grooves.) You can play a groove using constant structure over any chord and still make it sound interesting.

Figure 10-5 (at the start of Track 73) shows a typical Motown groove that works well over a major or dominant tonality. (This one even works for a minor tonality.) When you play the groove, start it with your pinkie.

Figure 10-5:
Motown groove using constant structure for major and dominant tonalities.

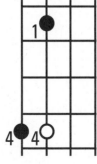

Figure 10-6 (at 0:22 on Track 73) shows a busy Motown groove using common tones for dominant and minor tonalities. This groove also sports chromatic tones in the second measure (a classic *groove tail*) that lead back to the beginning of the groove (see Chapter 6 for an explanation of the *groove tail*). Start the groove with your pinkie.

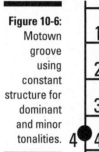
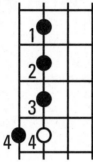

Figure 10-6: Motown groove using constant structure for dominant and minor tonalities.

Notice how the grooves in Figures 10-5 and 10-6 each have a slight variation in the second measure. This variation is a Jamerson trademark. You can hear the variation when you listen to the grooves on Track 73.

Fusion: Blending Two Styles into One

Fusion is the merging of two or more styles of music. Fusion generally refers to the combination of rock rhythms and jazz harmonies, but any combination of styles is possible. Fusion-style bass playing is intricate and complex, and full of nervous energy and fast notes; its deep grooves allow you to really rock the joint. In this section, I show you bass grooves that use every trick in the book: scale tones, dead notes, chromatic tones, and plenty of sixteenth notes.

Figure 10-7 shows a busy fusion-style groove that you can play over either a major or dominant chord (Ionian or Mixolydian mode). Notice the use of dead notes and the chromatic tones that make the groove more interesting. Start the groove in Figure 10-7 with your middle finger; no shifts of the left hand are necessary (or desired). The groove is extremely busy, hitting all 16 of the sixteenth notes in the measure.

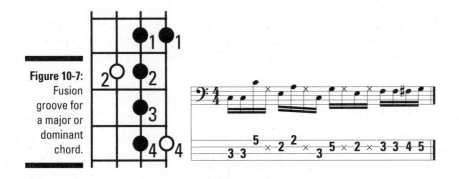

Figure 10-7:
Fusion
groove for
a major or
dominant
chord.

The groove in Figure 10-7 (at the start of Track 74) is challenging to play, so take your time with it. The ease with which you'll be able to play it in a band will be well worth the extra effort now.

Figure 10-8 (at 0:33 on Track 74) shows a fusion-style groove for a dominant chord (Mixolydian mode). Start this groove with your middle finger.

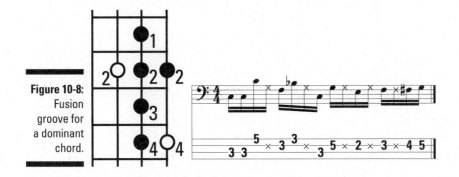

Figure 10-8:
Fusion
groove for
a dominant
chord.

Many fusion-style tunes have an extended section of just one chord. With this type of tune, you don't have to move your groove from chord to chord. You can use a groove that covers all four strings of your bass to really expand your harmonic range. Figure 10-9 (at 1:06 on Track 74) shows such a groove. This groove, which is based on a Mixolydian mode (for a dominant chord), requires no shifting if you start it with your middle finger. It may take a bit of effort to get it under your belt — I mean fingers — but it's well worth it.

Figure 10-9:
Fusion groove covering four strings on a dominant chord.

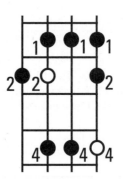

On Track 74, you can hear how the busy bass grooves in Figures 10-7 through 10-9 interact with equally busy drum parts. They're typical fusion grooves for both bass and drums.

Fusion grooves can be incredibly busy and complex while still having a fleeting feeling about them. They seem light and kind of skip along. To achieve this effect, pepper your fusion grooves generously with dead notes, which lighten up the wall of notes and give your groove some much-needed dynamic variety.

A brief history of fusion from the bass player's view

With the dawn of fusion in the 1970s, the role of the bassist was pushed to the forefront. Groups such as Return to Forever, with their astonishing bassist Stanley Clarke, and Weather Report, with the incredible bassist Jaco Pastorius, took bass playing to stratospheric heights. Suddenly bassists were expected to play blistering sixteenth-note grooves and perform solos like horn players. This era also saw the emergence of the *fretless bass* (a bass guitar without frets) — thanks to Jaco — as well as basses with more than four strings, such as the great session player Anthony Jackson's six-string contrabass guitar (with the addition of a low B string and a high C string) and the five-string (with a low B), which was a spinoff of Jackson's invention.

Funk: Light Fingers, Heavy Attitude

Funk is not only a collective term for funk styles; it also refers to a particular style of playing. *Funk style* is normally percussive in sound and is often played with a thumb (slap) technique (see Chapter 2). But playing finger-style works just as well in producing the percussive sound of funk. Flea (of the Red Hot Chili Peppers) and Victor Wooten (who plays with Béla Fleck and the Flecktones) are two excellent thumbers. Francis Rocco Prestia (of Tower of Power) is a master of finger-style funk. Marcus Miller (a solo artist) is great at using both finger-style and thumb technique.

Funk style emphasizes rhythm. The note choices are often *neutral* (they work for more than one tonality). Figure 10-10 is an example of a funk groove that's intended to be played by slapping. Of course, when your thumb starts to blister from all that slapping, you can always play the groove using finger-style. This particular groove moves through a little mini-progression (a sequence of chords) that's common in funk.

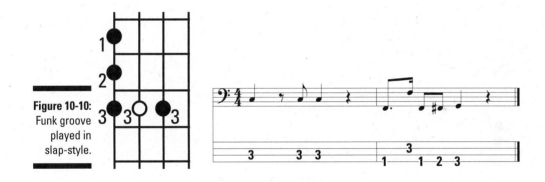

Figure 10-10:
Funk groove played in slap-style.

On Track 75, you can hear a distinct difference in the way the groove from Figure 10-10 sounds compared to the other grooves in this section, due to the fact that it's slapped (thumb style) and popped — the index finger snaps the top notes (see Chapter 2 for an explanation of slap-style playing).

You can try the slap technique on almost any of the other grooves in this section, though I'd recommend getting comfortable with playing them using finger-style first.

Figure 10-11 (at the start of Track 76) shows a funk groove that can be played over a dominant or minor chord. It has an aggressive attitude. Start the groove with the index or middle finger of your left hand.

Figure 10-11:
Funk groove for a dominant or minor tonality.

Figure 10-12 (at 0:27 on Track 76) shows a funk groove that can be played over a major tonality. (It also works over a dominant tonality.) This groove represents a happy-sounding funk. This happy sound isn't common, but sometimes the happy funk tunes have a way of sneaking up on you, so be ready. After all, where do you think the term *slap-happy* came from?

Figure 10-12:
Funk groove using a major tonality.

The groove in Figure 10-13 (at 0:57 on Track 76) is a heavier funk groove in a minor tonality with a couple of chromatic tones added. (**Remember:** The more notes in a funk groove, the lighter the groove; the fewer notes in the groove, the heavier the groove.) Start this one with your pinkie or ring finger to keep the shifts to a minimum.

Figure 10-13:
Heavy funk groove using a minor tonality.

Figure 10-14 (at 1:26 on Track 76) shows a heavy funk groove in a major or dominant tonality. While the major tonality isn't commonly found in funk, it's a good idea to be prepared in case you encounter one. Instead of defining this groove as a blatant major by adding a 3, you can avoid the 3 altogether by substituting the 6 (a neutral note). Start this groove with your pinkie to keep the shifts to a minimum.

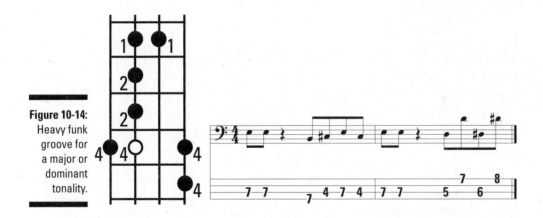

Figure 10-14:
Heavy funk groove for a major or dominant tonality.

In Figure 10-15 (at 1:55 on Track 76), you have a funk groove that fits over both minor and dominant chords and is played in finger-style. (I suggest using finger-style when you have a lot of fast-moving notes in a groove.) Start this groove with your pinkie or ring finger.

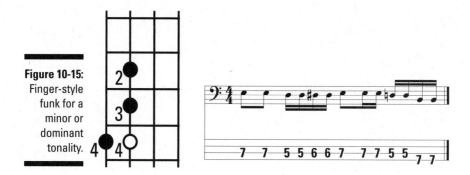

Figure 10-15:
Finger-style
funk for a
minor or
dominant
tonality.

Figure 10-16 (at 2:21 on Track 76) shows you a finger-style funk groove in a major tonality (the counterpart of the groove from Figure 10-15). Start it with your pinkie.

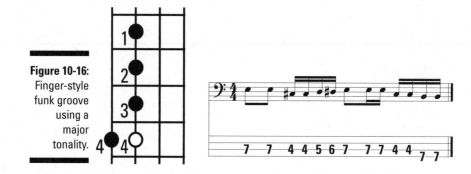

Figure 10-16:
Finger-style
funk groove
using a
major
tonality.

No matter how you play the grooves in this section, make them funky. Practice them with a metronome (see Chapter 4) and make them precise — and above all, enjoy!

Listen to the slight variations in Figures 10-11 through 10-16 on Track 76. Figure 10-11 sounds dominant or minor, whereas Figure 10-12 is definitely major; Figure 10-13 is minor, and its counterpart in Figure 10-14 is major or dominant; Figure 10-15 is minor or dominant, and Figure 10-16 is major. These differences may be difficult to distinguish at first, but with frequent listening, you can train your ear to hear the differences among major, minor, and dominant immediately.

Hip-Hop: Featuring Heavy Funk with Heavy Attitude

Hip-hop entered the music world in the 1990s. This style features a fat ("phat") bass groove that sounds more laid-back than some of the other funk styles. Hip-hop is all about the message; the bass groove provides an important but unobtrusive accompaniment to the vocals. Although the bass line isn't busy, it's well timed and repetitive. The feel and attitude are the most important features of the hip-hop groove. Raphael Saadiq is a well-known hip-hop bassist; he's best known for his work with D'Angelo and Tony Toni Tone.

Figure 10-17 (at the start of Track 77) shows a hip-hop-style bass groove. Start the groove with your ring finger.

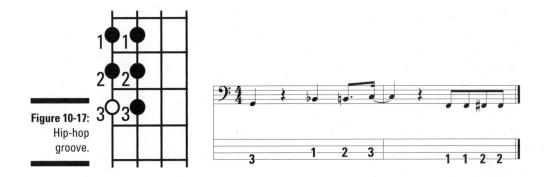

Figure 10-17: Hip-hop groove.

The tonality in hip-hop is often minor, but it may occasionally be a dominant tonality. Notice that the groove doesn't move much from its starting chord. The tone is usually much darker than the bright funk style.

Figure 10-18 (at 0:26 on Track 77) shows another groove in hip-hop style, this one for a minor or dominant tonality. Start this groove with your middle finger.

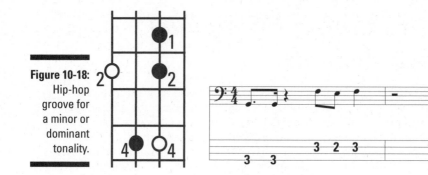

Figure 10-18: Hip-hop groove for a minor or dominant tonality.

Figure 10-19 (at 0:52 on Track 77) features a groove for a major or dominant tonality; it's for the happy hip-hoppers. Start this groove with your middle finger.

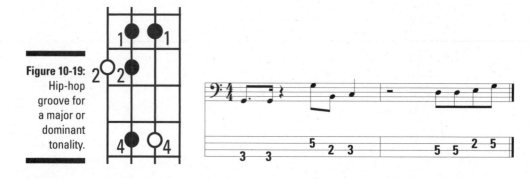

Figure 10-19: Hip-hop groove for a major or dominant tonality.

As you listen to the grooves from Figures 10-17 through 10-19 on Track 77, notice the long spaces between each note. Hip-hop grooves often use lots of space and only a few notes.

A synthesizer is sometimes used to play (or even double) the bass groove in hip-hop, but nothing grooves like the real thing.

Knowing What to Do When You Just Want to Funkifize a Tune

You wanna bring in da funk? But how? That's a loaded question. You need a groove that does the funk genre justice and at the same time is ambiguous enough to fit over just about any chord. Voilà! I present to you the slam-dunk-funk-R-&-B/Soul-always-makes-people-happy groove that gets the job done. When you're in a pinch and don't know what to play on a song, whip out the hip little groove in Figure 10-20 to hold down the bottom. Chances are you'll be right on the money with it.

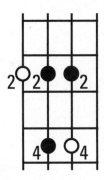

Figure 10-20: Generic funk groove and song.

Try out this one-size-fits-all groove by playing it along with Track 78, which is a pretty standard song for the funk genre. The song's harmony changes between dominant and minor, but your groove pattern doesn't change at all. (For more on dominant and minor scales, check out Chapter 5.) You simply move the pattern to the new root, and you're ready to get funky.

Chapter 11

Sampling International Flavors: Bass Styles from Around the World

In This Chapter

▶ Swaying and moving to Brazilian beats

▶ Spicing up Afro-Cuban grooves

▶ Jammin' with island rhythms reggae and calypso

▶ Throwing in some American flavor with ska

▶ Warming up to African grooves

▶ Connecting to world beat

▶ Access the audio tracks and video clips at www.dummies.com/go/bassguitar

Ah, imagine: Cool ocean breezes, white-sand beaches, palm trees, and, of course, the sound of great bass grooves with native flavor. In this chapter, you discover how to play bass grooves that come from such exotic locales as South America, the Caribbean, and Africa. Rhythm is the all-important ingredient for bass grooves in these international styles. The harmony itself is often fairly simple.

All the grooves in this chapter provide you with a whole new way to use rhythm. So the next time you feel like visiting an exotic location, grab your bass instead of your sunscreen and check out these places musically.

Bossa Nova: Baskin' in a Brazilian Beat

If you've ever heard "Girl from Ipanema," you're familiar with bossa nova. Antonio Carlos Jobim, who wrote "Girl from Ipanema," is one of the great composers of bossa nova tunes. Bossa nova music (native to Brazil) has a light, swaying quality and a sensuous, easygoing groove. *Bossas* (short for bossa nova tunes) are usually of medium tempo (if you find yourself shaking to a groove rather than swaying, it's probably too fast to be a bossa).

The bass line in bossa nova almost always employs a combination of the root and 5 (see Chapter 6), and it fits over all major, minor, and dominant chords. This allows you to play a very consistent bass groove.

Figure 11-1 gives a common bossa nova groove for a major, dominant, or minor tonality. Start it with either your index or middle finger; it needs no shifting of your left hand.

Figure 11-1: Bossa nova groove for a major, minor, or dominant chord.

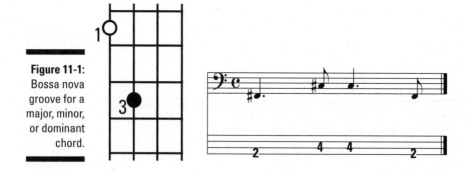

 When bossa novas are played as jazz tunes, you occasionally encounter *half-diminished* chords in which the 5 is flatted. In these cases, you can satisfy the harmonic requirements for the half-diminished chord by simply playing a groove with a root and a ♭5.

Figure 11-2 shows a groove in a half-diminished tonality using the Locrian mode (see Chapter 5 for more on modes). This groove is similar to the one in Figure 11-1, but the 5 is changed to ♭5 to accommodate the ♭5 in the chord. To avoid shifting, start it with your index or middle finger.

Figure 11-2: Bossa nova groove for a half-diminished chord.

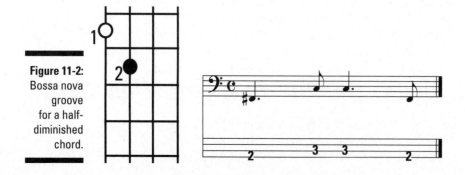

PLAY THIS!

You can listen to Figures 11-1 and 11-2 on Track 79 and Video 27. It's the typical sound of a bossa nova groove — swaying like the fronds on the palm trees by the ocean in a gentle breeze.

Samba: Speeding Up with Bossa's Fast Cousin

Samba is synonymous with the Brazilian carnival and is a huge part of the cultural identity of Brazil. Picture energetic dancers in colorful costumes quick-stepping through the streets of Rio de Janeiro and you get an idea of what samba encompasses.

The bass line for samba is harmonically simple. However, the notes are fast and the rhythm furious. Playing samba is like playing a bossa . . . at double speed.

The bass parts in Figures 11-3 and 11-4 are typical of modern samba grooves with their simple harmonic structure. Start both on your pinkie to save your hand from having to shift. The groove in Figure 11-4 has a note in the second beat that anticipates the third beat, giving the music a bit of extra urgency.

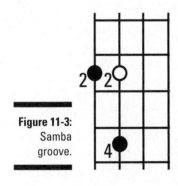

Figure 11-3:
Samba
groove.

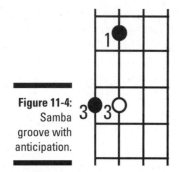

Figure 11-4:
Samba
groove with
anticipation.

You can listen to Figures 11-3 and 11-4 on Track 80 or Video 27.

Afro-Cuban: Ordering Up Some Salsa (Hold the Chips, Please)

Afro-Cuban music is a mixture of African and Cuban rhythms, with musical elements from Puerto Rico, the Caribbean, Africa, Brazil, and other parts of South America thrown in for good measure. Lincoln Goines and Andy Gonzales, two session players, are masters of this style. The Afro-Cuban style is often referred to as *Latin* or *salsa,* so don't be surprised when someone calls for salsa and expects to get the music instead of the sauce that goes with tortilla chips.

The bass groove in Afro-Cuban music often emphasizes the root and 5, but the *rhythmic syncopation* (notes played between the beats, on the offbeats) needs some practice to get under your skin. Afro-Cuban music has a fast-moving style, so buckle your seat belt.

The groove in Figure 11-5 (at the start of Track 81) starts on the first beat of each measure. It includes syncopation and fits over major, minor, and dominant tonalities. Start this groove with your index or middle finger to avoid shifting.

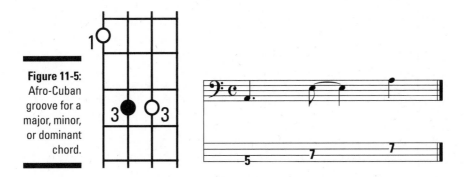

Figure 11-5:
Afro-Cuban
groove for a
major, minor,
or dominant
chord.

In Figure 11-6 (at 0:12 on Track 81), you have an Afro-Cuban groove that's similar to the one in Figure 11-5 (syncopation and all), but this one is played over a half-diminished chord. Start this groove with your index or middle finger.

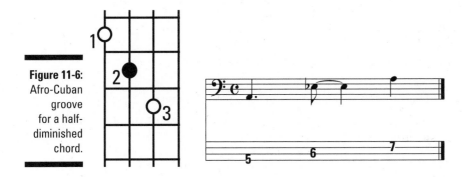

Figure 11-6:
Afro-Cuban
groove
for a half-
diminished
chord.

Figure 11-7 (at 0:18 on Track 81) shows another version of the groove in Figure 11-5, this time with syncopation added at the beginning of the measure. Playing notes off the beat provides a very cool feel after you get the hang of it. Start the groove in Figure 11-7 with your index or middle finger. You can use this Afro-Cuban groove for major, minor, or dominant chords.

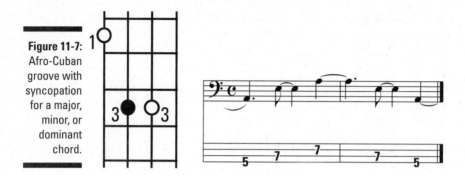

Figure 11-7: Afro-Cuban groove with syncopation for a major, minor, or dominant chord.

The groove in Figure 11-8 (at 0:41 on Track 81) uses the same syncopated rhythm as the one in Figure 11-7, but this time a ♭5 is substituted for the 5 to accommodate a half-diminished chord. Start this groove with your index or middle finger.

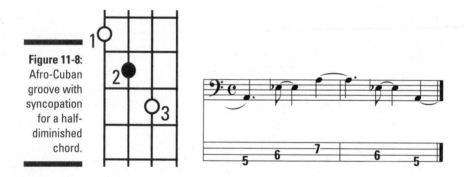

Figure 11-8: Afro-Cuban groove with syncopation for a half-diminished chord.

You can hear the grooves from Figures 11-5 through 11-8 on Track 81, or watch Video 27. Listen to how the groove starts *on* the beat in the first two examples and *off* the beat (with an anticipation) in the last two examples.

Reggae: Relaxing with Offbeat "Riddims"

Reggae music is most often associated with Jamaica and the Caribbean islands. The trademarks of reggae bass are a thuddy sound (short, dark notes) and syncopation — offbeat rhythms (usually spelled and pronounced "riddims" by reggae musicians).

Aston "Family Man" Barrett (who played with Bob Marley) and Robbie Shakespeare (who played with Peter Tosh) are two giants of reggae bass. Modern bassists, such as P-Nut of the group 311, also play this style to perfection.

With reggae, you often hear a lot of *space* (rests when the bassist isn't playing). Figure 11-9 (at the start of Track 82) shows an example of a reggae groove with a lot of space. This groove fits over a minor chord, which is common to reggae music. Start this groove with your index finger to avoid shifting, and keep the length of each note short.

Figure 11-9:
Reggae groove for a minor chord.

If you want to play the groove in Figure 11-9 over a major or dominant chord, you need to change the ♭3 in the chord to a 3.

Figure 11-10 (at 0:30 on Track 82) shows a reggae groove that's more on the happy side. It's for a major or dominant chord. Start the groove with your pinkie.

Figure 11-10:
Reggae groove for a major or dominant chord.

Sometimes you may hear a reggae bass groove that has a flurry of notes. Figure 11-11 (at 0:56 on Track 82) shows you such a groove, which is structured in a tonality that fits over major, minor, and dominant chords. You can start this groove with either your index or middle finger.

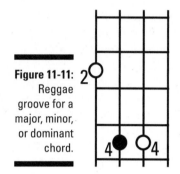

Figure 11-11: Reggae groove for a major, minor, or dominant chord.

The *drop-one* technique, in which the bassist doesn't play on the first beat of the measure, is signature reggae. Figure 11-12 (at 1:20 on Track 82) shows you a drop-one reggae-style bass groove. Start this groove with your middle finger. When listening to the groove shown in Figure 11-12, notice how the drummer hits on the *downbeat* (the first beat of the measure), and the bassist follows on the next eighth note.

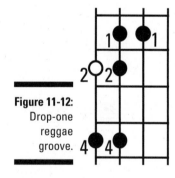

Figure 11-12: Drop-one reggae groove.

Track 82 starts with four clicks and then a four-beat drum intro before the bass comes in. The rhythm in Figures 11-9 through 11-12 is unpredictable and keeps the listener guessing. Watch me play these grooves in Video 28.

Use the previous reggae grooves as a blueprint for creating your own and listen to a lot of reggae bands for inspiration. Better yet, take your bass with you on a vacation to Jamaica!

Calypso Party Sounds: Dancing through the Groove

Caribbean calypso is driving and a lot of fun. The feel emphasizes the down-beats of the measures, with an occasional syncopated note (where the note comes in a little sooner than expected), giving the groove a lift and a certain lightness. Listen to Harry Belafonte for this sound. His music may be decades old, but it still sounds fresh and is the primary representative of calypso music.

The calypso groove in Figure 11-13 uses notes that fit over a major or domi-nant chord, and it implies a *progression* (a sequence of chords). Notice the heavy use of *downbeats* (notes played on the beats) and the syncopation in the middle of the measure (going into beat 3). Start the groove with your middle or index finger.

In Figure 11-14, you have a calypso groove that uses notes common to major, minor, and dominant chords. Start this groove with your middle finger.

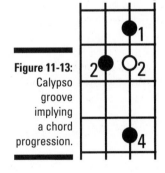

Figure 11-13:
Calypso groove implying a chord progression.

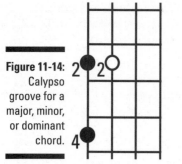

Figure 11-14:
Calypso
groove for a
major, minor,
or dominant
chord.

It's party time on Track 83. The calypso grooves in Figures 11-13 (at the start) and 11-14 (at 0:24) are laced with plenty of percussion, and the bassist is busy as well, driving this music at a good clip. You can see me playing these grooves in Video 28.

Combining Reggae and Rock: The Distinct Sound of Ska

Ska is a motley combination of Caribbean and American styles. Think of it as mixing the offbeat "riddims" of reggae with the driving force of rock. (See Chapter 8 for more on rock music.) Ska is very *up-tempo* (fast) and filled with high energy. Sting (most famous for his work with the Police) has been a prime force in ska music, playing some of the most memorable ska bass parts, which are often quite busy.

The ska groove in Figure 11-15 is an example of a busy bass line using notes that fit over major, minor, or dominant chords. No shifting is necessary. You can start this groove with your index or middle finger.

Figure 11-15:
Ska groove
for a major,
minor, or
dominant
chord.

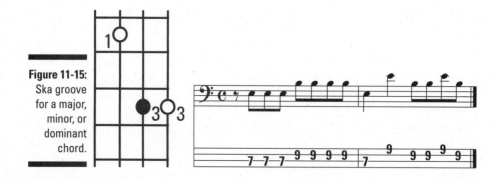

As you listen to the bass groove from Figure 11-15 (at the start of Track 84), notice that the groove doesn't start on the first beat of the measure, which is often the case in ska.

In Figure 11-16 (at 0:15 on Track 84), you have a ska groove that can be played over a major or dominant chord; you get to play it on the downbeat of the measure. Start this groove with your middle finger.

Figure 11-16:
Ska groove
for a major
or dominant
chord.

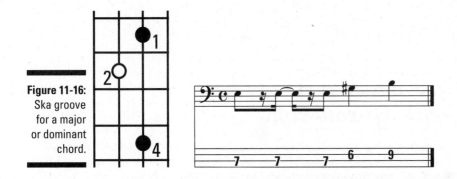

The minor version of the groove in Figure 11-16 is shown in Figure 11-17 (at 0:37 on Track 84). If you start this groove with your index finger, you don't have to shift your left hand.

Figure 11-17:
Ska groove
for a minor
chord.

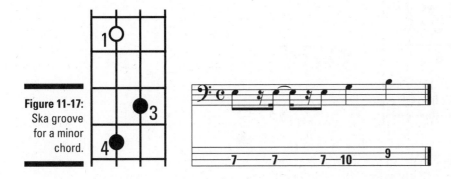

The sound of the ska grooves in Figures 11-15 through 11-17 can be heard on Track 84. Or watch me play them in Video 28. Notice the exotic rhythms combined with the steadiness of rock.

African Grooves: Experimenting with Exotic Downbeat Grooves

African music is an exotic blend of native rhythms with European and Caribbean influences. Bakithi Khumalo, whose bass playing is a wonderful example of South African style, recorded some excellent bass lines with Paul Simon. Richard Bona and Etienne Mbappé are bass stars hailing from Cameroon, where the only thing bigger than bass is soccer. I explore African grooves from South Africa and Cameroon in the following sections.

Grooving on a steady beat, South African–style

The groove in Figure 11-18 gives an example of how a South African groove can say a lot with few notes. This groove fits perfectly over a major or dominant chord and implies a simple progression. Start with your middle finger to avoid shifting, and don't even try to sit still when playing.

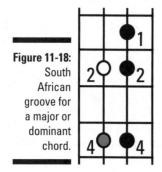

Figure 11-18: South African groove for a major or dominant chord.

As you listen to the groove in Figure 11-18 (at the start of Track 85), notice how the bass and drums interact to give it a downbeat quality.

In Figure 11-19 (at 0:20 on Track 85), you have a South African groove that uses *neutral notes* — root, 5, and 2 in the next higher octave — notes that fit over major, dominant, and minor chords. This groove does require a small shift in your left hand, but it's an easy one if you start with your index finger.

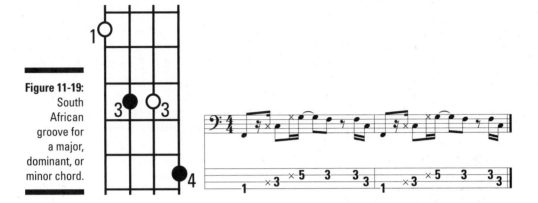

Figure 11-19:
South African groove for a major, dominant, or minor chord.

On Track 85, you hear the sound of the South African grooves shown in Figures 11-18 and 11-19. Notice how the bass drum is played on all four beats to steady this rhythm. I play these grooves in Video 29.

Checking out the bass groove styles from Cameroon

A famous African style from Cameroon is the Makossa, one of the most popular forms to come out of Africa. This style originated in the port town of Douala and spread all over the continent, influencing numerous additional styles. It's percussive and very lively.

Figure 11-20 (at the start of Track 86) is a nice example of a Makossa groove, using roots and 3rds of the chords in the progression. The harmonic lines of a Makossa are often rather melodic and simple, primarily using roots, 3rds, and 5ths of the chord. This progression is typical of African music.

Figure 11-20: Makossa groove.

In Figure 11-21 (at 0:40 on Track 86), you get to explore a seriously rhythmic Makossa groove. Pay close attention to the duration of each note and make sure you catch the downbeats.

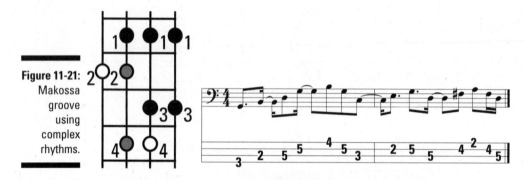

Figure 11-21: Makossa groove using complex rhythms.

One of the trademarks of grooves from Cameroon is the two-over-three feel. The grooves are in 6/8 (six eighth notes per measure). The bass drum emphasizes every third note, making it feel as if the groove is in two while the bass player implies all six eighth notes.

Listen (and then play) to Track 87 for Figures 11-22 and 11-23. Or watch me in Video 29. These are Bolobo grooves that utilize the two-over-three feel. Bolobo tunes are very popular throughout Cameroon and are often sung by children.

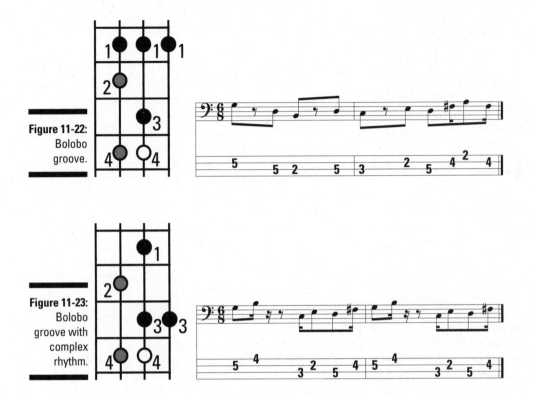

Figure 11-22: Bolobo groove.

Figure 11-23: Bolobo groove with complex rhythm.

The Bikutsi groove is another fine example of what can be done with two-over-three. Bikutsi is very jerky, highly energetic music and translates into something like "beat the earth," which implies foot stomping. Women have a dominant role in this type of music, dancing and singing at special gatherings of the village.

Figures 11-24 and 11-25 show two representative grooves of the Bikutsi style, the latter figure being a bit more rhythmically complex than the former — and that's saying something.

You can hear Bikutsi grooves in Figures 11-24 and 11-25 on Track 88 or Video 29.

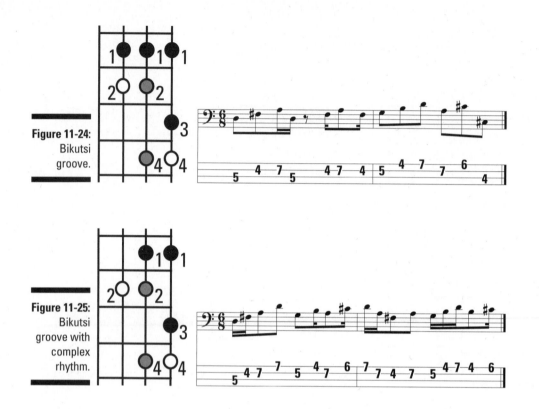

Figure 11-24: Bikutsi groove.

Figure 11-25: Bikutsi groove with complex rhythm.

Music without Borders: Grooving to the World Beat

World beat refers to any style of folk music from around the world (African, Latin American, or Caribbean, for example) that's fused with Western rock or other pop influences. It's certainly no easy task to be up on every one of the latest world beat styles, so in this section, I provide you with one groove that you can count on as a default when someone asks you to play in the style of an obscure African tribal celebration.

The pattern in Figure 11-26 gives you a great starting point toward getting the music going. This song uses chords that are common to the world beat genre (just listen to "Pata, Pata" by African artist Miriam Makeba or "Pressure Drop" by

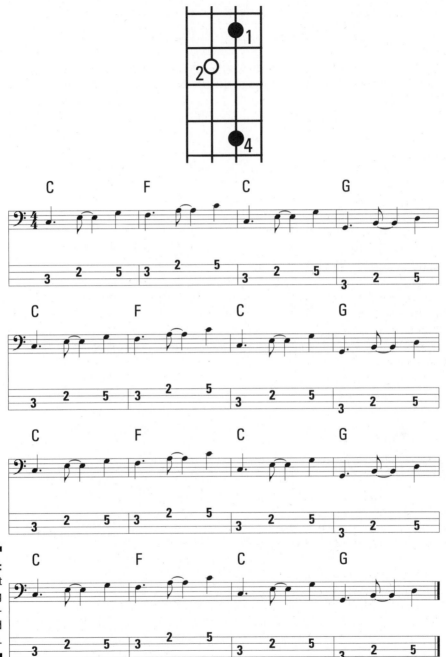

Figure 11-26: World beat song using a typical chord progression.

Jamaican group Toots & the Maytals; both songs use the same chords). You're certain to encounter this chord progression again and again in your world beat travels, so get comfortable with how this groove feels under your fingers.

Play along with Track 89 or Video 30 to hear how well the pattern in Figure 11-26 moves through the rhythm and harmony of the song.

Chapter 12

Playing in Odd Meters: Not Strange, Just Not the Norm

In This Chapter

▶ Sashaying through the waltz

▶ Dealing with beats in 5/4 and 7/4 time

▶ Syncopating odd meter

▶ Access the audio tracks and video clips at www.dummies.com/go/bassguitar

*W*hen you say that something is odd, you're implying that it's out of the ordinary or unusual. In music, that implication generally holds true; playing in an odd meter refers to playing a tune that doesn't have the usual four beats per measure. The word *odd* also refers to uneven numbers. Each measure in odd meter has an odd number of beats. For example, a tune may have three, five, seven, or more beats per measure. So is playing in odd meter a daunting task? Not at all. You don't even have to count past three. In this chapter, I show you how to handle odd meters with ease and bass — er, grace.

In addition to listening to the audio tracks mentioned in this chapter, you can watch me play many of the examples of odd meter in Video 31.

An Odd-Meter Oldie but Goodie: The Waltz

The waltz is the most common of all odd-meter styles. In fact, the waltz is so common that it's not thought of as being in odd meter at all. A waltz has three quarter notes per measure (thus the 3/4 symbol at the beginning of the staff in Figures 12-1 and 12-2), and your count is **1**-2-3, **1**-2-3, and so on. (***Note:*** You accent the bold numbers.) You frequently encounter the waltz in musicals and jazz, so it's a good idea to be ready with grooves tailored to the waltz.

The waltz is a technical breeze for the bass player; you usually play only one or two notes per measure, but you have to remember to keep counting. Figure 12-1 shows a typical waltz accompaniment for the bass. Simply play the root or 5 on the first beat of the measure. This accompaniment fits over major, minor, and dominant chords and adds a little walk-up at the end of the four-bar phrase.

Figure 12-1:
Waltz accompaniment for a major, minor, or dominant chord.

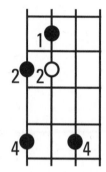

 TIP

If you want to spice up your waltz a little, add a note (such as the 5) on beat 3 — the last beat of each measure. Three-quarter time is so common and so easily recognizable that, by the time you hit the fifth measure or so of the waltz, you don't even have to think about the rhythm. Three-quarter time feels natural.

Figure 12-2 shows a waltz accompaniment that's spiced up with an extra note on the third beat and that includes the same walk-up as the previous figure. This example is a bit fancier than the one in Figure 12-1 because of the added note, but it's still simple. It fits over major, minor, and dominant chords.

Figure 12-2:
Waltz accompaniment using two notes for a major, minor, or dominant chord.

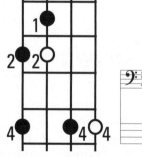

On Track 90, you hear a waltz, the most common odd-meter accompaniment in music (see Figures 12-1 and 12-2). The first example consists of simply a note on the first beat of each measure; the next adds a second note, a leading tone, on the last beat of the measure. Both of the four-bar phrases end with a walk-up, a very common occurrence in a waltz.

The sound of the waltz evokes images of imperial ballrooms in the heart of Europe, filled with ladies dressed in floor-length ball gowns and gentlemen in tuxedos turning in circles to the music. Yeah, these guys were party animals, too . . . well . . . sort of.

Beyond the Waltz: Navigating Beats in Odd Meter

The structure of any measure in odd meter can be divided into groups of two beats and three beats. That's right; it's just a matter of twos and threes. For example, if you have to count to seven in a measure, break it up into groups of two beats and three beats. Instead of counting 1-2-3-4-5-6-7, count in any of the following ways:

- ✔ 1-2-3-1-2-1-2
- ✔ 1-2-1-2-1-2-3
- ✔ 1-2-1-2-3-1-2

The number of beats is the same, but dividing the count into sets of two and three makes the phrasing manageable.

When choosing the notes you play for tunes in odd meters, select notes that fall naturally into groups of two and three, and connect the groups rhythmically and harmonically. I explain how to do this in the following discussion on odd meters in 5/4 and 7/4, the two most common odd meters besides the waltz. This concept of grouping the notes works for any type of odd meter.

5/4 meter: Not an impossible mission

When you play a tune in 5/4 meter, you have five beats (five quarter notes) per measure instead of the usual four. If you've ever watched the TV show *Mission: Impossible* and heard its distinctive musical theme, you've heard a tune in 5/4. You can think of 5/4 as either a group of two beats followed by a group of three, or as a group of three beats followed by a group of two. Take a look at Figure 12-3 to see how the beats are grouped.

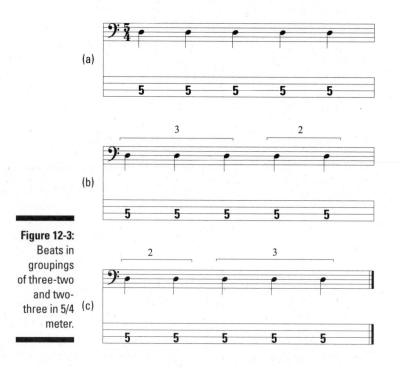

Figure 12-3:
Beats in groupings of three-two and two-three in 5/4 meter.

You can translate these groupings into music by playing your notes as a group of two beats followed by a group of three beats, or vice versa.

Listen to Track 91 to hear Figure 12-3. Part (a) starts the track, (b) is at 0:14, and (c) is at 0:29.

You can count the groove in Figure 12-4 as **1**-2-3-**1**-2 or as **1**-2-**1**-2-3 (accenting the bold numbers). Some of the beats in this groove consist of two eighth notes, which equal one quarter note to make the groove . . . well, a groove. The notes in the groove in Figure 12-4 fit over minor and dominant chords.

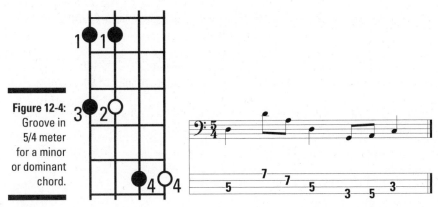

Figure 12-4:
Groove in
5/4 meter
for a minor
or dominant
chord.

You can hear Figure 12-4 at the 0:43 mark of Track 91.

The groove in Figure 12-5 shows a clear three-two grouping in 5/4 meter. Some of the quarter notes are divided into eighth notes, which doesn't change the meter at all. When you look at this figure, notice the following:

- ✔ The first group of notes (the group of three) consists of one quarter note plus four eighth notes, which equal three quarter notes (beats).
- ✔ The second group (the group of two) consists of two quarter notes.
- ✔ The combination equals five beats in all, the equivalent of five quarter notes.

The notes fit over minor and dominant chords.

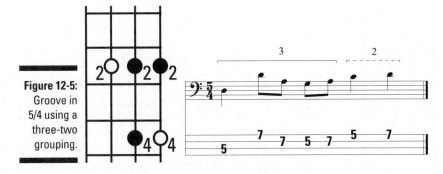

Figure 12-5:
Groove in
5/4 using a
three-two
grouping.

You can hear Figure 12-5 at the 0:55 mark of Track 91.

Figure 12-6, on the other hand, shows you a clear two-three grouping in 5/4 meter. When you look at this figure, notice that

- ✔ The first group of notes (the group of two) consists of two quarter notes.
- ✔ The second group of notes (the group of three) consists of six eighth notes.

The notes fit over minor and dominant chords.

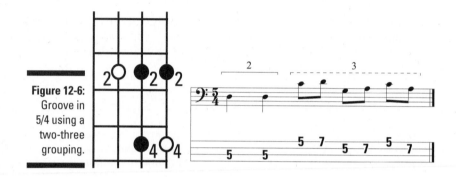

Figure 12-6: Groove in 5/4 using a two-three grouping.

You can hear Figure 12-6 at the 1:16 mark of Track 91.

If you want to get really fancy with your 5/4 meter, you can subdivide your beats into sixteenth notes, which requires some funky finger work (see Chapter 4 for more information). Figure 12-7 shows a groove in a two-three grouping using sixteenth notes. The notes in this groove fit over both minor and dominant chords, so you don't have to worry about the tonality too much.

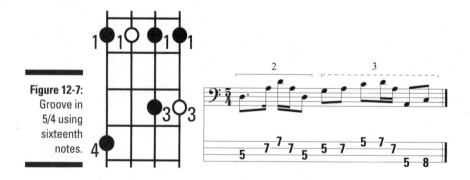

Figure 12-7: Groove in 5/4 using sixteenth notes.

You can hear Figure 12-7 at the 1:39 mark of Track 91.

Take a groove you know and make it grow

A really great way to get into this odd-meter thing smoothly is to take a groove you're already comfortable with, a groove in 4/4 for example, and then add a beat (you have a slew of beat combinations to choose from in Chapter 4).

Take the groove in Figure 12-8a as an example. If you play this as a 4/4 groove, it's pretty manageable. If you want to convert it into a 5/4 groove, add a beat. Now choose a subdivision for your beat, such as two eighth notes. Tag those two eighth notes onto the end of the original 4/4 groove and voilà! You've created the smooth 5/4 groove in Figure 12-8b; in fact, it's the same groove as in Figure 12-7. Kind of like being even-tempered and odd-timed.

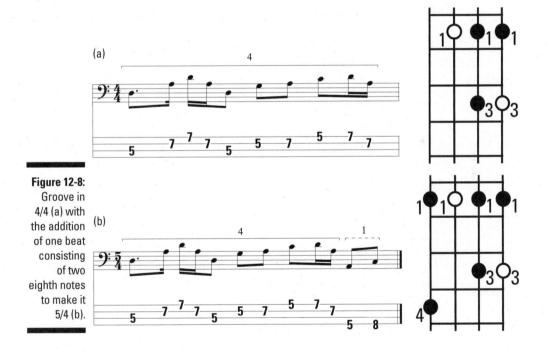

Figure 12-8: Groove in 4/4 (a) with the addition of one beat consisting of two eighth notes to make it 5/4 (b).

You can listen to the grooves in Figures 12-3 through 12-7 on Track 91. The grooves in Figure 12-8 are on Track 92. The first thing to pay attention to is the count-off. You hear five clicks before any of the grooves start. This sets you up to count everything in five. Figure 12-3 demonstrates how you can group the notes by *accenting* certain ones (playing a note louder). Next, you hear the note choices that allow your groove to fit over minor and dominant chords, followed by the sound of a 5/4 groove with groupings as shown in Figures 12-5 and 12-6. Finally, there's the fancy sixteenth-note groove in 5/4 as shown in Figures 12-7 and 12-8, which takes some getting used to but is a great way to play odd meter and keep the listener mesmerized.

With the examples in this section, you can see that playing a solid groove in 5/4 meter isn't such an impossible mission (should you choose to accept it).

7/4 meter: Adding two more beats

The 7/4 meter works the same as 5/4 meter (explained in the preceding section), but it has two more beats per measure. Form groups of two and three notes, adding up to seven, and you're all set to embark on the creation of a perfectly fine bass groove in 7/4. The song "Money," by the group Pink Floyd, is a successful tune in a 7/4 meter.

The possible groupings of beats for a measure in 7/4 are three beats plus two beats plus two beats — in any order. Take a look at Figure 12-9 to see the different groupings of beats in 7/4 meter.

You can translate these groupings into music by combining your notes into two groups of two beats and one group of three beats. Group the notes any way you like.

Count the groove shown in Figure 12-10 as **1**-2-3-**1**-2-**1**-2, **1**-2-**1**-2-3-**1**-2, or **1**-2-**1**-2-**1**-2-3 (accenting the bold numbers). The notes in this groove fit over minor and dominant chords.

(a)

(b)

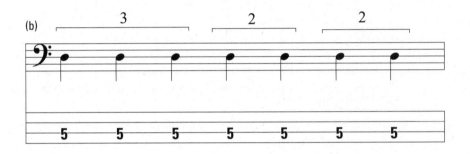

(c)

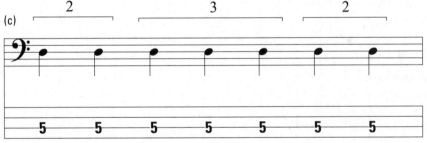

Figure 12-9:
Beats in
groupings
of three-
two-two,
two-three-
two, and
two-two-
three in 7/4
meter.

(d)

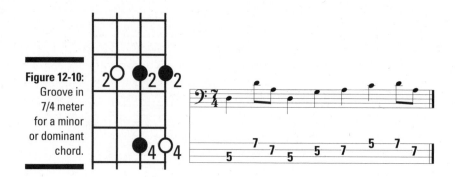

Figure 12-10: Groove in 7/4 meter for a minor or dominant chord.

The groove in Figure 12-11 is a clear three-two-two grouping in 7/4 meter. As you look at this figure, notice the following:

- ✔ The first group (three beats) consists of a quarter note (the first beat) followed by two eighth notes (the second beat) and another quarter note (the third beat).

- ✔ The second group (two beats) consists of four eighth notes.

- ✔ The third group (two beats) consists of one quarter note followed by two eighth notes.

The notes in this groove fit over minor and dominant chords.

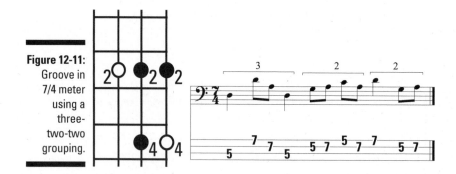

Figure 12-11: Groove in 7/4 meter using a three-two-two grouping.

Figure 12-12 shows a clear two-three-two grouping in 7/4 meter. When you look at this figure, notice the following:

- ✔ The first group (two beats) consists of a quarter note and two eighth notes.

- ✔ The second group (three beats) consists of six eighth notes.

- ✔ The last group (two beats) consists of two quarter notes.

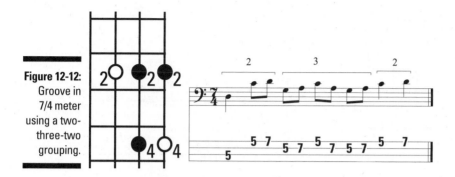

Figure 12-12:
Groove in
7/4 meter
using a two-
three-two
grouping.

The notes in this groove fit over minor and dominant chords.

Figure 12-13 shows a two-two-three grouping in 7/4 meter. When you look at the figure, notice the following:

- ✔ The first group (two beats) consists of a quarter note and two eighth notes.
- ✔ The second group (two beats) consists of two eighth notes and a quarter note.
- ✔ The third group (three beats) consists of six eighth notes.

The notes fit over minor and dominant chords.

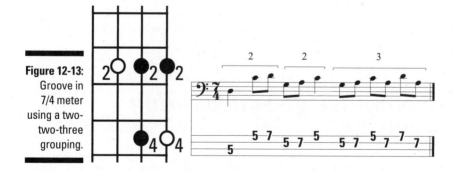

Figure 12-13:
Groove in
7/4 meter
using a two-
two-three
grouping.

And if you're brave, here's a 7/4 meter groove subdivided into sixteenth notes for some mind- and finger-boggling playing. Figure 12-14 shows a groove in a two-two-three grouping that uses sixteenth notes. The notes in this groove fit over minor and dominant chords.

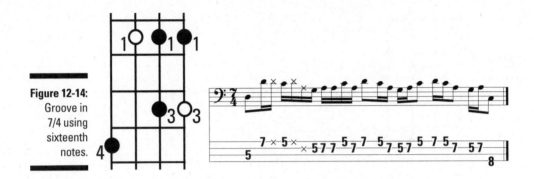

Figure 12-14:
Groove in
7/4 using
sixteenth
notes.

Listen to Track 93 for the sound of the grooves from Figures 12-9 through 12-14. First, you hear the count-off of seven clicks, letting you know you're in 7/4 meter, and then you hear seven even notes on the bass. Then, you hear the different grouping possibilities given in Figure 12-9 (at the start of the track), followed by a groove that uses notes to fit over minor and dominant chords (Figure 12-10, at 1:12 on the track). Next, listen to how the drums set up the groupings. You can hear the different pitches in the count-off to help you follow the groupings in Figures 12-11 (at 1:27), 12-12 (at 1:44), and 12-13 (at 2:00). Finally, you can listen to (and by all means play) the groove in Figure 12-14 (at 2:17) that uses all those fancy rhythms, in the form of sixteenth notes.

The trick to playing a song with rapidly changing chords in odd meter is to keep the groove structure simple and consistent. After all, the rhythm alone gives the listeners, as well as the musicians, plenty to chew on. I highly recommend making your groove ambiguous (see Chapter 13) and constant in structure (see Chapter 6) so you can move through the odd-meter chords with relative ease and grace.

Complex Simplicity: Syncopation and Subdivision

In the previous section, you work out with odd-meter grooves that are cleanly grouped into beats, with every phrase starting on the beat. However, in the real odd-music world, you can also find odd-meter grooves that *syncopate* beats (see Chapter 4) and that subdivide them into eighth notes.

The concept of the three-two groupings never changes. You may have to count eighth-note rhythms in groups of three and two, but the principal stands. The same holds true for combining different odd-meter measures, as in playing a measure of 6/4 followed by a measure of 7/4. Group them into threes and twos, and all is . . . odd.

Syncopating in odd meter

When you add syncopation to beats in an odd-meter groove, the groove can lose some of its stiffness and become a really smooth odd little thing. Let go of the thought of a groove as being in odd meter. Just remember that you've played all these groupings before, nothing new.

Figure 12-15 presents a 5/4 groove that has a few very cool syncopations in the first half and then brings things around to the beginning via a busy groove tail (see Chapter 6 for groove tails). Listen to Track 94 for this one.

Figure 12-15: Groove in 5/4 using syncopation.

Adding an eighth

Some odd-meter grooves add only half a beat, an eighth note, rather than the full beat, a quarter note. This gives you a whole new world of fresh possibilities for your three and two groupings. Count this groove in eighth notes.

The rhythms in Figure 12-16 give you five prime choices for eighth-note combinations for your grooves. Not that many, but they do pack a punch.

Figure 12-16:
Eighth-note
combina-
tions.

And how does this translate into a groove? Check out Figure 12-17 on Track 95 and marvel at an 11/8 groove. This translates into five-and-a-half beats if you're thinking of it in quarter notes, so keep your odds even with the eighth note.

Figure 12-17:
Groove in
11/8.

Dealing with the rush

Every now and then a band comes along that can't seem to make up its mind which odd-meter groove to use, and then they combine a whole bunch of them in the same song. The bands Rush, Yes, and Dream Theatre are examples.

Geddy Lee (the bass player in Rush) and his bandmates have been using odd-meter grooves successfully for a very long time. Just listen to "Limelight" or "Free Will" and you can hear that square-dancing to these rhythms would be pretty impossible.

Their music sounds sophisticated and daring and yet very smooth. Look at Figure 12-18, and mentally group the 6/4 and the 7/4 bars, and then listen to Track 96 and play along. You can see that they're not all that difficult technically; it's all in the rhythm.

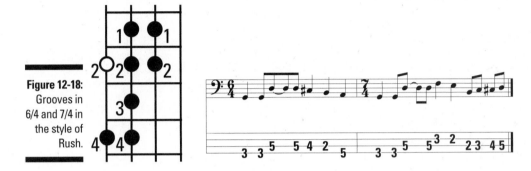

Figure 12-18: Grooves in 6/4 and 7/4 in the style of Rush.

Figure 12-19 is a typical odd-meter song (in this case, in 5/4) that has a different chord for each measure. Notice how the bass groove in this song shifts from the first pattern to a new pattern for the *bridge* (the middle section of the song) to differentiate it from the rest of the music. Both bass grooves, however, are ambiguous as well as constant in structure. You just need to make sure you have both grooves solidly under your fingers so you can shift from one chord to the next with ease.

Listen to Track 97 to hear how danceable an odd-meter song can sound. Grab your bass and play along as you read the music in Figure 12-19.

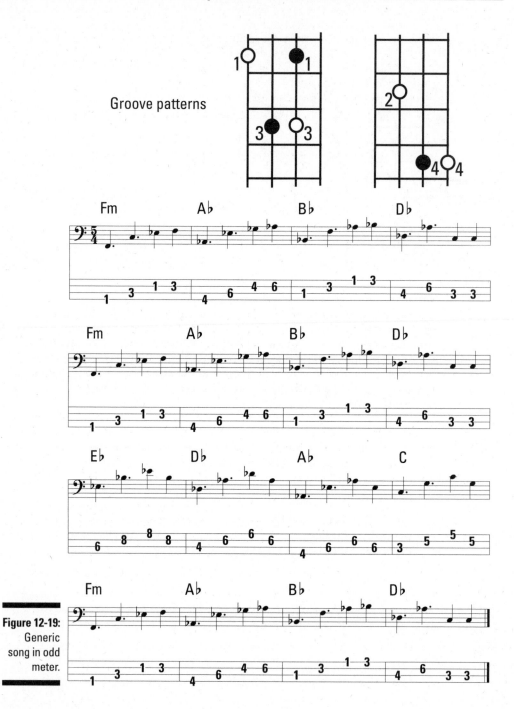

Figure 12-19: Generic song in odd meter.

Chapter 13

Groovin' in a Genre: It's All About Style!

In This Chapter

▶ Exploring different ways to play a song

▶ Knowing when to blend (or not)

▶ Access the audio tracks and video clips at www.dummies.com/go/bassguitar

*I*magine that you're invited to a luau, and on the big day you show up in shorts and a colorful T-shirt with a big lei around your neck. Seems appropriate enough, right? However, as you enter the party, you catch a glimpse of all the other guests wearing their finest tuxedos and ball gowns. It turns out that your expected poolside BBQ is actually a formal dinner party. You stick out like a fresh ink stain on a wedding dress; you certainly *won't* blend in with this crowd.

Music genres (jazz, world beat, rock, and so on) work on the same premise — certain elements in each groove indicate which genre you're playing in. If you play your groove in the wrong genre — a funk groove in a country tune, for example — prepare to audition for a new gig. But if you master a few basic grooves for each genre and learn to use the appropriate one for your band's interpretation of a tune, get ready to dump your day job for a lucrative career as an in-demand bass player. In this chapter, I demonstrate the simple but crucial steps you can take to ensure that you're always in style, no matter what genre you're asked to play in.

Each genre may include several different styles that are closely related. Visit Chapters 8 through 12 to find out more, including appropriate grooves for each.

Playing Grooves in Each Genre: One Simple Song, Many Genres Strong

The song in Figure 13-1 uses a standard chord progression that's a common sequence in many tunes. You can find this exact same chord sequence, or large portions of it, in plenty of songs in different genres, from pop to shuffle. I use this same chord progression in every example throughout this chapter, but each rendition of it sounds distinctly different, depending on the genre of groove being played over it.

Note: I don't include country and world beat as individual genres in this section because they're technically part of pop and Latin, respectively. I also don't include jazz because traditionally it doesn't groove (it most likely walks).

Root placement for song

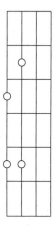

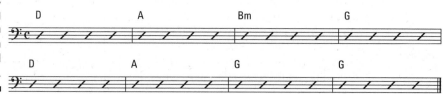

Figure 13-1:
Song
notation
with
standard
progression.

As you change the groove from one genre to the next throughout this chapter, notice how the whole character of the song changes without affecting the harmony or tempo. (For more on harmony and tempo, check out Chapters 4 and 5.) It's the core elements of each groove that define the genres.

Check out Video 32 to see me playing the various genre grooves covered in the following sections.

Pop: Backing up the singer-songwriter

Playing space (playing sparingly) is the name of the game when you're performing in the pop genre. A simple, uncluttered *accompaniment* (the bass line you play to support a soloist) is your best choice. Most important is the groove skeleton (see Chapter 6 for a thorough discussion of the groove skeleton). The two notes making up the groove skeleton are hit on beat 1 and on the *and* of beat 2 (Chapter 4 provides an explanation on how to count the different parts of a beat). All the other notes of the groove fall on eighth notes and lead smoothly to the next chord in the progression.

Take a look at Figure 13-2 for the bass part in a pop tune and listen to Track 98 for the sound of it. Play along with the recording and just enjoy the mellow vibe of this genre. This also works well in a country tune, which is another style in the same genre.

Place your fretting hand so you don't have to shift. In other words, check out the grid and make sure you can reach all the notes without moving to another position.

Rocking by the quarter or eighth note

Playing this chapter's standard progression in the rock genre requires some minor changes, but they yield major results. In Track 99, listen to how the same song transforms instantly when you play your groove skeleton right on beats 1 and 2. The same song, at the same tempo, with the same progression all of a sudden has much more of a punch to it — it has a rock sound. The notes after the groove skeleton are eighth notes and lead to the next chord in the progression. Figure 13-3 shows the rock bass part to this song. Get your rockin' attitude ready and play along with Track 99.

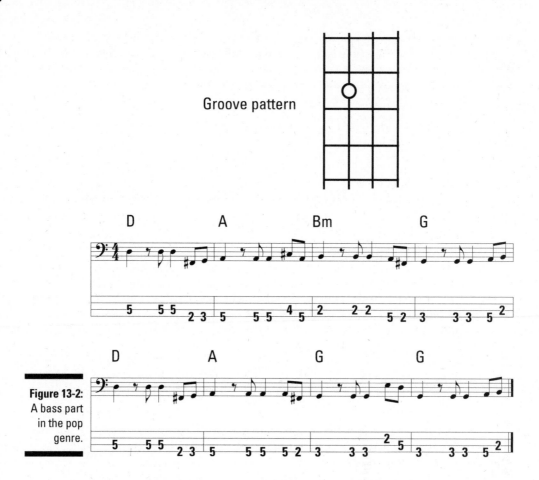

Figure 13-2: A bass part in the pop genre.

You can add some urgency to the rock genre by playing a groove skeleton that includes notes on beat 1 and on the *and* of 1, making this an eighth-note rock. All the other notes stay pretty much the same as in the quarter-note rock. Keep your hand in position; no shifting is required (or desired).

Listen to Track 100, and take a stab, er, pluck at the bass part shown in Figure 13-4.

R & B/Soul, with or without the dot

In the R & B/Soul genre, things get a bit funkier. Two different groove skeletons are used most commonly to evoke this genre. One is the same as the eighth-note rock genre, in which the notes are played on beat 1 and on the *and* of 1.

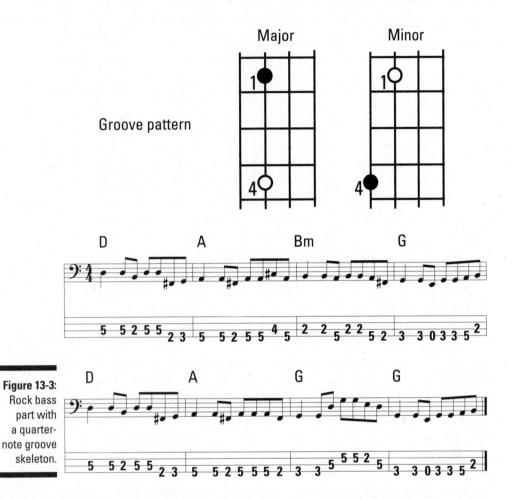

Figure 13-3: Rock bass part with a quarter-note groove skeleton.

You can hear on Track 101 that this version sounds a heck of a lot funkier and busier — almost percolating. The reason is the placement of the notes *following* the groove skeleton, especially the groove *apex* — the note immediately following the groove skeleton. (Refer to Chapter 6 for an explanation of the groove apex.) These notes create a sixteenth-note feel, falling on the *e* or *a* of the second beat (for the abc's of *1 e and a,* see Chapter 4); the rest are in eighth-note rhythms. Have a go at it with the help of Figure 13-5.

To get a grip on sixteenth-note rhythms and all their subdivisions, practice playing the patterns in Chapter 4.

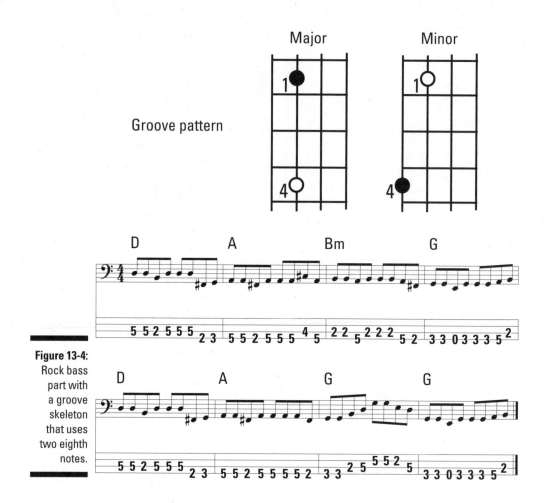

Figure 13-4:
Rock bass
part with
a groove
skeleton
that uses
two eighth
notes.

Adding a dot to the first note of the R & B/Soul groove skeleton (see Chapter 4 for an explanation of the *dot*) is an even clearer indication that you're about to enter Soul City. Your groove skeleton is now on beat 1 and the *a* of 1. In addition, your follow-up notes, including the groove apex, are still in the sixteenth-note rhythms of *e* and *a*. It's hard to believe you're still playing the same old tune at the beginning of this chapter, isn't it?

You can prepare yourself for the dotted R & B/Soul groove skeleton by evenly counting *1-e-and-a-2-e-and-a,* and tapping your hand against your thigh on the 1 and on the *a* of 1, and then not tapping on anything else. This gives you a good sense of the feel you're going for.

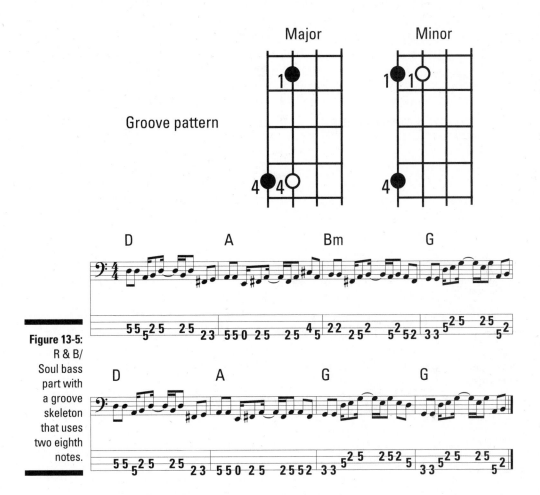

Figure 13-5:
R & B/
Soul bass
part with
a groove
skeleton
that uses
two eighth
notes.

Take a peek at Figure 13-6 while you're listening to Track 102. And, by the way, do try to control that twitch in your foot that's letting you know you're really feelin' the groove.

Make sure you play the rhythm of the first two notes cleanly and crisply; it's a very particular feel that's not easy to catch right away. The trick is to make sure you complete this rhythmic phrase directly before beat 2 comes around.

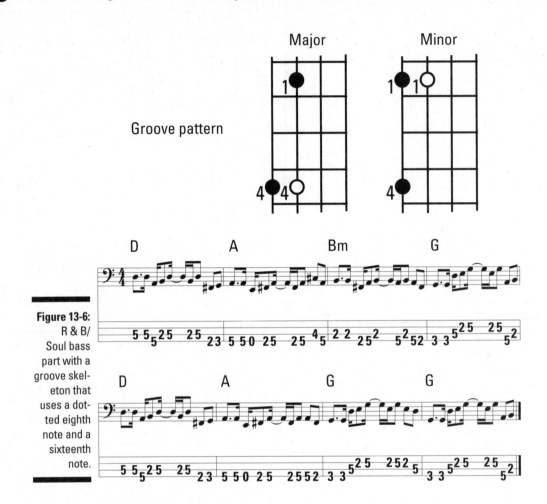

Figure 13-6:
R & B/
Soul bass
part with a
groove skel-
eton that
uses a dot-
ted eighth
note and a
sixteenth
note.

Feeling da funk

Bring on da funk! It's time to really get down. Funk is a genre that can be busy or sparse, but it's most definitely performed with a sixteenth-note feel. Signaling a funk groove with two sixteenth notes upfront as your groove skeleton leaves no doubt in anyone's mind that your intentions are . . . funky! The notes following the groove skeleton are placed onto the *e* and *a* of any of the beats in the sixteenth-note rhythms. Keep your notes short and crisp — no lingering allowed.

Pick up some outrageous sunglasses to get you into the mood, but don't put them on until you've checked out Figure 13-7 for your typical funk groove. Track 103 sounds it out for you. Grab your new shades and play along.

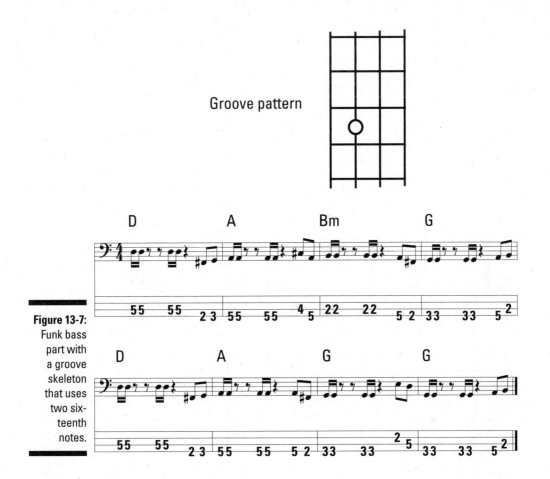

Figure 13-7: Funk bass part with a groove skeleton that uses two sixteenth notes.

Don't confuse funk with slap playing. Funk is a genre based on rhythm and harmony; slap is a technique sometimes used for funk. Check out *slap technique* (also called *thumb-style*) in Chapter 10. Although funk is often played with slap technique, use of the index/middle finger technique is more common (see Chapter 2). Familiarize yourself with both and then choose your preference on a case-by-case — or rather song-by-song — basis.

Layin' down some Latin grooves

Latin bass parts are one of the most easily recognizable musical figures in world beat and you won't have trouble finding people to play with. The standard Latin groove is a predictable root-5 pattern, as shown in Figure 13-8 (for more on roots and 5ths, check out Chapter 2).

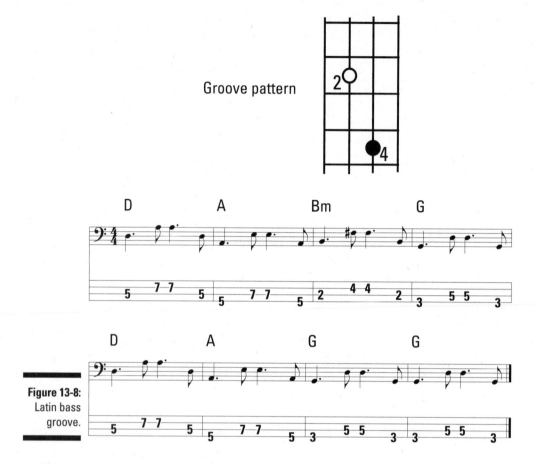

Figure 13-8:
Latin bass
groove.

Listen to Track 104, and you can instantly hear a bass groove you've probably heard hundreds of times before ("Girl From Ipanema," anyone?). The groove skeleton hits on beat 1 and the *and* of beat 2.

Be sure to leave lots of space in your groove for the two dozen percussionists who want to play with you on the Latin stuff.

When you're feelin' blue, shuffle

The shuffle genre is most often expressed in the blues style. With only three subdivisions per beat (triplets) instead of four (sixteenth notes), the shuffle has a much more relaxed feel than, say, funk style.

You can instantly recognize a shuffle by its lopsided feel — each beat is subdivided into three equal parts: The first two parts of the first beat are assigned to the first note you play, and the third part of the beat is assigned to the second note. The resulting rhythm is long, short, long, short, and so on (sort of like a drunkard limping back to his room after a bar brawl).

Figure 13-9 gives you the lowdown on the high art of the shuffle, using the same old tune that's used in all the other genres in this chapter, but, boy oh boy, does the same old tune sound different as a shuffle. Check it out on Track 105. And if your lover (or dog) has left you alone and blue, feel free to play along.

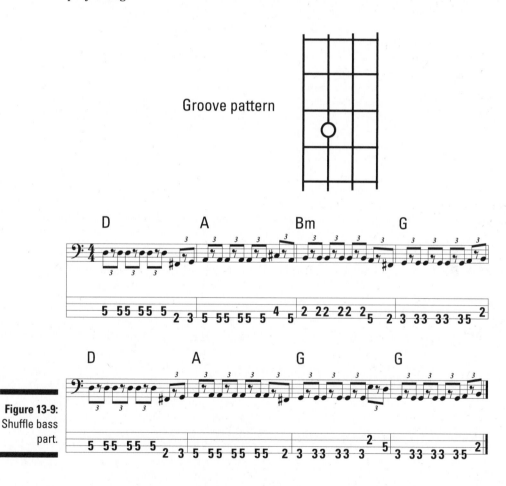

Figure 13-9: Shuffle bass part.

To Blend or Not to Blend: Knowing How to Fit In

Blending a bass line means choosing the notes you play so they support the song perfectly without being overly noticeable. It's almost like the hidden beams in the ceiling of a modern house — you don't see them, but if they weren't there, the roof would collapse.

A *bold groove,* on the other hand, has a much more obvious role in a tune. It's more akin to the exposed beams of an old colonial house. They, too, serve to hold up the roof, but they're obvious and also ornamental; they're a major part of the aesthetics.

No matter what genre you're playing, being able to choose between blending unobtrusively into a song with your bass rumbling in support, or playing a bass line that's so distinct that you can't even imagine the song without it, is a powerful skill to have as a bass player. Grooves that blend and grooves that are bold both have their proper place in music, and both are equally respected when they're used appropriately. Here's the lowdown on when to use each of them:

✔ **Blending grooves:** You use a blending groove when you're playing a supportive role in a song, when you're trying to stay out of the way of the vocals or a melody instrument, or when you're just not all that familiar with the particular song (or musicians you're playing with).

Think of the song "Soul Man" (either the version by Sam & Dave or the one by the Blues Brothers — they're both played with Donald "Duck" Dunn on bass). The bassist plays a perfectly complex yet unobtrusive groove. It blends so well that it's kind of difficult to think of what *exactly* the bass is doing.

✔ **Bold grooves:** Playing a bold groove thrusts you into a leadership position; you're leading the song, and your bass part has a much more authoritative and unyielding quality. This means, of course, that you have to be *very* familiar with the song.

The Beatles' "Come Together" (with Paul McCartney on bass) is a perfect example of a bass line that really sticks out, creating a secondary melody to the song. It doesn't blend in at all.

The following sections give you the goods on how you can create both kinds of lines. Video 33 shows me playing both blending and bold grooves.

Just blending in: How to do it

A blending bass groove is a favorite device of session bassists, who may play in hundreds of recording sessions per year. After all, this type of groove is the perfect vehicle to support a song without diverting attention from the melody and words.

You can achieve the desired blending effect as a bass player by keeping your notes low. Yes, I know, it's kind of a no-brainer — it *is* a bass. What I mean is keeping the notes you use to flesh out the groove *below* the root of the groove skeleton (see Chapter 6 for a definition of the groove skeleton). In other words, after you establish the groove skeleton, play the follow-up notes *lower* than the root.

Take a look at Figure 13-10 to see how the notes for the blending groove on Track 106 are positioned. The root of the chord is the highest note and then the groove dips, only to emerge again at the root for the beginning of the next round of the groove.

Figure 13-10:
A blending
groove.

The bold and the beautiful: Creating a bold groove

When you want to capture the ear of your audience, create a bold groove by choosing a sequence of notes that rise. Let your notes soar upward. After you establish the groove skeleton, play the follow-up notes *higher* than the root (instead of lower).

When you choose to create a bold groove, it's usually a good idea to settle on a firm, repetitive groove and to pick notes that complement the melody. Your upper notes are much closer to the range of the melody and can easily clash if they aren't related to the same chord (check out Chapter 5 to make sure they are).

Take a look at Figure 13-11 to see how to create a bold groove; notice that the notes after the groove skeleton are higher. Listen to Track 107 to hear the impact of this groove.

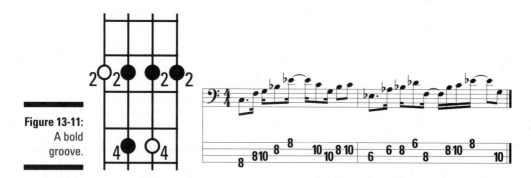

Figure 13-11:
A bold
groove.

Blending and bolding by genre

The choice of using a blending groove versus a bold groove falls squarely on *your* shoulders as the bass player. You're the one to choose which kind of groove to go for, but you don't want to use a groove arbitrarily. You need to follow certain broad guidelines, and as you gain experience, you develop an ear for what's needed. Both types of grooves work in all genres.

Rock, for example, may call for a blending or a bold groove, depending on the particular style of the tune. For example, a pop style (singer-songwriter) usually needs a blending groove, because the words need to be understood. A progressive rock tune, on the other hand, is much more likely to sport a bold groove. Both styles are part of the rock genre but call for very different groove types.

In other cases, the choice between using a blending versus a bold groove is even more subjective. Take R & B/Soul, for example. Some songs have a busy but blending bass groove (the Temptations' "Cloud Nine" is an excellent example), while others have an equally busy but bold groove (the Four Tops' "Bernadette" comes to mind). Both songs are part of the same genre (R & B/ Soul) and even the same style (Motown), yet one has a blending groove while the other is bold. As you gain more experience in playing bass, the choice between whether to use a blending or a bold groove becomes easier.

Signing off with a flourish

Putting your own stamp on a groove is just like writing a letter. In a letter, you take care of all the important points you need to cover and then sign it at the end. It's the same with bass grooves.

A sign-off is usually in contrast to the rest of the grooves in a phrase and signals that a large four- or eight-bar phrase is about to be completed. Some musicians refer to this as a *turnaround.* This is your flourish, your personal signature. You use this element to alert the other players and the listeners that you're about to start a new phrase (for an explanation of phrases, check out Chapter 4).

You can sometimes tell who the bass player is by listening to his or her signature at the end of a phrase. Jaco Pastorius, for example, signs off very differently than Paul McCartney, and Donald "Duck" Dunn does it quite differently than Pino Palladino.

Go ahead and take some liberties at the end of a phrase; after all, it's *your* signature. Just make sure you're back in time for the beginning of the next phrase.

Take a look at Figure 13-12 for some cool sign-offs and listen to Track 108 or Video 34 to hear them implemented at the end of each four-bar phrase. You may also think of the ornamental flourish of your sign-off as a very fancy *groove tail,* which you can check out in detail in Chapter 6.

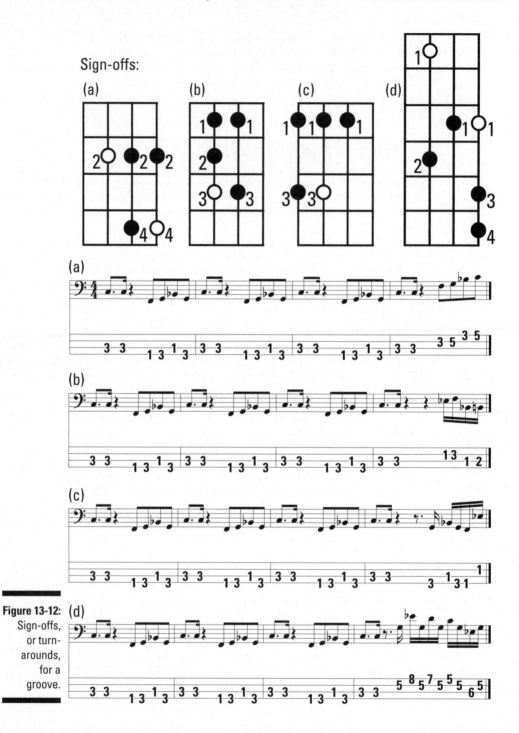

Figure 13-12: Sign-offs, or turn-arounds, for a groove.

Chapter 14

Eight Degrees of Separation: The Beatles' Solution

In This Chapter

▶ Playing straight and syncopated rhythms, Beatles'-style

▶ Using a little Paul McCartney inspiration for your bass grooves

▶ Access the audio tracks and video clips at www.dummies.com/go/bassguitar

*T*hink about this: You're trying to come up with a bass part to a song, but you're not even sure how to start the process — where do you begin? Fortunately, thanks to a certain Beatle, you have eight distinctly different templates you can use to create the perfect bass part to a song. All you have to do is pick your favorite template.

Paul McCartney has a unique place in the development of modern bass. Not only is he a highly accomplished bassist, but he's also a multi-instrumentalist and, most important, a prolific composer. All of this enables him to view a song in its completeness — its melody, harmony, lyrics, you name it. McCartney's unique perspective allows him to create bass lines that fit perfectly for each song. If you listen closely to McCartney's bass lines, you discover that he uses only eight templates, and he has the track record to prove that they work.

In this chapter, you get to explore the thought process of one of the most influential bass players of all time and adopt his techniques. All you have to do to create a classic bass line is ask yourself "What would Sir Paul do?"

You can watch me play all eight templates in Video 35.

Playing Your Rhythm Straight or Syncopated

Two of the most common approaches to a killer bass line are the *straight* and *syncopated* rhythmic styles. In both cases, the harmony of the bass part stays pretty much on one note, usually the root. Where they differ is in their rhythm. In straight rhythm, the notes are played on the beat; in syncopated, some of them are played between the beats. The effects are quite different.

Pumping eighth notes

Pumping eighth notes is a common bass style in pop, rock, hard rock, punk, and songs with a driving beat. The Beatles' tune "Get Back" is a perfect example, as are "Please Please Me" and "Back in the USSR." Beyond The Beatles, you can listen to U2's Adam Clayton laying it down on "Beautiful Day" and to Pink on "Try." What may surprise you is that you can also use this style for slower songs, like Sting's "Every Breath You Take."

You can play this technique by evenly subdividing the beat (the quarter note), effectively doubling the feel of the tempo, and pumping eighth notes without actually playing the chords any faster. You're simply doubling the number of hits per chord. To make this technique even more interesting and to give the music a lift, you can practice occasionally striking the next chord an eighth note early. It's a harmonic syncopation rather than a rhythmic one (see Chapter 10 for syncopation).

Check out the song in Figure 14-1. First, pump eighth notes, changing the root at the beginning of each new chord; then play it again, occasionally moving to the new chord an eighth note early and see how you like the sound.

On Track 109, you can hear the song in Figure 14-1. The chords don't change, nor does the tempo, but occasionally the bass plays an eighth note a little earlier than the chord officially changes, giving the music a less regimented feel.

Syncopating the bass beat

Playing a syncopated bass part requires you to skip occasional beats and to play in between others. Musicians often refer to this method as "singer-songwriter" accompaniment, and it's one of the most commonly used bass lines. The Beatles use it on "Ticket to Ride," "And I Love Her," and "In My Life." You can also hear this technique played on Bruce Sringsteen's "Badlands," Van Morrison's "Brown Eyed Girl," and The Mamas & The Papas' "California Dreamin'."

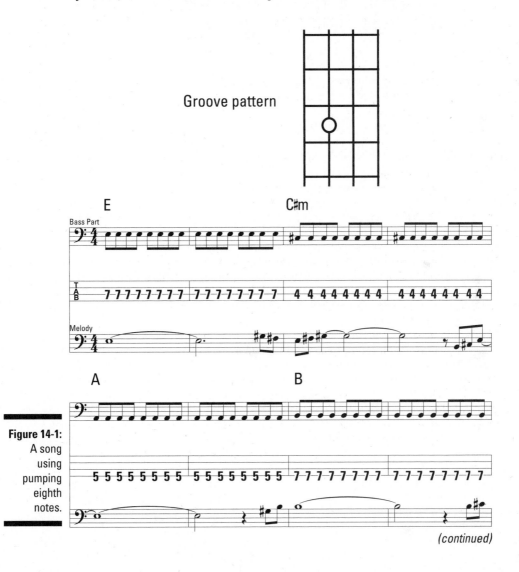

Figure 14-1:
A song using pumping eighth notes.

(continued)

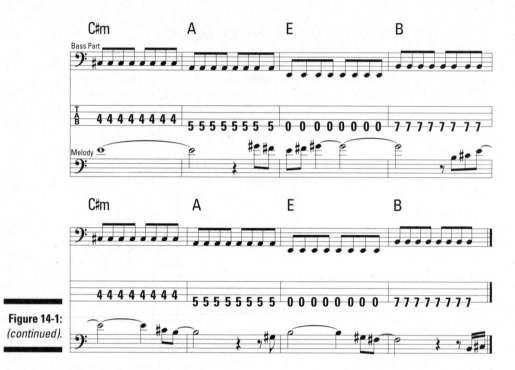

Figure 14-1:
(continued).

On some tunes, you may hear the bass part as simply syncopation on one note; on others, you hear syncopation that has a more active harmony, with other chord tones thrown in. Check out Figure 14-2 for an example of both in the same song. The first time through, the bass part includes only the roots of the chords; the next time around, it includes chord tones. Both are syncopated.

Play Track 110 to hear the song in Figure 14-2.

Figure 14-2:
A song using syncopation.

(continued)

Figure 14-2:
(continued).

Making Harmonic Choices

The bass player in a band has the opportunity to fill out the harmonic spectrum of a song — to make different harmonic choices. Sometimes you can contribute to a song in such a way that the bass part becomes an integral part of the song (I mean, could you ever imagine "Come Together" without that signature bass riff?).

Feeling fine (with roots and 5ths)

Playing roots and 5ths in a bass line is standard fare in country songs, but it's by no means limited to this style. You can hear a root-5 pattern in The Beatles' songs "I Feel Fine," "Love Me Do," "From Me to You," and even in the sophisticated "Help." Playing the root and 5 for each chord allows you to use the same fingering anywhere on the neck, so it's easy to move the pattern around. Not surprisingly, this technique is well represented in country-tinged tunes, such as Pure Prairie League's "Amie" or Credence Clearwater Revival's "Lookin' Out My Back Door." Even bossa novas use this device; just listen to Horace Silver's "Song for My Father."

You can play the root once and follow it with the 5. You can also play the root twice and then follow it with the 5 and make the bass part busier as the song progresses. You even can play the 5 either above or below the root to provide a fresh sound. Check out Figure 14-3 and listen to Track 111 for some examples of how to play the root-5 pattern.

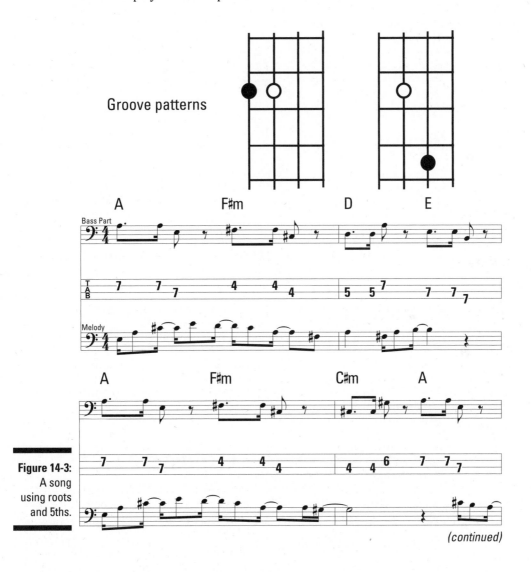

Figure 14-3: A song using roots and 5ths.

(continued)

Figure 14-3:
(continued).

Walking along Penny Lane

Walking a bass line in a rock or pop song is a little different from walking in a jazz tune but, oh, so effective. A walking line is such an ear-catcher that it could detract from the song, drawing the listener's attention from the lyrics and melody to the bass; and then how would you describe to anyone what song you just heard? Sing them the bass part? The way around this is to build a walking bass line and then repeat it *exactly* each time you play through the same section of the song. In this way, the listener knows what to expect from the bass and starts focusing on the lyrics and melody instead.

You also want to avoid *chromatic leading tones,* because they give the bass line a jazzy feel. Instead, use *dominant* and *diatonic* leading tones (see Chapter 9).

"Penny Lane," "Eight Days a Week," and "All My Loving" are prime examples of beautifully constructed walking bass lines by Paul McCartney. Also check out Stevie Wonder's fantastic "I Wish," Queen's "Crazy Little Thing Called Love," and The Black Eyed Peas' "Let's Get It Started." See Figure 14-4 and have fun walking yourself through Track 112.

Figure 14-4:
A song using a walking bass line.

(continued)

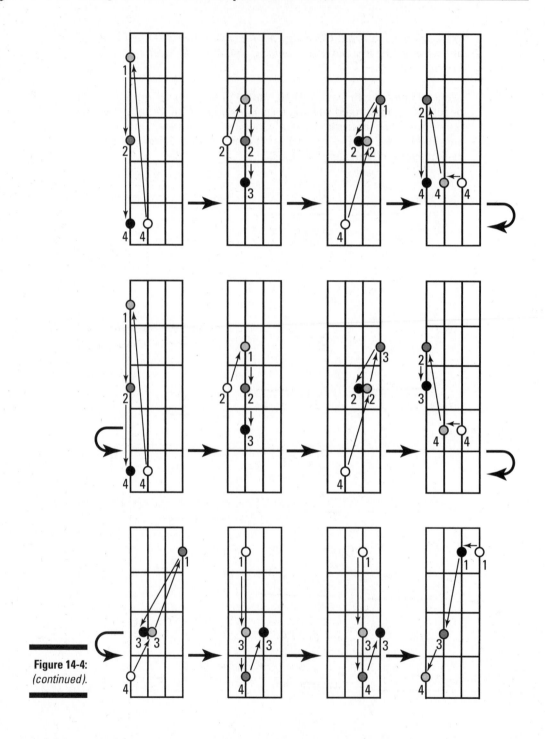

Figure 14-4: (continued).

When you construct a walking bass line, one of your goals is to keep your hand in position as much as possible. Doing so helps smooth your bass part.

Coming together to move with the groove

Creating a fitting groove to a song is what bassists do most often. It's also the most complex accompaniment technique and could fill a whole chapter by itself — oh, wait a minute, I actually describe it in detail in Chapter 6. All you have to do is choose the style of the groove (Chapters 6 and 13 are your friendly guides for this) and decide whether to make your groove bold or blending (see Chapter 13).

Playing grooves works best when the song doesn't have a lot of fast-moving chord changes. You can exploit a groove most effectively when staying on one chord for a while. Make sure your groove stays fairly consistent throughout the song and that all the chords relate to one another . . . in a groovy fashion.

Paul McCartney's groove style is well represented in "Come Together" (one of the most famous bass grooves in history), "Ob-La-Di, Ob-La-Da," and "Lady Madonna." Other tunes that use this groove style include a fabulous version of "Wild Nights" by John Mellencamp (with the fabulous Me'Shell Ndegeocello on bass) and the Eagles' "Hotel California" — and don't forget Elvis's "Hound Dog."

Figure 14-5 shows you a song that uses one groove that moves with the changing chords. Play along with the song on Track 113 and come up with your own.

Day-tripping in perfect agreement: Unison

Double your pleasure when you double your line (musical phrase) with someone else, usually the guitar player or the keyboardist. Unison is very popular in hard rock and progressive rock styles, but it was also used much earlier by Paul McCartney in tunes such as "Day Tripper" (where he doubles the guitar line) and the more subtle "Drive My Car" (he doubles the guitar on that one as well). In playing in unison, you mirror the *exact* same musical phrase that one or more of your bandmates is playing, so it's a really good idea to get together before a gig or jam to rehearse the phrase, note for note, matching each other as closely as possible.

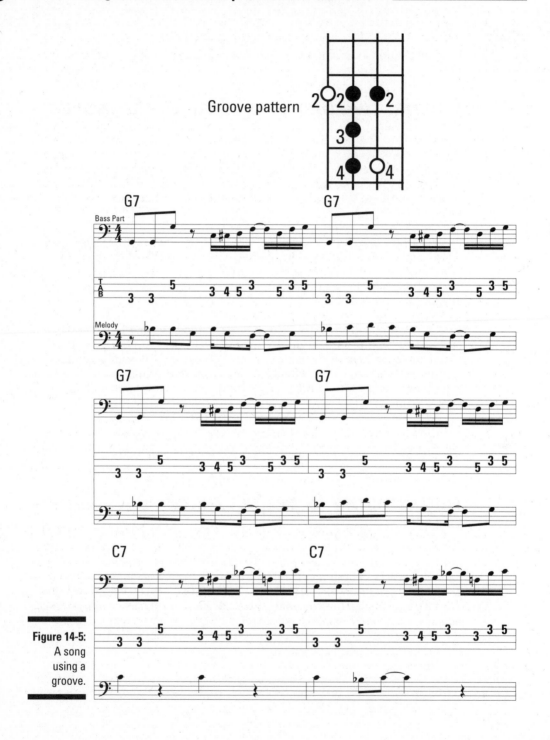

Figure 14-5:
A song
using a
groove.

Some other unison lines include the famous Led Zeppelin song "Black Dog" (bass and guitars play in unison), as well as the Jackson 5's "I Want You Back" (bass and piano play the unison line on that one). You can also check out AC/DC's "You Shook Me All Night Long;" listen to the bass doubling all the hits of the guitar chords.

Figure 14-6 is a song that requires a unison accompaniment, so get together with one of your bandmates, listen to Track 114, and learn the line, note for note. The effect is a wall of sound played in perfect agreement. Well, as they say, the band that plays together, stays together (or something like that).

Figure 14-6:
A song using unison accompaniment.

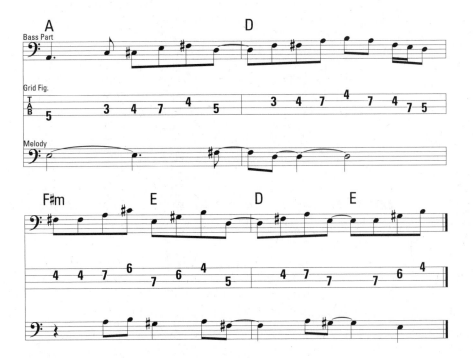

Playing something to counter the melody with

Luckily for the bass world, Paul McCartney was one of the lead vocalists in The Beatles, and he learned to take the entire song — melody, lyrics, and all — into consideration. Most people want to hear the melody and lyrics of a song; they don't want the bass in the way. Sir Paul developed an uncanny feel for when to get busy on bass and when to lay back and just support the vocals.

The countermelody method for accompanying a song sounds immensely complex, but it's really very straightforward: Play a simple line when the melody is busy, and get busy when the melody is simple (or even pauses entirely). This method creates a beautiful and effective balance between the high and the low register of the song.

A prime example of the perfect interplay between the melody and bass, with the bass as a countermelody, is The Beatles' song "Something." (And don't get into arguing with your bandmates "Hey, let's play 'Something.'" "Okay, but what?" Many hours of valuable rehearsal time have been lost on this one.) Listen to the song carefully, and you hear how the bass kicks in when the vocals take a breather.

The same holds true for McCartney's bass parts in "Lucy in the Sky with Diamonds" and "Hello, Goodbye." Other examples are Paul Young's version of "Every Time You Go Away" (with Pino Palladino laying down an amazing bass part) and Jaco Pastorius's soaring bass line on Joni Mitchell's version of "Goodbye Pork Pie Hat."

Playing the countermelody on bass is a highly individualized approach to accompanying a tune. Everyone has a unique way of embellishing a melody, so don't be shy — get busy, just not when the melody is. Try out your best stuff by playing along with Track 115 and check out Figure 14-7.

Inverting while your bass gently weeps

What do Johann Sebastian Bach, Procol Harum, Percy Sledge, Elton John, and, oh, yeah (or rather "yeah, yeah, yeah"), The Beatles have in common? Highly successful songs that take advantage of inversions via a descending bass line. Quite an assortment of genres, isn't it? Bach's "Orchestral Suite No. 3 in D major" is the inspiration for Procol Harum's "A Whiter Shade of Pale." Same device for "When a Man Loves a Woman," by Percy Sledge, and in parts of "Rocket Man," by Elton John. As for Paul McCartney's contributions, they include "While My Guitar Gently Weeps," "Dear Prudence," and "Cry Baby Cry."

Inverting a chord means playing a non-root of the chord on the bass, but to make it really effective, you need to consider the following:

- **The attack:** Any time you begin with a non-root of a chord in the bass, the impact is a little softer than playing the root. This softer attack is sometimes exactly what the song needs.

- **The voice leading of the bass line:** You want to look for notes that are close to the one you played immediately previously. For example, if you play a C and your next chord is a G, you can play a B in the bass (the 3 of G) and move only a half step down (one fret). This process is called *voice leading* and makes a song move very smoothly through the harmony. The chord notation would show G/B, the G being the chord and the B the bass note that you play.

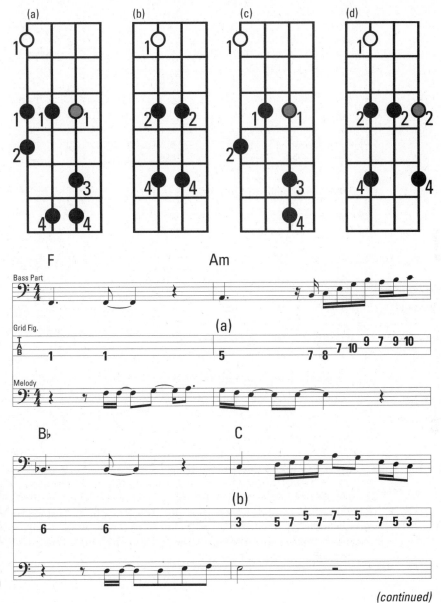

Figure 14-7:
A song using a counter-melody.

(continued)

Figure 14-7: *(continued).*

Make sure to check out Chapter 5 for inversions and harmonic structures. Figure 14-8 shows a typical chord chart that just cries out for inversions in the bass part (also shown). Listen to Track 116 and have fun "Bach-ing" it out.

Whether you're a raving Beatles fan or you just can't deal with the mop heads, taking advantage of McCartney's bass-accompanying genius is a great way to explore different options for creating a bass part for any tune. It comes in really handy when you work with a composer who hires you to record one of his songs and tells you he wants you to play something "slip-pery, slinky" (huh?) as a bass part. Just think of which Beatles' tune reminds you most closely of the tune you're about to record, and, all of a sudden, you just may come up with the next classic "slippery, slinky" bass line, perhaps something like "Come Together."

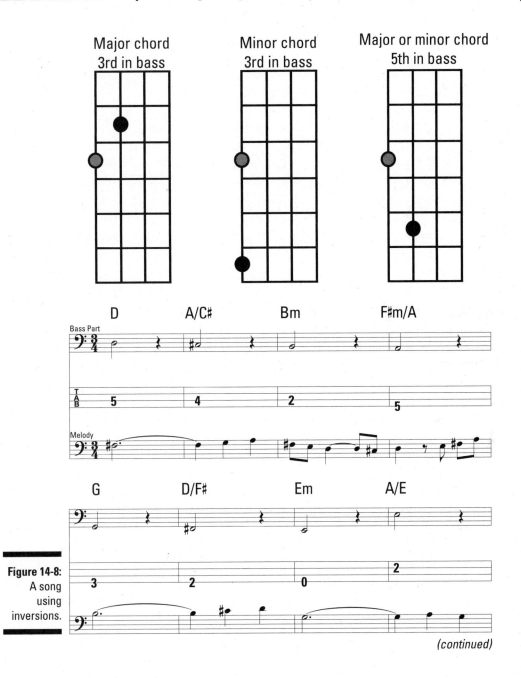

Figure 14-8:
A song using inversions.

(continued)

Figure 14-8: *(continued).*

Part V
Buying and Caring for Your Bass

In this part...

- ✔ Assess what to look for when you're buying a new bass.
- ✔ Discover how to choose your amp and speaker for your bass.
- ✔ Distinguish between essential and nonessential accessories.
- ✔ Get the scoop on changing the strings on your bass guitar.
- ✔ Perform basic maintenance to keep your bass in top form.

Chapter 15

Love of a Lifetime or One-Night Stand? Buying the Right Bass

In This Chapter

▶ Identifying your bass-ic needs and wants

▶ Keeping an eye on your budget

▶ Shopping for your bass

▶ Commissioning a bass from a luthier

*B*uying a bass guitar is an exciting and rewarding experience, but it can also be a bit daunting. You're about to commit a lot of hard-earned cash to the purchase of your bass. You're also about to commit yourself to becoming a true bassist. Instead of borrowing a friend's instrument or renting one from the local music store, you're now getting your very own personal bass guitar.

Buying the right bass is a personal choice that only you can make; it's also a choice that you can make only every once in a while (unless you're independently wealthy), so choose wisely. This chapter helps you make the tough decisions when buying a new bass guitar. It also prepares you to step bravely into that music store as a bass player who knows exactly what to look for.

Assessing Your Needs Before You Buy

The single most important question to ask yourself before buying a bass is: "What do I want in a bass?" The following are some key points to consider when choosing your new instrument:

> ✔ **Feel:** The bass needs to feel good to you. Actually, it needs to feel good to your hands. You don't have to be an expert to determine whether a bass is right for you. Just pick it up and play a few notes. If the bass responds to your touch and doesn't feel awkward or stiff, it's a good candidate. Play lots of different basses when you shop so you have some

way of comparing the different models. Play a high-end (expensive) model for comparison as well (those $15,000 basses usually feel *very* good), and then see whether you can find a less expensive model that feels similar (or just buy the $15,000 one).

✔ **Sound:** The bass needs to sound good to you and to the people you play with. (Of course, you can always find other people to play with.) It needs to have a clear, clean *bottom end* (low frequencies — what did you think the term meant?). If you want to alter the tone of the bass and dirty it up, fine. But make sure that you start out with a clean bottom, er, tone.

✔ **Looks:** Looks are a distant third behind feel and sound. I had a bass that played like a dream and sounded like Thor, the god of thunder, had come down from the heavens . . . and it had the most obnoxious purple finish on the body, with grass-green silk windings on the strings to top it off. I was happy to buy it. (I used it mostly for recording, where nobody would see me.) Don't sacrifice tone or playability for looks. You can always have the bass refinished. Of course, if possible, pick a bass you also enjoy looking at (or rather, you enjoy being seen with).

Here's a really good piece of advice: Don't settle. If you find a bass that sounds great but doesn't feel good in your hands, don't buy it. If you find a bass that feels wonderful but sounds like a buzz saw, don't buy it. You *can* have the best of both worlds; you just have to look for it.

Also, keep in mind that bass guitars are versatile instruments. You want to be able to play your bass during the afternoon jazz cocktail hour at the local cafe before rushing off with it to play the rock 'n' roll set at the local pub in the evening. Then you can get up the next morning and use the same bass to record a country song at the studio. So set your buying priorities without worrying about what style of music you want to play.

Thinking long-term: Moving in together

Some fledgling bassists feel that they have to *earn* that special bass. In other words, before buying their dream bass, they feel that they need to deserve it. Don't buy into that line of thinking. You need to determine only whether your level of commitment is strong enough, and nobody knows that better than you. If you're convinced you're going to be playing bass for the rest of your life, or at least for the next few years or so, get the best bass you can afford (as long as it fulfills the criteria I explain earlier in this chapter). A great bass encourages you to play more, which in turn makes you a better player.

In the long run, buying a good instrument right from the start is more cost-effective than constantly trading in mediocre instruments without ever buying the one you really want. Every time you trade in a used bass, you lose money. Make your bass yours, for better or for worse, in sickness and in health.

Thinking short-term: Help me make it through the night

If you aren't sure that you want to be a bassist, or if you're just temporarily filling the bass chair for a band, go for a bass that feels good and has a good tone (and, yes, there's a difference between good and great), but don't break your bank account.

You can choose from a wide variety of bass guitars in the economy price range, and some of them are quite good. If you find that bass playing is growing on you, you can always get a better one later and keep the first one as a backup.

How many strings are too many?

Today's bassists face a variety of choices when selecting a bass. Not only do you have a huge selection of brand names to consider, but you also have to decide whether to buy a traditional four-string bass or go for the extended range of a five-string bass, six-string bass, or beyond.

In the mid-1970s, Anthony Jackson — a top New York City session player best known for his work with Steely Dan, Chaka Khan, and Paul Simon — conceived of, and had luthier Carl Thompson build, a six-string contrabass guitar with an extra high string and an extra low string. Soon after, other players saw his design and adapted the idea of adding a lower fifth string to compete with the extra low sounds of the keyboard bass on records. (After all, nobody plays better bass than a bassist.) The resulting five- and six-string configurations allow bassists to reach lower notes for groovy, synth-like (or synthesizer-like) bass lines, the high notes for clearer soloing and filling, and everything in between. Take a look at Figure 15-1 for some exotic six-string basses.

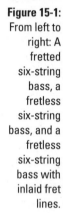

Figure 15-1:
From left to right: A fretted six-string bass, a fretless six-string bass, and a fretless six-string bass with inlaid fret lines.

Photo by Steven Schlesinger

To determine how many strings your bass guitar should have for the styles of music you want to play, figure out whether you need to venture into the extreme low and high registers frequently. If you play a lot of dance or hip-hop, a five-string bass with its extra low string may be right for you. If you want to get into fusion jazz, a six-string bass may be the answer for extensive soloing on the high string. However, a four-string bass can fulfill the bass function just as well for any genre. So, like most of the other items on your shopping list, the number of strings becomes a question of personal preference.

Because the strings on five- and six-string basses are tuned to have the same tonal relation to each other as the strings on the four-string bass, all the fingering grids in this book are relevant to them as well.

To fret or not to fret

Fretless basses, which have no frets on the fingerboard, have a distinctive sound (sort of a growl). When you play a fretless bass, you press the string directly onto the wood, just as you would on an upright (double) bass. In place of the frets, the neck has *markers* either on the top, where the frets would be, or on the side of the fingerboard.

If you're just beginning to play and you're buying your first bass, I advise you not to get a fretless bass. A fretted bass is easier to play in tune; its frets cut off your string precisely at the correct note, whereas on a fretless bass your fingers are responsible for finding the correct intonation. You may consider a fretless bass as your second bass when you reach the intermediate level or beyond. You may even want to use a fretless bass as your primary instrument after you become a more seasoned player.

Listen to recordings by Jaco Pastorius and Pino Palladino to hear masters of the fretless bass. You can read more about Pastorius in Chapter 19.

Needs Are One Thing . . . Budget Is Quite Another

You need to decide how much money you can afford to spend on a bass so you still have some left for an amp, a cable, and a few other essentials (see Chapter 16). You can certainly play a bass guitar without an amp — you just won't be able to hear it . . . and neither will anyone else.

If you feel that your commitment level is strong, buy a bass that can keep up with you throughout your playing career. Such an instrument will cost anywhere from about $700 to . . . well, the sky's the limit. If you're just starting out and aren't sure whether bass playing is for you — are you serious? *Of course* it's for you! — you can get package deals that include a bass guitar and an amp for about $400. Beginner basses start at just under $200.

The lower your budget, the more important it is for you to try out several basses of the same brand before you settle on one. In the lower price ranges, the quality is inconsistent, even within the same brand. Some instruments may fall apart fairly quickly, while others may last for years and sound and feel great.

Checking out magazines, such as *Bass Player* and *Bassics,* for articles that review and compare the quality of various basses is a good idea. You also can find reviews on bass websites like TalkBass.com and ActiveBass.com. Talk to as many bass players as you can and ask them what they recommend (and why). If you're lucky enough to have a bass-centric music store in your area (even if it means a three-hour trip to get there), go and talk to whoever runs the bass department. And plan to play a lot of basses before deciding which one to purchase. You may get lucky and find a diamond in the rough.

A Trip to the Bass-Mint: Where to Shop for Your Bass Guitar

You can get your perfect bass from many different sources, be it large music stores, small mom-and-pop shops, the Internet, retiring musician friends, or bass-playing tenants who left in a hurry. In this section, I provide some ideas to help make your search fruitful and time efficient.

Buying a bass is best done over the course of several days. This time frame allows you to compare different basses and their prices, and it also keeps you from falling prey to impulsive shopping. This decision may well change your life, so take your time.

Hitting the music stores

Visiting the biggest music store in your area, where you can look at (and listen to) the most basses in one place, is the best way to start your search. You can check out the small music stores after you've settled on a bass. You may want to bring a friend who can listen objectively and provide moral support. If this friend knows more about basses than you do, that's even better. Just remember, *you're* the one who's going to play it, so make sure you choose what's best for you.

When you come face to face with a salesperson, say that you're looking for a bass guitar and that you'd like to try a few. Ask to check out a Fender Precision and a Fender Jazz. These basses are considered the standards for comparison. They sound great for any style of music, they look great, and they're real workhorses, too. If you can afford them, stick with the Fender basses made in America; their quality is better than the quality of the imported models. Even if these basses are beyond your present budget, they give you a standard to compare other prospective basses to.

The salesperson is going to ask you what you're looking to spend, so come in knowing your budget. Also, prepare yourself to walk out of the store bassless (leave your wallet at home if you have to). Before you plunk down all your savings from the past six months, you still have work to do. This first trip is your intelligence-gathering mission. You're trying to get an idea of which bass feels and sounds best to you.

When you're ready to try out a new bass, first give it a once-over. Check to see whether the finish is even and all the seams are tight (especially where the neck joins the body). Also make sure the strings are evenly spaced on the fingerboard: The G string should be about the same distance from the edge of the fingerboard as the E string, and all the strings should be about the same distance from each other. Take a look at Figure 15-2 to see evenly spaced strings on a fingerboard.

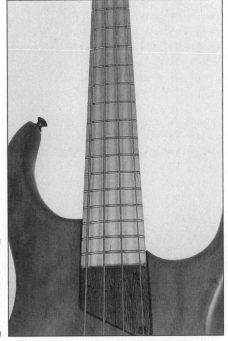

Photo by Steven Schlesinger

Figure 15-2:
Evenly
spaced
strings on a
fingerboard.

When you have the bass guitar in your hands, check to see whether the neck is securely attached to the body of the instrument. The neck can be attached to the body in one of three ways:

- ✔ **Bolt-on:** The neck is screwed onto the body with large screws.
- ✔ **Set-in (or glued-in):** The neck is seamlessly glued into the body.
- ✔ **Neck-through:** The neck continues through the entire body of the bass, and the body wings are glued to the sides of the neck piece.

If the neck is bolted on, be sure that the neck doesn't shift when you push and pull it from side to side. (Don't try to break it; just move it lightly.) The neck and the body need to be solidly joined.

After you determine whether the bass is solid, ask the salesperson whether you can plug the bass into the best bass amp in the store to get the truest response from the instrument. Tune up the bass (see Chapter 2) and start playing. Play every fret on every string so you can make sure the frets don't have high spots that make the strings buzz.

Next, play some music. If you've been practicing the grooves in Part IV of this book on an old or borrowed bass, see what it feels like to play some of them on the new bass. If bass playing is new to you, just play a few notes and listen to the sound. Do you like it? Does it feel good? When you finish testing the bass, move on to the next one. After you try all the basses in your price range (and maybe some that are beyond your price range), thank the salesperson and leave. Make sure you know which models you like best and what they cost.

Try to resist the urge to buy a bass during your first trip to the store. You should take all the information you gather and mull it over carefully before deciding which bass to buy. You may want to search out some other stores to see what else is available.

Consulting newspaper ads

After doing some testing and research in your favorite music store, you can check the classified ads in your local paper to see whether someone is selling the bass model you're looking for. As a general rule, newspaper ads state a price that leaves some wiggle room, so you may want to negotiate to get the price down. Even if you can afford the stated price, negotiating gives you more cash for buying your amp.

Be very careful to meet the seller, try out the bass, and make sure all the parts are working before kissing your hard-earned money goodbye. Unlike a store, no guarantees are offered when buying a bass through a classified ad. However, you may find an excellent instrument at a very reasonable price.

Visiting online shops and individual online ads

Thanks to the Internet, you can be in Seattle reading about a very cool bass that's patiently waiting in southern Florida for someone just like you. However, I advise you not to buy a bass on the Internet without trying the model in a local store first.

When you have a pretty good idea which bass feels and sounds the best to you in the store, concentrate on that model when you shop online. Get prices from the online stores and see whether your local music store can beat them. If you feel comfortable buying your bass online and can get a significantly better price, go for it. Make sure you can return the bass if it isn't as good as the one in the store.

Sometimes getting a *service agreement* (which you can get only from a store) for your bass is worth a little extra money. With a service agreement, the store's technician will set up your bass for free every six months or so. (A *set-up* for your bass is the equivalent of a tune-up for your car.)

Some online stores and bass websites also have classified sections where individuals can sell used or new basses. Individual online ads really aren't much different from newspaper ads; the only difference is that they cover a much vaster geography than newspaper ads. To protect yourself, you should do the following before buying from an individual who posts an online ad:

✔ Make sure the seller is reputable (many online sites rate their sellers).

✔ Don't buy anything from anyone who gives you a bad feeling. For example, you should steer clear if someone says "I'll ship you this bass while your check is on the way. . . . Oh, and could you make it out for a little more to round the number off? I'll send you the change in cash."

✔ Stick with the better-known sites, such as eBay. They have a system in place to minimize the possibility of fraud. Reputable bass websites that have "for sale" sections include www.basscentral.com, www.bassnw.com, and www.talkbass.com.

✔ Try to stay local, if you can. Sometimes you get lucky and a bass player in the next town is looking to sell just the bass you're looking for.

✔ Make sure you contact the individual who's selling the bass *before* you buy. A phone call is a must! You need to know that this person actually exists.

If you're able to get all your bass questions answered from a very knowledgeable salesperson at your local music store and you end up liking a particular bass, I'd highly recommend buying the bass from this place rather than going for the same model online, even if it's a little more expensive. You're supporting someone who has a wealth of information and who has experience in the bass world. By building a relationship with such a person, you ensure that this bass place stays in business and that you have access to the kind of advice you need when you move up to the next model or when you need accessories.

When Money Is No Object: Getting a Custom-Made Bass

If you have enough money at your disposal to go to a *luthier* (a stringed-instrument maker), that's a great route to take. A luthier can make an instrument especially for you. You need to tell him what styles of music you like to play (even if the answer is "all of it"), how many strings you need, and whether you want to go fretless or fretted. (For more information, see the section "Assessing Your Needs Before You Buy," earlier in this chapter.)

When you commission a bass from a luthier, you can also pick the color of your bass. However, because the wood on custom-made instruments is usually very beautiful, you may just want to go with the natural finish. (After all, you don't spray-paint a Rolls Royce.) The rest is best left to the luthier. He knows which wood types sound best for the bass you desire.

You may have to wait a while until your bass is ready (usually between six months to three years), but let me tell you, the wait is well worth it. A custom-made instrument is one for a lifetime (and beyond), and meeting someone who's as passionate about building a bass guitar as you are about playing it is a wonderful experience.

Buying a bass comes down to this: What feels good to you? When you buy a bass, you build a relationship, so make it a good one.

Chapter 16

Getting the Right Gear for Your Bass Guitar

....

In This Chapter

▶ Amplifying your bass

▶ Outfitting your bass

....

Most bass guitars have a solid body. Unlike instruments that have a hollow body, which acts as a resonating chamber (a cavity that resonates when notes are played, making the notes audible), solid-body instruments are inaudible without amplification. And because the notes that bassists play are so low, they need a good amount of amplification.

To share your bass grooves with the world — or even with the person right next to you — your bass guitar needs to be connected to an amplifier and speaker. So you need to take a trip to the music store; and while you're there, you may as well pick up a few other items for your permanent bass arsenal.

This chapter tells you exactly what you need to be a fully functional bassist, ready for any playing situation. So take this book with you when you head out to the music store . . . and don't forget your wallet.

Making Yourself Heard: A Primer on Amplifiers and Speakers

The *amplifier* (or *amp* for short) is the unit that boosts the electronic signal of your bass and sends it to the *speaker*, which takes the signal and converts it into sound. The speaker is just as important as the amp. In fact, if you don't have a speaker attached to the amp, nobody will be able to hear you.

Guitarists can start out with a little 15-watt practice amp, but bassists don't have this option, because low notes require a lot more power than high notes. So you need to practice a little fiscal irresponsibility when purchasing your amp: You need to spring for a larger, more expensive one.

Going with a combo or separate amp and speaker

The choice of combo or amp and speaker depends on whether you prefer to carry one large pack or a couple of medium-sized ones. You can amplify your bass in two basic ways:

- **With a separate amp and speaker:** The amp and speaker come as two separate units and are connected via a *speaker cable.* The advantage of buying separate units is that you can get an amplifier from a company known for making good-quality amps and a speaker from one that specializes in speakers. Additionally, the separate amp and speaker are more powerful, and they allow you to mix and match different amps and speakers.

- **With a combo amp:** A *combo amp* houses both the speaker and the amplifier in one unit, eliminating the need for a separate speaker. The combo amp is more portable than a separate amp and speaker. (You need to carry only one piece, as opposed to two.)

Take a look at Figure 16-1 for an example of a combo amp and of a separate amp and speaker.

Figure 16-1:
A combo amp (left) and a separate amp and speaker (right).

Photos by Steven Schlesinger

I recommend you start with a combo amp that has between 50 and 100 watts of power (it'll run you anywhere from $200 to $1,000). That's enough for practicing at home, rehearsing in the garage (get the car out first), and playing at the local pub. (Hint: Madison Square Garden is *not* a local pub, even if you live in New York City.) If you start playing at bigger venues — parties and weddings, for example — go for a performance amp and speaker with at least 300 watts. Yes, they're pricey (from $400 to $2,500 and beyond), but they're well worth it. You want to feel the rumble, don't you?

Opting for solid state or tubes

When buying an amplifier, you have a choice between solid state and tube amplification. Here's the lowdown on each:

✔ *Solid state amplification* refers to technology that uses transistors and/or microchips for amplification.

✔ *Tube amplification* refers to technology that uses vacuum tubes for amplification (like the red, glowing tubes in the back of old radios).

Selecting between solid state and tube amplification is a personal choice, although some people swear by one or the other. Try several different amps (using *your* bass) at a music store to see which sound you prefer; you'll notice a subtle difference between the two. Bear in mind that solid state amps usually weigh less (often *much* less) than tube amps.

If you don't have a strong preference for either solid state amps or tube amps, go for the solid state. It's usually less expensive for comparable power and quality, and it requires less maintenance. (A tube amp needs to have its tubes replaced every couple of years.)

Picking a speaker size

Amplifiers have a variety of speaker sizes, whether separate or part of a combo amp. Bass speakers that are 10 or 15 inches in diameter are best. Some speaker cabinets have a combination of different speakers as well. For example, the cabinet may have a 15-inch and a 10-inch speaker in the same enclosure.

The larger the speaker, the more boom you hear in the sound; the smaller the speaker, the clearer the tone (but with less of the bass sound). Try different ones with your bass to find out which you prefer. You may want to start out with a 15-inch speaker and eventually graduate to a cabinet that has four

10-inch speakers. (Or you may want to go with the Grateful Dead's famous "wall of sound," which is several stories tall.) Just remember that you're the one who has to move all this equipment; you probably won't be able to count on your singer for help. Fortunately, speakers have been getting lighter with the advent of neodymium designs, so moving your speaker cabinet doesn't have to be like moving a fridge anymore — well, for a price.

Setting the tone

Every amp has a control panel (see Figure 16-2) with a few knobs for adjusting the sound. Most control panels are similar from amp to amp. Here's a quick rundown on what the knobs are used for:

- **Volume:** This knob raises or lowers the volume of your bass.

- **Bass:** This knob raises or lowers the low frequencies. If you don't have enough bass, the tone sounds tinny and weak; if you have too much, the tone sounds boomy and undefined.

- **Mid:** This knob adjusts the midrange tone. If you don't have enough midrange, the tone sounds undefined; however, too much midrange and the tone honks (not a pleasant sound). Sometimes amps have one knob for *high* mid and another for *low* mid.

- **Treble:** This knob adjusts the high tone. If you don't have enough high, the tone sounds dull; if you have too much high, it sounds piercing.

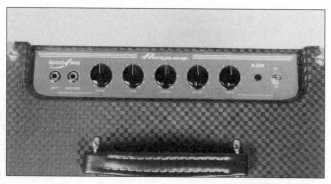

Figure 16-2:
The control panel of a bass amplifier.

Photo by Steven Schlesinger

Experiment with different settings, and keep in mind that you have to readjust your settings to compensate for the unique acoustical qualities of the room in which you're playing. Be sure to listen carefully to your sound during the sound check.

When experimenting with the sound of your amp for the first time, start out with all the knobs *flat* (no added bass, treble, or mids); then adjust the tone on your bass guitar until you have it roughly where you like the sound. After that, tweak the knobs on the amp, one by one, to enhance the sound.

Needs, Wants, and Nonessentials: Rounding Out Your Equipment

Certain items are required for your career as a bass player; they simply come with the territory. Other items can make your life a lot easier if you have them. Finally, some items are just the icing on the cake; you won't miss a performance if you don't have them. This section covers these three types of equipment.

You can complete your arsenal at any time, but the essentials, along with the amp and speaker, are, well, essential. Fortunately, the essentials don't wear out quickly, so you'll have them for years and years of joyful bass playing.

Must-haves: Cases, gig bags, and more

You need to be able to transport your bass safely from place to place, and you may have to do this during a blazing heat wave, a tropical monsoon, or a snowstorm. (For example, I recorded part of the audio tracks for this book in New York City during one of the biggest blizzards of the decade; the basses were safely in their cases while I was slogging through the storm on the way to the studio.) Two types of cases — hard-shell cases and soft-sided gig bags — give your bass ample protection.

Most basses come with a hard-shell case to protect it from the elements as well as from anyone bumping into it. A hard case is great for traveling because other bags and suitcases may end up loaded on top of your precious bass.

If you live in a city and take public transportation, or you walk a lot, you may want to carry your bass in a gig bag. A *gig bag* is a soft case that protects your instrument from the elements but doesn't offer a lot of protection from people (or vehicles) bumping into it. However, hauling your bass in a gig bag is a lot easier than toting your bass around in a hard case: You carry a gig bag like a backpack, leaving your hands free to sign autographs for your adoring fans.

Whether you go for a hard case or a gig bag, you need to put several other items in the carrying case (along with your bass). Here are the items you need to carry with you (see Figure 16-3):

- ✔ **Cable:** You need a cable to connect your bass to the amp. Without a cable, the best amp in the world won't be able to give you any sound.

- ✔ **Strap:** A strap helps you hold your bass while you're playing. The only other way to hold your bass in the proper position is to glue it to your belly. Ouch!

- ✔ **Electronic tuner:** An electronic tuner helps you tune your bass, especially in a noisy environment. You also may want to carry extra batteries (or even a tuning fork) in case the batteries in your electronic tuner give out. (See Chapter 2 for more information about tuning.)

- ✔ **Extra set of strings:** Bass strings rarely break. But if they do break in the middle of a performance, you want to be ready. (Refer to Chapter 17 for details about changing strings.)

- ✔ **Rubbing alcohol and cleaning cloth:** You want to keep your strings nice and bright, don't you? (Chapter 18 discusses cleaning your bass.)

- ✔ **Wrenches and screwdrivers:** Put together a toolkit with the essentials to help you fix your bass when you're in a bind. However, if the problem is beyond the light repair discussed in Chapter 18, let a professional instrument repairperson handle it.

- ✔ **Metronome:** You may want to take your metronome, in case you get a chance to practice when you're traveling. Even if you don't bring your metronome, make sure you own one.

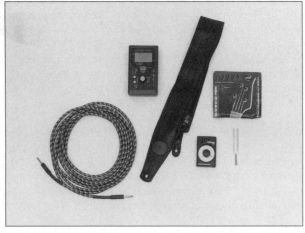

Figure 16-3:
Contents of
a bass bag.

Photo by Steven Schlesinger

Definite maybes: Useful effects, gadgets, and practice items

Some items make your life as a bass player easier (and sometimes more fun), but often you can function without them.

Bassists generally prefer a clean sound, so they aren't as likely as guitar players to use all kinds of *effects* (gadgets that alter the sound). However, here are two useful effects items (shown in Figure 16-4) that bassists do often use:

- ✔ **A chorus unit:** A *chorus unit* makes your bass sound like two basses played simultaneously.

- ✔ **A volume pedal:** A *volume pedal* lets you adjust the volume with your foot, even in the middle of a tune.

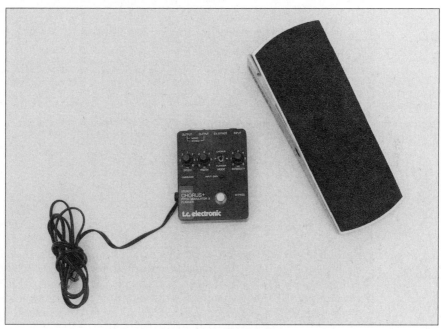

Figure 16-4:
A chorus unit and a volume pedal.

Photo by Steven Schlesinger

For those long hours of practicing, you also may find the following items useful (see Figure 16-5):

- ✔ A stand for your bass
- ✔ A stool for proper posture while playing
- ✔ A music stand to hold your charts (or this book)

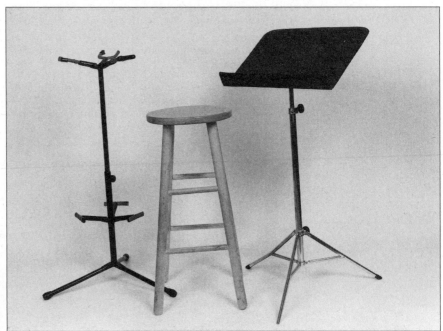

Figure 16-5:
A bass stand, a stool, and a music stand.

If you still have some cash to burn, get a good *headphone amp* (an amp that allows you to hear your bass over headphones). Figure 16-6 shows a headphone amp. With one of these, you can play at all hours of the day or night without disturbing anyone. A wide variety of headphone amps are available, ranging in price from $30 to $300. The better the unit, the better your sound — and the more you'll want to practice. Some headphone amps (like the JamHub) even enable you to plug in with your guitar-playing friends, and you can all rock out without waking the family dog.

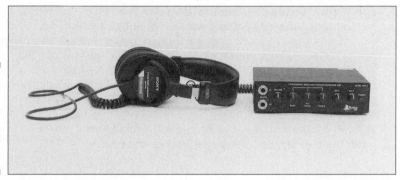

Figure 16-6:
A profes-
sional
headphone
practice
amp.

You can find most of the items in this section at any large music store. You may have to buy the stool from a furniture store and the headphone amp online, but the really large music stores usually have everything you need.

Extras: Effects pedals

As a bass player, your job is to hold down the groove and keep the sound of the band tight, and that's best accomplished with a clean sound from the bass. But for a little special effect during a bass groove or solo, you may want to audition some other pedals besides the chorus unit and the volume pedal (both described in the previous section). Here are examples of other effects pedals you may want to use:

- **Flanger/phase shifter:** These devices create a whooshy, swirly sound, similar to the Hammond organ.

- **Digital delay:** This device creates an echo of the notes you play. You also can use the digital delay unit to record a short, rhythmic phrase that repeats as you play over it.

- **Distortion:** This device distorts your sound, making it rough and dirty. Distortion is mostly used for guitars, but basses can use it, too. This device is great for hard-rock tunes.

- **Envelope filter:** This device makes your bass sound like a funky keyboard bass. It makes it sound as though a synthesizer is playing the bass part.

- **Octave pedal:** This device doubles your bass notes (either an octave above the note you're playing or an octave below).

✔ **Multi-effects unit:** A multi-effects unit is an all-in-one effects unit. It can be programmed to alter your bass sound in several ways at the touch of a foot pedal. Keep in mind, though, that a unit like this requires a lot of homework on your part. You have to find sounds you like, program them, and listen to how they work when you're playing in a band. You may find some cool sounds along the way. Just don't get carried away; you're the *bass* player, not the *guitar* player.

You can get these items at most large and small music stores, or you can order them online or through mail-order companies.

Chapter 17

Changing the Strings on Your Bass Guitar

In This Chapter

▶ Removing old or damaged strings

▶ Attaching new strings

▶ Keeping your new strings in good condition

*W*hat kind of strings do you use?

I dunno. They came with the bass.

Some bassists think that you don't need to change the strings on a bass until they unravel — and then you need to replace them only if you absolutely need that particular string. If this were true, you'd be waiting a long time to change your strings, and eventually the only sound you'd get out of your poor old strings would be a dull thud.

The fact is, bass strings need to be changed regularly. The dirt from your fingers and the dust particles from the air wear them out. In addition, they get metal fatigue from being under constant tension. (Hey, come on! Don't *you* get fatigued when you're under constant tension?) Old strings lose their *brightness* (clarity of sound) and *sustain* (length of time that a note rings out); they get sticky and become difficult or even impossible to tune. So in this chapter, I lead you step by step through the painless process of changing the strings on your bass.

Always replace all your strings at the same time. The strings wear at the same rate. So when you replace them all simultaneously, you ensure that they all sound the same; in other words, you ensure that one doesn't sound clearer than the others.

Knowing When It's Time to Say Goodbye

How do you know when it's time to replace your strings? Here are some clues that signal a change is necessary:

- ✔ **The strings show wear and tear.** You can see dark spots along the strings, probably as a result of dirt stuck in the windings of the steel. You also may see corrosion (or rust spots) on the strings.

- ✔ **The strings sound dull and lifeless.** Your notes don't *sustain* (ring out for an extended length of time), and hearing an exact pitch is difficult. Playing a harmonic for tuning also is a challenge. (See Chapter 2 for more on tuning with harmonics.)

- ✔ **The strings feel sticky and stiff.** Unless you ate a cinnamon roll before playing your bass, this is a sure sign of trouble. (As with swimming, you should always wait at least a half-hour to play bass after eating a cinnamon roll.)

- ✔ **Jimmy Carter was president when you last changed your strings, or you just can't remember *when* you last changed them.** In other words, if you've lost count of how many decades it's been since you've changed your strings, do it *now!*

Off with the Old: Removing Bass Strings

Before you can put new strings on your bass, you need to remove the old ones. The quickest way to remove your old bass strings is simply to take wire cutters (sturdy ones — bass strings are pretty thick) and cut the string at the thin section, between the *tuning post* (the round metal post that has one end of the string wound around it) and the *nut* (the little bar near the tuning posts that has a groove for each string; see Chapter 1).

If you're afraid that the string is going to whip across your face and leave a scar (imagine trying to explain that one), turn the tuning head to loosen the tension of the string before cutting it. Just remember which size string is connected to which tuning post. After cutting the old string, pull the coiled part off the tuning post, and then pull the other part through the bridge. Take a look at Figure 17-1 to see what this process looks like.

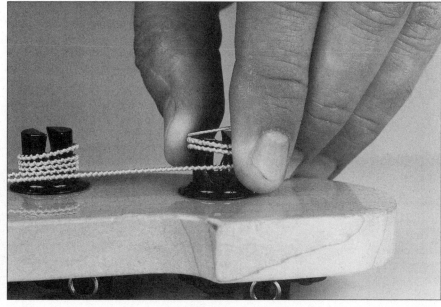

Figure 17-1:
Cutting the
string and
pulling the
coiled part
from the
tuning post.

Photo by Steven Schlesinger

If you want to save your strings as an emergency set (in case one of the new strings breaks), don't cut the string. Just release the tension until you can grab the coiled end and pull it off the tuning post. Straighten the end of the string as best you can, and then pull the entire length through the bridge (see Figure 17-2).

One common myth says that you should change only one string at a time to maintain tension in the neck. I disagree. Take 'em off. Take 'em all off. Your bass can handle it, and removing all the strings at once gives you access to your fingerboard and pickups for some basic cleaning. (See Chapter 18 for info on how to clean your bass.)

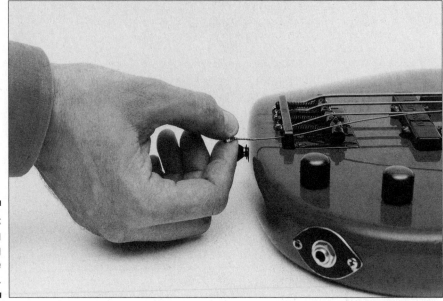

Photo by Steven Schlesinger

Figure 17-2:
Pulling
the string
through the
bridge.

On with the New: Restringing Your Bass

After you clip the old strings and clean any grime off the fingerboard, renew the voice of your bass by adding brand-new strings. You need to be in a clean and comfortable environment for this task. After all, why put on new strings if you're going to get sawdust all over them as soon as you're done? Be sure to lay your bass on a clean towel before restringing it.

Have wire cutters nearby when you restring your bass. You'll need to cut the new strings down to size.

You attach strings to your bass at two points:

- ✔ The bridge
- ✔ The tuning posts

New strings are usually coiled in envelopes. The envelopes are numbered according to string size (the thickest string has the highest number). With most basses, the new string has to be pulled through a hole in the bridge, so that's the place to start. Here's a step-by-step guide to changing the strings of your bass guitar:

1. **Put a towel on the floor in front of you and lay the bass on it, with the neck pointing to the left (to the right if you're left-handed).**

2. **Remove the old strings.**

   See the previous section for instructions on how to remove the old strings.

3. **Take the thickest string out of its envelope (make sure you leave the string coiled) and take a look at it.**

   Notice that it has a ring (called a *ball*) at one end; the other end is pointed, with its tip wrapped in silk. Figure 17-3 shows you what a coiled string looks like.

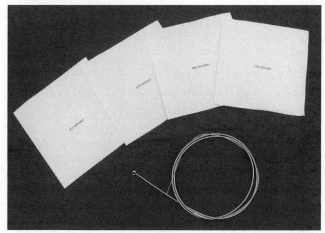

Figure 17-3:
Coiled
string with
envelopes.

Photo by Steven Schlesinger

4. **Straighten the string and push the pointed end (the one without the brass ring) through the hole that's nearest you on the bridge.**

   Each string goes into a separate hole. Pull the string through the proper hole, toward the nut. As you pull it through, make sure the ball at the end of the string comes to rest against the bridge. Figure 17-4 shows how to perform this step.

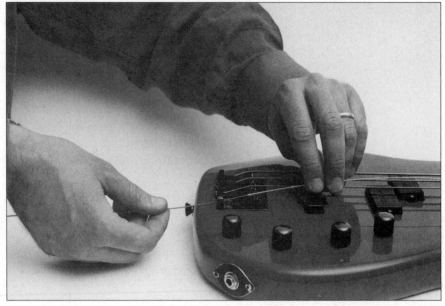

Figure 17-4:
Pulling
the string
through the
bridge.

Photo by Steven Schlesinger

5. **Pull the string until it's resting against its designated tuning post.**

   The post has a groove that crosses the top and also has a hole in its center. Make sure you have enough string to extend 4 to 5 inches beyond the tuning post. This extra length ensures that your string is long enough to wind several times around the tuning post (so the string doesn't slip when tightened).

6. **With your wire cutters, snip off any excess string 4 to 5 inches past the post (see Figure 17-5).**

   Cut only from the part of the string that's wrapped with silk. Never cut the thick part of the string itself (the metal). If you cut this part of the string, it will simply unravel.

7. **Take the tip of the string (now freshly cut) and stick it straight down into the hole in the center of the tuning post, bending the string to the side so it rests in the groove at the top of the tuning post.**

   Hold the string in place at the tuning post with your right hand. Figure 17-6 shows you how to perform this step.

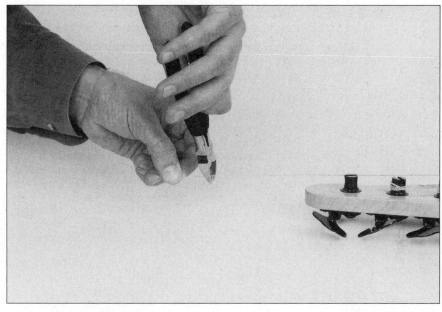

Figure 17-5:
Cutting the
string to
size.

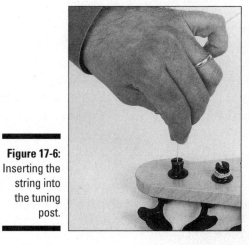 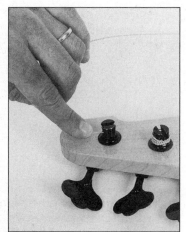

Figure 17-6:
Inserting the
string into
the tuning
post.

8. **Turn the tuning head with your left hand to increase the tension of the string.**

   Make sure the string winds *down* the post (you can guide it with the fingers of your right hand). This downward winding increases the slight bend (breaking angle) of the string against the nut and ensures that the string sits firmly in its groove on the nut, giving the notes better sustain.

   At the same time, make sure the other end of the string runs over the proper *saddle* (a small moveable part that has a groove for the string to fit into) at the bridge. Figure 17-7 shows a properly wound string, and Figure 17-8 shows how the strings lie over the saddle.

Figure 17-7:
Windings of
a string at
the tuning
post.

Photo by Steven Schlesinger

9. **Repeat the entire process for all the other strings, moving from thick to thin.**

   Some basses have *string retainers* that hold the two thinnest strings close to the *headstock* (the top part of the neck). Pass the two thinnest strings under the string retainers before tightening them. Now tune them

Figure 17-8:
The strings
at the
saddle.

up. You need to go through the tuning process (described in Chapter 2) several times right then and there, because the strings stretch out and the neck bends forward under the increased tension. When your strings are in tune, you're ready to play.

Turn the tuning heads to wind up the strings. Don't wrap the strings around the tuning posts by hand; if you do it by hand, the strings will twist and lose their ability to sustain notes.

You can get many happy playing weeks (even months) out of your new strings. Just keep them reasonably clean so you don't have to change them too often. New bass strings come at a price: $15 to $40 for a four-string set.

Ensuring a Long Life for Your Strings

After you get those new strings onto your bass, you want to do all you can to keep them in good, working condition, right? Well, increasing the life of your strings is easier than you think. All you have to do is follow two basic rules:

✔ Wash your hands before you touch your strings.

✔ Don't let anyone else touch your strings unless he washes his hands first.

The natural oils and sweat on *clean* hands are hard enough on your bass strings. If you indulge in a greasy roast chicken or change the oil in your car before your next rehearsal, all that grease, grime, and dirt ends up on your strings. This kind of debris shortens string life drastically. So wash those paws before you play.

Chapter 18

Keeping Your Bass in Shape: Maintenance and Light Repair

. . . .

In This Chapter

▶ Cleaning your bass

▶ Repairing just the bass-ics

▶ Adjusting the neck and bridge

▶ Putting together a bass toolkit

▶ Storing your bass safely and properly

. . . .

Bass guitars are like their owners — tough, hard, and rugged — but only on the surface. Deep down, basses (like their owners) yearn for some tender, loving care and affection and, of course, for some appreciation.

Despite the most careful handling and the best of care, your instrument is bound to collect battle scars. If you play your bass a lot, it needs to be cleaned regularly, and certain parts will need replacing from time to time — or at least tightening and adjusting. This chapter tells you what maintenance you can easily do yourself and what maintenance is best left to your friendly, neighborhood instrument repairperson.

Cleaning Your Bass, Part by Part

Cleaning your bass is the most basic of maintenance jobs, and the first step is to wash your hands. No, really, I'm not kidding! The finish on the wood and hardware shows every fingerprint. So the least you can do is keep those fingerprints clean; don't enhance them with grime. The next few sections walk you through cleaning the various parts of your bass, one by one.

The body and neck

Clean the body of your bass the way you clean your favorite antique furniture — very carefully. You can polish the finish with a cloth (such as an old sweatshirt), but use *guitar polish* (available in a spray bottle at any music store or online) rather than furniture polish. Guitar polish gets dust and dirt off your instrument and leaves your bass looking well cared for.

Apply a squirt or two of the polish to the cloth and work it into the fabric. Then rub your bass down — work on the body (front and back) and on the back of the neck. Your bass will love it. Keep the polish away from the strings and the fingerboard, though; I deal with them a little later.

The hardware

The *hardware* consists of all the brass and metal parts attached to the wood, with the exception of the frets and pickups. The tuning heads, bridge, and strap pins are all considered hardware. Rubbing the hardware down with a dust cloth helps keep it shiny. If too much dirt builds up on the hardware, you can use a mild brass polish from the supermarket to clean the metal. Make sure that the polish isn't abrasive and that it doesn't get onto the wood because it will mar the finish.

The pickups

When it comes to cleaning your bass, the pickups are in a category all by themselves. A lot of dust accumulates where the wood meets the metal of the pickups (see Chapter 1 for a picture of the pickups on a bass guitar).

Whatever you do, don't use any liquids for this part of the cleaning. Pickups are electronic, and they can't deal with liquid. The liquid can cause them to short out, making it necessary to replace them.

Of course, getting new pickups every four weeks is one way to keep them clean. Otherwise, use dry cotton swabs to clean the area where your pickups meet the wood.

The fingerboard

The fingerboard consists of two major parts:

- ✔ The long wooden strip on the front of the neck
- ✔ The metal frets embedded in the long wooden strip

These two parts are made of very different materials, so each needs to be cleaned in its own special way. You can clean them only after removing your old strings and before restringing. (See Chapter 17 to find out how to restring your bass.)

The wood

Because the wood on your fingerboard is normally exposed, it's prone to drying out. To restore the wood to its original luster, use a dry cloth to get rid of the dirt, and then place a few drops (no more than five or so) of finger-board oil (which you can get from your local music store or online) on a clean cotton cloth and work it into the wood. The wood absorbs fingerboard oil easily, so let the oil dry thoroughly before rubbing down the fingerboard again to remove any excess oil. Apply oil to the wood every time you change the strings, or at least every other time.

The frets

You can use a jewelry polishing cloth that has polish already soaked into it (available in any supermarket) to polish the frets. The cloth is inexpensive, and your frets will sparkle with joy (maybe not as bright as diamonds, but you never know).

When polishing the frets, don't use an abrasive jewelry polish that you have to pour out of a bottle. That stuff is rough on the wood of the fingerboard.

The strings

Yes, the strings need to be cleaned as well. After all, they take the most abuse. After the strings are on the bass, you can simply wipe them with a dry cotton cloth after you've finished playing. However, using a couple drops of rubbing alcohol (available in any pharmacy) on a cotton cloth is even better.

Let the alcohol sink into the cloth for a few seconds. Then put a moist section of the cloth between your index finger and thumb and pinch one string at a time, rubbing the cloth up and down along the string's length. Check out Figure 18-1 for the proper method for cleaning bass strings.

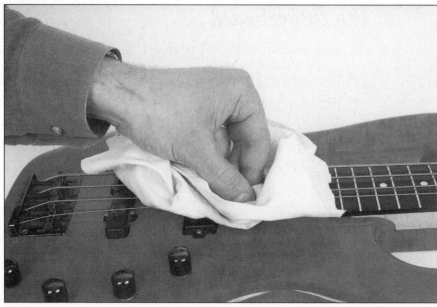

Photo by Steven Schlesinger

Figure 18-1:
Cleaning the
strings.

Don't get any of the alcohol on the wood; it'll dry it out.

Making Minor Repairs to Your Bass

You can do your own minor repairs to your bass to keep it in top-notch playing
condition — tweaking a few screws, touching up a bit of finish, soldering a couple
of electronic connectionszzzzzzzzzzzap! . . . well, maybe not the electronics.

The taming of the screw(s)

The parts of the bass guitar are held together in two ways: with glue and with
screws. A *luthier* (a person who builds stringed instruments) uses specific
glues for each type of wood on the bass. If anything that's supposed to be
glued comes apart, take your instrument to a qualified repairperson.

If, on the other hand, a piece of hardware comes loose or starts rattling, you
can simply screw it back where it belongs. Just remember one thing: Your
bass has an array of different-sized screws. Most of the screws are of the
Phillips variety. Buy a set of screwdrivers at the hardware store and make sure

you have a perfect fit for each screw on your bass. Why do I say that? The reason is simple: If you force a screwdriver that doesn't fit into a screw, you'll end up stripping the head of the screw . . . and then you're really screwed.

If you don't feel comfortable turning the screws on your bass, don't mess around. Take your precious instrument to a qualified repairperson.

Taking care of the finish

The *finish* is the thin layer of lacquer that seals the wood of your bass. The finish usually is glossy; it looks beautiful when the instrument is new. The finish also serves a function: It protects the wood from severe changes in humidity. Low humidity makes the wood brittle and prone to cracking; high humidity causes the wood to swell and warp.

Collisions between your bass and other objects (such as the drummer's cymbals) may leave dings or cracks in the finish. If you want that perfect look back, you have to take your bass to a pro for refinishing, which can be costly. If you're not overly concerned with the look, or you think that battle scars are cool, seal the cracks with colorless nail polish. You can also try to match your bass's color with a small bottle of model paint from a toy store.

Be vigilant in protecting the *back* of your bass neck. If you scratch it, you'll be able to feel the scratch when you're playing. If the scratch is shallow, try to get it out by rubbing the entire neck up and down with 0000-grade (superfine) steel wool. Sand the entire length of the neck. The steel wool will give the back of the neck a nice satin feel. If you still feel the scratch, have a repairperson refinish the neck of your bass.

Don't get too used to just sanding the scratches off the neck of your bass. Each time you sand the neck, even with the finest-grade steel wool, you take a layer of finish off. Eventually, none of the finish will be left, and you'll need to get the neck refinished. Of course, you'll be better off if you don't get your bass neck scratched in the first place.

Leaving the electronics to the experts

If you hear crackling when you turn any of the knobs, it may be a minor problem. Just turn the knobs vigorously back and forth to eliminate the crackling. If that doesn't do the trick — you guessed it — take it to a pro.

With the advent of high-tech basses that feature complex pre-amps and pickups, I don't recommend touching the electronics. Take your bass to a pro to have any electronic problem fixed — unless, of course, you have a graduate degree in electrical engineering.

Adjusting the Bass Guitar

Your bass is a sturdy instrument, but every now and then it needs some slight adjusting. As the weather changes from season to season (provided you live in a location that has seasons), the wood in your bass also changes. The neck tends to bend or straighten slightly, causing the strings to either pull away from the frets or rest against them; at times this makes playing almost impossible.

You can counter the forces of nature by

✔ Tweaking the *truss rod* (a metal rod that runs inside the length of the bass neck)

✔ Adjusting the *saddles* (the little, moving metal parts of the bridge that have grooves for the strings to lie across)

Providing relief to the truss rod

The truss rod controls the curvature of your bass neck. Because the strings need space to vibrate freely over the entire length of the fingerboard, your bass neck has to have a slight *relief* (curve) to give them room. Now, notice that I said *slight* relief. If the relief is too great, the *action* (the space between the strings and frets) will be too high, and you'll need arms like Popeye's to press down the strings.

How much action is enough to keep the strings vibrating while still making them easy to press down? To check your action, press the E string (the thickest one) down at the first fret with your left hand. At the same time, press the E string down at the last fret with your right hand. The space between the E string and the neck (between the 7th and 12th frets) should be about the thickness of a credit card (finally, a good use for credit cards). You can have a little more space if you prefer, or slightly less space if you play very lightly.

To adjust the action, you need to turn a screw in the truss rod, which changes the curvature of the neck. The screw is located either on the headstock or at the other end of the neck. Turn the truss rod only between one-quarter and one-half of a turn per day. You need to allow the wood to settle before doing any more adjustments.

On some basses, you have to remove the neck from the body to reach the screw of the truss rod. Don't attempt to loosen the screws at the back of the bass that hold the neck in place without first loosening the tension of the strings. Otherwise, the neck will snap off, stripping away the wood that holds the screws.

In most cases, you can adjust the truss rod with the small Allen wrench that comes with your bass. If you lose this wrench, you can get another from your local music store or the bass manufacturer. On other basses, the screw of the truss rod requires a Phillips screwdriver, which may not come with the bass. (You can buy it at the hardware store.) Here's how to adjust the truss rod:

- ✔ If you have too much space between the E string and the neck, insert the Allen wrench or Phillips screwdriver into the screw and tighten the truss rod by turning the wrench or screwdriver clockwise.

- ✔ If your strings buzz when you play on the first four frets (near the headstock), you need to loosen the truss rod by turning the wrench or screwdriver counterclockwise.

Take a look at Figure 18-2 to see how to adjust a truss rod.

Figure 18-2:
Adjusting the truss rod.

Photo by Steven Schlesinger

Use only the specific wrench or screwdriver that fits into your truss rod. If you don't have the proper tool, get one from your local music store or the manufacturer of the bass. Don't try to force the truss rod with anything that doesn't quite fit. If you strip the truss rod, it'll cost you.

Raising and lowering the bridge

You also can adjust the action of your bass by moving the saddles on the bridge. The saddles can be lowered or raised by turning the screws at the top with an Allen wrench. When you adjust the saddles, you lower or raise the string height (the action). Figure 18-3 shows how to adjust the saddles.

Figure 18-3:
Adjusting
the height of
the saddles.

Photo by Steven Schlesinger

Getting your bass set up by a repairperson initially is a good idea. After you get your bass back from the repairperson, take note of how high he or she set the saddles and how the strings feel. From then on, you can fine-tune your bass by comparing it to the original setup.

You also can use the saddles to correct the intonation of your bass. If you hear your bass going out of tune when you play on the very high or low frets, you need to adjust the intonation. To do this, find a screwdriver that fits the screws at the back of the bridge. Turning these screws moves the saddles back and forth. Read the following steps and check out Figure 18-4 to find out how to adjust the saddles to correct the intonation:

1. **Play the harmonic of one of the strings at the 12th fret, and tune that pitch to a tuner.**

   When the harmonic of the string is in perfect tune, play the same string by fretting it at the 12th fret, and compare the pitch of the note with the pitch of the harmonic. They should be the same. (See Chapter 2 for how to play a harmonic.)

2. **If the fretted note is sharp compared to the harmonic, lengthen the string by tightening the screw.**

   Moving the saddle away from the neck lengthens the string. Now tune the string again using the harmonic. Compare the pitch of the harmonic with the fretted note, and keep adjusting the saddle until both the harmonic and the fretted note are in tune.

3. **If the fretted note is flat, shorten the string by loosening the screw to move the saddle toward the neck.**

   Tune the string using the harmonic, and keep adjusting the saddle until both the harmonic and fretted note are in tune.

4. **Repeat this process with all the strings.**

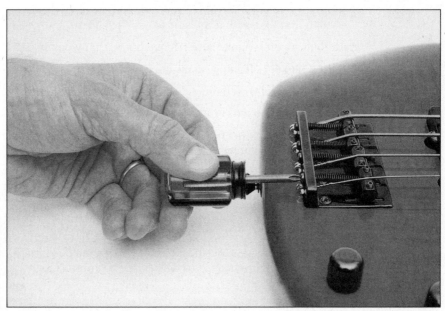

Figure 18-4:
Adjusting the intonation.

Photo by Steven Schlesinger

Be patient and take your time when you're adjusting your bass. It needs to be done only about four times a year (as the seasons change), but you have to take a whole afternoon to do it right, especially if you're adjusting your bass for the first time. The process will bring you closer to your instrument — you know, bass bonding.

Assembling a Cleaning and Repair Tool Bag

Before you attempt any of the adjustments or cleaning procedures I cover in this chapter, you need to make sure you have all the required tools. Start assembling a tool set just for your bass. Here's a list of what needs to be in a bass tool bag (see Figure 18-5):

- Truss-rod wrench (usually the Allen wrench that comes with your bass)
- Screwdrivers and Allen wrenches for every screw on the bass

    A multi-screwdriver tool is okay, but you can get more leverage with separate screwdrivers. Make sure you have a screwdriver or Allen wrench that fits each of the screws for the saddle.

- Rubbing alcohol (make sure it's in a bottle that won't leak)
- Cotton rags for cleaning (make sure to replace them once in a while)
- Super-fine steel wool
- Colorless nail polish (or a color that matches your bass)
- Electronic tuner (this needs to be part of your tool set if you adjust the intonation yourself)
- Wire cutters for changing your strings (make sure you always have a spare set of strings with your bass)
- Jewelry polish cloth for polishing the frets

Be sure to keep your bass tools separate from your household tools so they won't get lost or damaged. Besides, basses can get jealous if they find out that *their* truss-rod wrench was used to tighten the bathroom faucet.

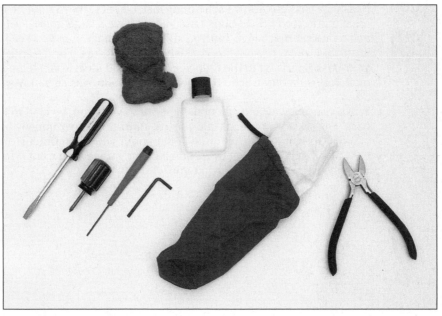

Photo by Steven Schlesinger

Figure 18-5:
Contents of
a bass tool
bag.

Storing Your Bass

Keeping your bass guitar happy is really quite simple. If you're comfortable, your bass will be comfortable. You want to keep it out of direct sunlight, and you want to keep it out of the snow — at least for any extended period of time. The safest place to keep your bass is in its case, but then it can be kind of a hassle to get to when inspiration strikes. If you want to keep your bass handy, place it on a sturdy bass guitar stand, preferably with the strings covered by a soft cloth. Just make sure you set it up in a safe corner of the room that doesn't get a lot of traffic. (In other words, don't place it in the path of the family dog, which just happens to be a clumsy Saint Bernard.)

If you have a *gig bag* (a soft, padded carrying pack), you can store your bass in it when you're not playing. The gig bag gives your bass some protection (actually a good gig bag can give the bass a *lot* of protection), and it also allows you to get to your bass relatively easily.

Nearly all bass guitars are solid-body instruments (they're not hollow), making them quite sturdy. Solid-body bass guitars have a large tolerance for humidity and temperature change, but you still need to make sure you keep your bass in an area with a reasonable, consistent temperature. For example, keeping your bass right next to the fireplace isn't a good idea. Room temperature with moderate humidity will do the trick, making your bass as happy as a clam.

When you go away and can't take your bass with you, be kind to it. Put your bass in its case and keep it in a climate-controlled environment. You can stand it upright in a closet or lay it flat under your bed. Don't store your bass in a damp basement or an uninsulated garage. You want it to still love you when you come back, don't you?

Part VI
The Part of Tens

Enjoy an additional Part of Tens chapter online at www.dummies.com/extras/bassguitar.

In this part...

- Get introduced to some of the pioneers of the bass guitar.

- Appreciate some of the contributions to the bass world.

Chapter 19

Ten Innovative Bassists You Should Know

In This Chapter

▶ Getting to know some great bassists

▶ Seeing who's responsible for influencing the bass world

Certain bass players have made a lasting mark on the entire bass world, regardless of which genre of music they play. These innovators advance the instrument to new levels, influencing everyone who follows in their footsteps. Each of the bass players in this chapter has a unique style; it isn't easy to say how these giants have influenced one another (it's sort of like saying, "Which came first, the magnetic pickup or the steel string?"), so I simply put them in alphabetical order by last name.

You sure can benefit from listening to these masters of the bass world. If you want to explore any of these bassists' styles yourself, I include samples of their groove styles on my website, www.PatrickPfeifferBass.com.

Stanley Clarke

Considered by many to be the liberator of the bass, Stanley Clarke pioneered the concept of the "solo bass album" in the early 1970s and brought the bass guitar (including his higher-pitched tenor and piccolo basses) from the back line to front and center in a featured melodic role that's usually reserved for guitarists and horn players. Clarke is best known for his work with the jazz-fusion group Return to Forever and for his solo projects. Signature Clarke tunes include "School Days" and "Lopsy Lu."

John Entwistle

John Entwistle's nickname (among others) was "Thunderfingers." He's best remembered as the bassist for the rock group The Who. From the mid-1960s to the early '80s, Entwistle developed a busy style of lead bass playing that included occasional explosive solos (and he was *loud*). He also performed as a solo artist. Brilliant signature Entwistle features include "My Generation" and "Who Are You." When called upon to play a solo on a rock gig, you can't do better than to draw on Entwistle for inspiration.

James Jamerson

James Jamerson is the father of modern electric bass. Between the early 1960s and the late '70s, he played on more number-one hits than Elvis, The Beatles, The Beach Boys, and the Rolling Stones . . . *combined*. He was the main bassist for the Funk Brothers, the legendary rhythm section for the Motown label. Some of his signature tunes are "I Heard It through the Grapevine" (check out the Gladys Knight version for some incredible bass playing) and Stevie Wonder's "For Once in My Life."

Carol Kaye

Carol Kaye is a true pioneer of the bass guitar, having played on literally thousands of studio recordings, including classics by The Beach Boys, Simon & Garfunkel, The Monkees, The Righteous Brothers, Ray Charles, and many, many more, along with movie and TV soundtracks by the dozens. You can hear her cutting loose on Quincy Jones's "Hicky-Burr" and on the Mel Tormé version of "Games People Play." One of her most famous bass parts is the theme for "Mission: Impossible" (the original TV series). Kaye was a member of the L.A. studio musicians' clique (later dubbed "The Wrecking Crew") of the 1960s and '70s, during the "California Rock Explosion."

Will Lee

Will Lee is living the dream of a bassist. He started his career as a top New York session player in the early 1970s. Lee records and performs with stars in musical genres that range from jazz (The Brecker Brothers), to rock and pop (Steely Dan, Barry Manilow), to soul (James Brown, D'Angelo), and everything in between. A musical chameleon whose super-precise bass lines enhance any contemporary style, he can be heard (and seen) most nights on the popular *Late Show with David Letterman.* He also tours with his Beatles cover band, The Fab Faux.

Paul McCartney

Perhaps the most famous bassist in history, Paul McCartney was one of The Beatles. He embarked on a solo career after The Fab Four's split in 1970. McCartney pushed the bass to new levels in rock and pop music by playing in a melodic style that embellished the vocals and melody of a tune (see Chapter 14 for a detailed analysis of his playing). Signature McCartney tunes include "Something" and "Come Together" (among many, many others).

Marcus Miller

A strong soloist and groove player, Marcus Miller is a multitalented musician and producer who just happens to play bass. Miller burst onto the scene in the late 1970s and never left. He mixes soul, R & B, hip-hop, funk, and contemporary jazz and comes up with original works of stunning beauty and depth. He's best known for his work with jazzers Miles Davis and David Sanborn, as well as for his studio work and solo projects.

Jaco Pastorius

Hailed as the greatest electric bassist in the world, Jaco Pastorius restructured the function of the bass guitar in music when he took the bass world by storm in the mid-1970s. He was truly unprecedented, performing audacious technical feats. Jaco (he's typically referred to by this name; his full name is John Francis Pastorius III) played both fluid grooves and hornlike solos with equal virtuosity, and he incorporated harmonics into his playing as an additional musical tool (along with the regular notes). He's best known for his work with the jazz-fusion group Weather Report and as a solo artist. Signature Jaco tunes include "Donna Lee," the beautiful "Continuum," and the blistering "Teen Town" (check out the live version on the album *8:30* by Weather Report).

Victor Wooten

Defying boundaries and categories, Victor Wooten is a modern bass virtuoso who came to fame in the late 1980s. Best known for his work with Béla Fleck and the Flecktones and as a solo artist, he's continually pushing the bass further and further into the limelight. Check out Wooten's bass playing on the CD *Live Art* with Béla Fleck and the Flecktones and on his solo album *Palmystery.* You also can hear him with two other fabulous bassists on this top-ten list: He plays with Stanley Clarke and Marcus Miller on the album *Thunder,* under the band name S.M.V.

X (Fill in Your Own)

This spot is yours to fill. Which bassist influenced you to pick up the bass (and this book) and made you want to play? Your bassist choice can be a world-famous (and fabulous) rocker like Adam Clayton, Sting, Geddy Lee, or Flea; a jazz virtuoso like Alain Caron, Gerald Veasley, or John Patitucci; or a famous (to bassists) studio player like Lee Sklar or Anthony Jackson . . . or even your talented next-door neighbor or your teacher.

I have my favorite picked out, but this choice is yours. Frankly, I have more than one picked out . . . but don't tell anyone!

Chapter 20

Ten Great Rhythm Sections (Bassists and Drummers)

In This Chapter

▶ Discovering great bassist-drummer combinations

▶ Listening to some examples in the styles of the pros

*T*he bass guitar, more than any other instrument, is at its best when tightly aligned with the drums. Together, the bassist and drummer develop the powerful grooves that drive the song by constantly listening and reacting to each other. In this chapter, I introduce you to ten classic bass-and-drum combinations (sorted alphabetically by the bass player's last name) that have enhanced a multitude of songs. If you listen to music at all (and I presume you do), you probably have heard most of these rhythm sections already. If you haven't, you should make a concerted effort to find recordings that feature these classic combinations — and then listen and enjoy!

On Track 117, you can hear brief examples in the styles of these masters. However, to get a sense of truly great bass grooves, you need to listen to the original recordings. Go directly to the source and get inspired by the same musicians who inspire me.

Bootsy Collins and Jab'o Starks

Bootsy Collins and Jab'o Starks are stellar as James Brown's rhythm section of 1970. Their work is one of the earliest examples of the complex interplay between bass and drums. Check out James Brown's recordings "Sex Machine" and "Super Bad" to hear their funky grooves. Figure 20-1 features a bass line in the style of their playing.

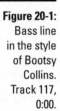

Figure 20-1:
Bass line
in the style
of Bootsy
Collins.
Track 117,
0:00.

Figure 20-1:
Bass line in the style of Bootsy Collins. Track 117, 0:00.

Donald "Duck" Dunn and Al Jackson Jr.

From the mid-1960s through the early '70s, Donald "Duck" Dunn and Al Jackson Jr. recorded many hits for a number of artists as members of the house band for the Stax/Volts record label. Stax was one of the ultimate R & B/Soul record labels, featuring artists Sam and Dave, Otis Redding, Isaac Hayes, and many more. Listen to "Soul Man" and "In the Midnight Hour" to hear their soulful R & B/Soul grooves. Figure 20-2 shows you an example of a bass line in the style of "Duck" Dunn.

Figure 20-2:
Bass line in the style of Donald "Duck" Dunn. Track 117, 0:15.

James Jamerson and Benny Benjamin

James Jamerson and Benny Benjamin combined to form the ultimate rhythm section for the Motown record label throughout the 1960s. Their playing can be heard on hits such as "I Was Made to Love Her" and "Going to a Go-Go." Check out Figure 20-3 for an example of Jamerson's style of playing.

Figure 20-3:
Bass line
in the style
of James
Jamerson.
Track 117,
0:26.

Jamerson & Benjamin

John Paul Jones and John Bonham

John Paul Jones and John Bonham are best known for their work in the band Led Zeppelin. Songs such as "The Lemon Song" and "Ramble On" exemplify their brilliant work from 1968 through 1980. Take a look at Figure 20-4 for an example of a bass line in the style of John Paul Jones.

Figure 20-4:
Bass line in
the style of
John Paul
Jones. Track
117, 0:52.

Jones & Bonham

Joe Osborn and Hal Blaine

Joe Osborn and Hal Blaine were members of an elite assortment of session players who recorded a staggering number of hits during the "California Rock Explosion" of the '60s (when an unusually large number of hits were recorded by bands in California). As part of the "Wrecking Crew," Osborn and Blaine laid down solid grooves for The 5th Dimension, Simon & Garfunkel, The Mamas and The Papas, The Monkees, and many more. Listen to "Vehicle" and "California Dreaming" for great examples of their diversity. Figure 20-5 shows an example of a groove in the style of Joe Osborn.

Figure 20-5:
Bass line in
the style of
Joe Osborn.
Track 117,
1:09.

Osborn & Blaine

Jaco Pastorius and Peter Erskine

Jaco Pastorius and Peter Erskine were both members of the pioneering jazz-rock-fusion group Weather Report during the high point of the band's popularity in the late 1970s. Their complex interplay of bass and drums can be found in such tunes as "Birdland" and "Teen Town" (the live recordings, not the studio recordings). Erskine later went on to play with Jaco's big band Word of Mouth. To call these two masters dynamic is truly an understatement. Check out Figure 20-6 for an example of a bass line in the style of Jaco Pastorius.

Figure 20-6:
Bass line
in the style
of Jaco
Pastorius.
Track 117,
1:22.

Pastorius & Erskine

George Porter Jr. and Zig Modeliste

The syncopated and rubbery style of George Porter Jr. and Joseph "Zigaboo" Modeliste represents New Orleans funk at its very finest. As members of The Meters from the late 1960s to the late '70s, Porter and Modeliste laid down some of the most memorable grooves in history in such tunes as "Cissy Strut" and "Funky Miracle." Figure 20-7 features an example of a bass line in the style of George Porter Jr.

Figure 20-7:
Bass line
in the style
of George
Porter Jr.
Track 117,
1:38.

Francis Rocco Prestia and David Garibaldi

The soul funk of the Oakland-based band Tower of Power was at its peak throughout the 1970s with the combination of Francis Rocco Prestia and David Garibaldi. Their solid sixteenth-note grooves can be heard on "Soul Vaccination" and "What Is Hip," displaying some of the best funk you'll ever hear. Figure 20-8 features a bass line in the style of Francis Rocco Prestia.

Figure 20-8:
Bass line
in the style
of Francis
Rocco
Prestia.
Track 117,
1:55.

Chuck Rainey and Bernard Purdie

The power and nuances of Chuck Rainey's and Bernard Purdie's playing drove some of the best music recorded in New York in the mid-1960s and '70s. This duo laid down the grooves for a diverse list of artists (from Aretha Franklin to Steely Dan). The Rainey-Purdie combination shines on tunes like "Until You Come Back to Me (That's What I'm Gonna Do)" and "Home at Last." Figure 20-9 shows a bass line in the style of Chuck Rainey.

Figure 20-9:
Bass line
in the style
of Chuck
Rainey.
Track 117,
2:14.

Rainey & Purdie

Robbie Shakespeare and Sly Dunbar

Robbie Shakespeare and Sly Dunbar are widely considered the premier bass-drum combination of reggae. Besides playing on dozens of records together, both were members of Peter Tosh's band in the late 1970s. Shakespeare and Dunbar played some of the most memorable reggae grooves in history on such tunes as "Mama Africa" and "Whatcha Gonna Do." In Figure 20-10, you can see a bass line in the style of Robbie Shakespeare.

Figure 20-10:
Bass line
in the style
of Robbie
Shakespeare.
Track 117,
2:40.

Shakespeare & Dunbar

Appendix

Audio Tracks and Video Clips

• •

*Y*ou've probably seen the "Play This!" icon scattered throughout the book. It refers you to more than 100 audio tracks and over 30 video clips that demonstrate various bass guitar tunes and techniques. This appendix provides you with a handy list of all the audio tracks and video clips you can access online.

If you've purchased the paper or e-book version of *Bass Guitar For Dummies,* 3rd Edition, you can find the audio tracks and video clips — ready and waiting for you — at www.dummies.com/go/bassguitar. (If you don't have Internet access, call 877-762-2974 within the U.S. or 317-572-3993 outside the U.S.)

What's on the Audio Tracks

Table A-1 lists all the audio tracks that accompany each chapter, along with any figure numbers if applicable. You also find several backing and play-along tracks to help you with your practice.

Table A-1		Bass Guitar Audio Tracks	
Track	Time	Figure	Description
1		n/a	Open strings for tuning
2		2-23	Open-string song
3		2-24	Closed-string song
4		3-3	Right-hand accents on E string
5		n/a	Right-hand string crossing
6		3-4	Left-hand permutations
7		3-6	Practice exercise for combining the right and left hands
8		4-2	E minor rock groove notation

(continued)

Table A-1 *(continued)*

Track	Time	Figure	Description
9		n/a	Playing to a metronome
10	0:00	4-8	Whole notes
	0:11	4-8	Half notes
	0:23	4-8	Quarter notes
	0:35	4-8	Eighth notes
	0:48	4-8	Sixteenth notes
	1:00	4-8	Eighth-note triplets
11		4-11	Values of notes and rests
12		4-12	Chunks of notes
13	0:00	4-13	Measure 1
	0:10	4-13	Measure 2
	0:18	4-13	Measure 3
	0:26	4-13	Measure 4
	0:34	4-13	Measure 5
	0:42	4-13	Measure 6
	0:50	4-13	Measure 7
	0:57	4-13	Measure 8
	1:05	4-13	Measure 9
	1:13	4-13	Measure 10
	1:21	4-13	Measure 11
	1:29	4-13	Measure 12
	1:37	4-13	Measure 13
	1:45	4-13	Measure 14
	1:53	4-13	Measure 15
	2:01	4-13	Measure 16
	2:09	4-13	Measure 17
	2:17	4-13	Measure 18
	2:25	4-13	Measure 19
	2:33	4-13	Measure 20
	2:41	4-13	Measure 21
	2:49	4-13	Measure 22

Track	Time	Figure	Description
	2:57	4-13	Measure 23
14		4-17	"Two Too Tight Shoes Blues" song
15	0:00	5-2	Major scale
	0:11	5-3	Natural minor scale
16	0:00	5-4	Major triad
	0:11	5-5a	Major triad accompaniment (a)
	0:35	5-5b	Major triad accompaniment (b)
	1:00	5-5c	Major triad accompaniment (c)
17	0:00	5-6	Minor triad
	0:10	5-7a	Minor accompaniment (a)
	0:34	5-7b	Minor accompaniment (b)
	0:59	5-7c	Minor accompaniment (c)
18		5-8	Song using triad accompaniment
19	0:00	5-9	Major 7th chord and Ionian mode
	0:11	5-9	Minor 7th chord and Aeolian mode
	0:24	5-9	Dominant chord and Mixolydian mode
	0:35	5-9	Half-diminished chord and Locrian mode
20		5-10	Song using boogie pattern
21	0:00	5-11	Major triad in root position
	0:08	5-12	Major triad inversion with the 3rd in the bass
	0:13	5-13	Major triad inversion with the 5th in the bass
	0:21	5-14	Minor triad in root position
	0:27	5-15	Minor triad inversion with the 3rd in the bass
	0:32	5-16	Minor triad inversion with the 5th in the bass
22	0:00	5-17	Major tonality: modes and chord
	0:24	5-17	Dominant tonality: mode and chord
	0:40	5-17	Minor tonality: modes and chord
	1:12	5-17	Half-diminished tonality: mode and chord
23	0:00	side-bar	Melodic minor scale
	0:09	side-bar	Harmonic minor scale
24		5-18	Major bass line with chromatic tone

(continued)

Table A-1 *(continued)*

Track	Time	Figure	Description
25		5-19	Minor bass line with chromatic tone
26		5-20	Major bass line with chromatic tone outside the box
27		5-21	Minor bass line with chromatic tone outside the box
28		5-22	Groove with dead notes
29		5-23	Dead note etude
30		5-24	Groove using the chord
31		5-25	Groove using the 7th chord
32		5-26	Groove using the Mixolydian mode
33		5-27	Groove using chromatic tones
34		5-28	Groove using dead notes
35		n/a	Figures 5-24 through 5-28 in sequence
36	0:00	5-30a	Harmonically ambiguous groove (a)
	0:10	5-30b	Harmonically ambiguous groove (b)
	0:23	5-30c	Harmonically ambiguous groove (c)
	0:35	5-30d	Harmonically ambiguous groove (d)
	0:50	5-30e	Harmonically ambiguous groove (e)
37	0:00	6-1a	Groove skeleton (a)
	0:15	6-1b	Groove skeleton (b)
	0:30	6-1c	Groove skeleton (c)
	0:44	6-1d	Groove skeleton (d)
	1:00	6-1e	Groove skeleton (e)
	1:15	6-1f	Groove skeleton (f)
38		6-2	Groove skeleton song
39	0:00	6-4	Creating a dominant groove
	0:35	6-5	Simple and complex dominant grooves
40	0:00	6-6	Creating a minor groove
	0:35	6-7	Simple and complex minor grooves
41	0:00	6-8	Creating a major groove
	0:36	6-9	Simple and complex major grooves
42		6-10	Creating a groove tail

Track	Time	Figure	Description
43		6-12	Mobile groove using constant structure
44		6-13	Mobile groove using chord tones
45	0:00	6-14	Groove with upper groove apex
	0:21	6-15	Upper groove apex exercise
46	0:00	6-16	Groove with lower groove apex
	0:17	6-17	Lower groove apex exercise
47	0:00	n/a	The sound of the bass drum
	0:04	6-18	Grooving with the bass drum
	0:16	n/a	The sound of the snare drum
	0:21	6-19	Grooving with the snare drum
	0:34	n/a	The sound of the hi-hat
	0:42	6-20	Grooving with the hi-hat
48	0:00	6-23a	Variation of a famous groove (a)
	0:29	6-23b	Variation of a famous groove (b)
	1:02	6-23c	Variation of a famous groove (c)
	1:32	6-23d	Variation of a famous groove (d)
	2:01	6-23e	Variation of a famous groove (e)
49	0:00	6-24a	Simplified variation of a famous groove (a)
	0:30	6-24b	Simplified variation of a famous groove (b)
	0:57	6-24c	Simplified variation of a famous groove (c)
50	0:00	7-1	Blues scale
	0:06	7-2	Blues-scale lick #1
	0:40	7-2	Blues-scale lick #2
	1:09	7-2	Blues-scale lick #3
51	0:00	7-3	Minor pentatonic scale
	0:07	7-4	Minor pentatonic lick #1
	0:40	7-4	Minor pentatonic lick #2
	1:09	7-4	Minor pentatonic lick #3
52	0:00	7-5	Major pentatonic scale
	0:07	7-6	Major pentatonic lick #1
	0:38	7-6	Major pentatonic lick #2
	1:06	7-6	Major pentatonic lick #3
53		7-7	Solo over chord chart

(continued)

Table A-1 *(continued)*

Track	Time	Figure	Description
54	0:00	7-8a	Eighth-note blues-scale fills
	0:37	7-8a	Eighth-note minor pentatonic fills
	1:14	7-8a	Eighth-note major pentatonic fills
55	0:00	7-8b	Triplet blues-scale fills
	0:49	7-8b	Triplet minor pentatonic fills
	1:39	7-8b	Triplet major pentatonic fills
56	0:00	7-8c	Sixteenth-note blues-scale fills
	0:45	7-8c	Sixteenth-note minor pentatonic fills
	1:28	7-8c	Sixteenth-note major pentatonic fills
57	0:00	8-1	Rock 'n' roll groove using the root
	0:11	8-2	Rock 'n' roll groove using chord notes
	0:23	8-3	Rock 'n' roll groove in minor using chord notes
	0:34	8-4	Rock 'n' roll groove using notes from the chord and mode
	0:46	8-6	Rock 'n' roll box groove
	0:58	8-7	Rock 'n' roll box groove in minor tonality
	1:10	8-8	Rock 'n' roll groove in a major 7th tonality
	1:21	8-9	Rock 'n' roll groove with a 6
58	0:00	8-10	Hard rock groove using only the root
	0:12	8-11	Hard rock groove using a minor chord
	0:26	8-12	Hard rock groove using notes from the minor chord and mode
	0:39	8-13	Hard rock box groove in a minor tonality
59	0:00	8-14	Pop rock groove using the root
	0:11	8-15	Pop rock groove in a major tonality
	0:23	8-16	Pop rock groove in a dominant tonality
	0:36	8-17	Pop rock box groove in a dominant tonality
60	0:00	8-18	Blues rock groove using the root
	0:10	8-19	Blues rock groove using notes from the chord
	0:21	8-20	Blues rock groove using notes from the chord and mode
	0:33	8-21	Blues rock box groove
61	0:00	8-22	Country rock groove using the root

Track	Time	Figure	Description
	0:12	8-23	Country rock groove using notes from the chord
	0:25	8-24	Country rock groove using the mode
	0:38	8-25	Country rock box groove
62	0:59	8-26	Generic rock song
63	0:00	9-1	Swing groove using a major pentatonic scale
	0:18	9-2	Swing groove using a Mixolydian mode
64		9-5	Walking bass using root-5 plus leading tone
65		9-6	Walking bass using chord tones plus leading tone
66		9-7	Walking bass using scale tones plus leading tone
67		9-8	Jazz blues walking pattern starting on E string
68		9-9	Jazz blues walking pattern starting on A string
69	0:28	9-10	Blues shuffle groove using the root
	0:19	9-11	Blues shuffle groove using a major chord
	0:39	9-12	Blues shuffle groove using a Mixolydian mode
	0:59	9-13	Blues shuffle groove using a minor mode
	1:18	9-14	Blues shuffle groove using a Mixolydian mode with a chromatic tone
	1:38	9-15	Blues shuffle groove in a minor tonality using a chromatic tone
70	0:00	9-16	Funk shuffle groove using only the root
	0:29	9-17	Funk shuffle groove for a dominant or minor chord
	0:58	9-18	Funk shuffle groove for a dominant or minor mode
71		9-19	Generic shuffle song
72	0:00	10-1	R & B groove in a major tonality
	0:27	10-2	R & B groove in a dominant tonality
	0:53	10-3	R & B groove in a minor tonality
	1:20	10-4a	R & B groove in a major tonality with chromatic tones and dead notes
	1:37	10-4b	R & B groove in a dominant tonality with chromatic tones and dead notes
	1:54	10-4c	R & B groove in a minor tonality with chromatic tones and dead notes

(continued)

Table A-1 *(continued)*

Track	Time	Figure	Description
73	0:00	10-5	Motown groove using a major or dominant tonality
	0:22	10-6	Motown groove using a minor or dominant tonality
74	0:00	10-7	Fusion groove in a major or dominant tonality
	0:33	10-8	Fusion groove in a dominant tonality
	1:06	10-9	Fusion groove in a dominant tonality covering four strings
75		10-10	Funk groove in slap-style
76	0:00	10-11	Funk groove in a dominant or minor tonality
	0:27	10-12	Funk groove in a major tonality
	0:57	10-13	Heavy funk groove in a minor tonality
	1:26	10-14	Heavy funk groove in a major or dominant tonality
	1:55	10-15	Finger-style funk groove in a minor or dominant tonality
	2:21	10-16	Finger-style funk groove in a major tonality
77	0:00	10-17	Hip-hop groove
	0:26	10-18	Hip-hop groove in a minor or dominant tonality
	0:52	10-19	Hip-hop groove in a major or dominant tonality
78		10-20	Funk song
79	0:00	11-1	Bossa groove
	0:18	11-2	Bossa groove for half-diminished chord
80	0:00	11-3	Samba groove
	0:27	11-4	Samba groove with anticipation
81	0:00	11-5	Afro-Cuban groove
	0:12	11-6	Afro-Cuban groove for a half-diminished chord
	0:18	11-7	Afro-Cuban groove with syncopation
	0:41	11-8	Afro-Cuban groove with syncopation for a half-diminished chord
82	0:00	11-9	Reggae groove in a minor tonality
	0:30	11-10	Reggae groove for a major or dominant chord
	0:56	11-11	Reggae groove for a major, minor, or dominant chord

Track	Time	Figure	Description
	1:20	11-12	Drop-one reggae groove
83	0:00	11-13	Calypso groove
	0:24	11-14	Calypso groove for major, minor, or dominant chord
84	0:00	11-15	Ska groove for a major, minor, or dominant chord
	0:15	11-16	Ska groove for a major or dominant chord
	0:37	11-17	Ska groove for a minor chord
85	0:00	11-18	South African groove for a major or dominant chord
	0:20	11-19	South African groove for a major, dominant, or minor chord
86	0:00	11-20	Makossa groove
	0:40	11-21	Complex Makossa groove
87	0:00	11-22	Bolobo groove
	0:33	11-23	Complex Bolobo groove
88	0:00	11-24	Bikutsi groove
	0:38	11-25	Complex Bikutsi groove
89		11-26	World beat song
90	0:00	12-1	Waltz using a single note in each measure
	0:15	12-2	Waltz using two notes in each measure
91	0:00	12-3a	Beats in 5/4
	0:14	12-3b	Beat grouping 1-2-3-1-2
	0:29	12-3c	Beat grouping 1-2-1-2-3
	0:43	12-4	Groove in 5/4 for a minor or dominant chord
	0:55	12-5	Groove in 5/4 using a 3-2 grouping
	1:16	12-6	Groove in 5/4 using a 2-3 grouping
	1:39	12-7	Groove in 5/4 using sixteenth notes
92	0:00	12-8a	Groove in 4/4
	0:20	12-8b	Converting a 4/4 groove into a 5/4 groove
93	0:00	12-9a	Beats in 7/4
	0:20	12-9b	Beat grouping 1-2-3-1-2-1-2
	0:38	12-9c	Beat grouping 1-2-1-2-3-1-2
	0:55	12-9d	Beat grouping 1-2-1-2-1-2-3

(continued)

Table A-1 *(continued)*

Track	Time	Figure	Description
	1:12	12-10	Groove in 7/4 for a minor or dominant chord
	1:27	12-11	Groove in 7/4 using a 3-2-2 grouping
	1:44	12-12	Groove in 7/4 using a 2-3-2 grouping
	2:00	12-13	Groove in 7/4 using a 2-2-3 grouping
	2:17	12-14	Groove in 7/4 using sixteenth notes
94		12-15	Groove in 5/4 using syncopation
95		12-17	Groove in 11/8
96		12-18	Groove in 6/4 and 7/4 mixed meter
97		12-19	Song in odd meter
98		13-2	Bass part in the pop genre
99		13-3	Bass part in the rock genre with a quarter-note groove skeleton
100		13-4	Bass part in the rock genre with eighth notes in the groove skeleton
101		13-5	Bass part in the R & B/Soul genre using eighth notes in the groove skeleton
102		13-6	Bass part in the R & B/Soul genre using a dotted eighth note and a sixteenth note in the groove skeleton
103		13-7	Bass part in the funk genre using two sixteenth notes in the groove skeleton
104		13-8	Bass part in the Latin genre
105		13-9	Shuffle bass part
106		13-10	Blending groove
107		13-11	Bold groove
108	0:00	13-12a	Sign-off using four eighth notes
	0:14	13-12b	Sign-off using four sixteenth notes
	0:25	13-12c	Sign-off using five sixteenth notes
	0:36	13-12d	Sign-off using eight sixteenth notes
	0:47	13-12a	Sign-off using four eighth notes
	0:58	13-12b	Sign-off using four sixteenth notes
	1:10	13-12c	Sign-off using five sixteenth notes
	1:21	13-12d	Sign-off using eight sixteenth notes

Track	Time	Figure	Description
109		14-1	Pumping eighth-note style accompaniment
110		14-2	Syncopation style accompaniment
111		14-3	Roots and 5ths accompaniment
112		14-4	Walking style accompaniment
113		14-5	Groove style accompaniment
114		14-6	Unison style accompaniment
115		14-7	Countermelody style accompaniment
116		14-8	Inversion style accompaniment
117	0:00	20-1	Bootsy Collins and Jab'o Starks
	0:15	20-2	Donald "Duck" Dunn and Al Jackson Jr.
	0:26	20-3	James Jamerson and Benny Benjamin
	0:52	20-4	John Paul Jones and John Bonham
	1:09	20-5	Joe Osborn and Hal Blaine
	1:22	20-6	Jaco Pastorius and Peter Erskine
	1:38	20-7	George Porter Jr. and Zig Modeliste
	1:55	20-8	Francis Rocco Prestia and David Garibaldi
	2:14	20-9	Chuck Rainey and Bernard Purdie
	2:40	20-10	Robbie Shakespeare and Sly Dunbar

What's on the Video Clips

Table A-2 lists all the video clips that accompany each chapter.

Table A-2		Bass Guitar Video Clips
Clip	Chapter	Description
1	2	Left hand fretting a note and right hand finger styles
2	2	Major scale grid / minor scale grid / open string scales E major, A major, E minor, A minor, F major, B♭ major
3	2	Song played on open strings and closed strings
4	3	Right-hand attack, sequence, accents, and string crossing
5	3	Left-hand permutations and right- and left-hand coordination

(continued)

Table A-2 *(continued)*

Clip	Chapter	Description
6	5	Triads
7	5	7th chords
8	5	Inversions
9	5	Modes and 7th chords
10	5	Groove box
11	5	Dead notes
12	6	Groove thought process
13	6	Groove skeleton
14	6	Creating your own groove
15	6	Groove tail
16	6	Groove apex
17	6	Groove creativity
18	7	Blues-scale licks
19	7	Grooves with fills
20	8	Rock groove development
21	8	Rock groove variations
22	8	Rock song
23	9	Swing groove
24	9	Walking lines
25	9	Blues and funk shuffles
26	10	R & B, Motown, and fusion
27	11	Bossa, samba, and Afro-Cuban
28	11	Reggae, calypso, and ska
29	11	African grooves
30	11	World beat song
31	12	Odd meter
32	13	Different musical genres
33	13	Blending and bold groove
34	13	Sign-offs
35	14	Beatles styles

Customer Care

If you have trouble downloading the companion files, please call Wiley Product Technical Support at 800-762-2974. Outside the United States, call 317-572-3994. You can also contact Wiley Product Technical Support at `http://wiley.custhelp.com/`. Wiley Publishing will provide technical support only for downloading and other general quality control items.

To place additional orders or to request information about other Wiley products, please call 877-762-2974.

Index

• Numerics •

3rd note, 135
4/4 meter, 261
4th note, 135
5/4 meter, 258–260
5th note, 135
5th-fret tuning method, 46–48
6th note, 136
7/4 meter, 262–265
7th chord
  groove using, 121, 135
  structures, 101–102
7th-fret tuning method, 48–50

• A •

accenting notes, 60–61, 262
accessories
  amplifier, 319–323
  cable, 324
  case, 323–324
  choosing, 20
  chorus unit, 325
  cleaning cloth, 324
  digital delay device, 327
  distortion device, 327
  electronic tuner, 324
  envelope filter, 327
  flanger/phase shifter, 327
  gig bag, 323–324
  headphone amp, 326–327
  metronome, 324
  multi-effects unit, 328
  music stand, 326
  octave pedal, 327
  rubbing alcohol, 324
  screwdrivers, 324
  speakers, 319–322
  stand for bass, 326
  stool, 326
  strap, 324

  strings, extra, 324
  volume pedal, 325
  wrenches, 324
accidentals, 88
accompaniment
  groove, 120–124
  major triad, 96–97
  minor triad, 97–98
  triad, 99
  unison, 299–301
active electronics, 15
ActiveBass website, 313
Aeolian mode
  minor scale relation, 112–113
  in R & B, 223
Aerosmith, 191
African style
  Cameroon styles, 249–251
  South African groove, 248–249
Afro-Cuban music
  groove for major, minor, or dominant
      chord, 240–241
  groove in half-diminished chord, 241
  groove with syncopation for half-
      diminished chord, 242
  groove with syncopation for major,
      minor, or dominant chord, 241
  syncopation, 240
Allman Brothers, 196
ambiguous groove, 218
amplifier
  basic description, 319
  choosing, 20
  combo, 320–321
  control panel, 322–323
  solid state, 321
  tube, 321
anatomy of bass guitar
  body, 14–15
  innards/guts, 15
  neck, 13–14
  sections, 12

apex, groove, 151–153, 162–163
arpeggio, 95
attack, inversions, 302
audio tracks
  bass guitar, 363–373
  listening to, 2
augmented chord, 100

• B •

back of neck, 14
backbeat, 154
band, bass player function in, 10–12
Barrett, Aston "Family Man" (reggae
    bassist), 243
bass drum, 154, 156
Bass knob, 322
bass line
  basic description, 32
  blending, 282–285
  groove representation, 120
  swing, 204
  walking, 205–214, 294–297
Bass Player magazine, 313
Bassics magazine, 313
bassist
  Adam Clayton (U2), 12, 191, 288
  Anthony Jackson (session player), 311
  Aston "Family Man" Barrett (reggae
    bassist), 243
  Berry Oakley (Allman Brothers), 196
  Bootsy Collins (James Brown band),
    357–358
  Carol Kaye (studio musician), 32, 354
  Chuck Rainey (session player), 222,
    361–362
  Dee Murray (pop rock bassist), 193
  Donald "Duck" Dunn (blues bassist), 196,
    214, 285, 358
  Flea (Red Hot Chili Peppers), 33, 229
  Francis Rocco Prestia (Tower of Power),
    27, 361
  Geddy Lee (Rush), 191, 268
  George Porter Jr. (Meters), 360–361
  Jaco Pastorius (Weather Report), 27, 228,
    285, 360
  James Jamerson (Funk Brothers), 27, 225,
    354, 358–359

Joe Osborn (studio musician), 32, 359–360
  John Entwistle (The Who), 12, 191, 354
  John Myung (Dream Theatre), 191
  John Paul Jones (Led Zeppelin), 191, 359
  Larry Graham (slap-style bassist), 33
  Louis Johnson (slap-style bassist), 33
  Marcus Miller (solo bassist), 33, 229
  Milt Hinton (upright bassist), 205
  Paul Chambers (upright bassist), 205
  Paul McCartney (The Beatles), 19, 32, 163,
    193, 287–289, 294–297, 301–302, 304
  Pino Palladino (pop rock bassist), 193
  P-Nut (modern bassist), 243
  Raphael Saadiq (hip-hop bassist), 233
  Ray Brown (upright bassist), 205
  Robbie Shakespeare (reggae bassist),
    243, 362
  Ron Carter (upright bassist), 205
  Roscoe Beck (blues bassist), 214
  Stanley Clarke (Return to Forever), 33,
    228, 353
  Tom Hamilton (Aerosmith), 191
  Tommy Cogbill (session player), 222
  Tommy Shannon (blues bassist), 214
  Victor Wooten (Béla Fleck and the
    Flecktones), 33, 229, 356
  Will Lee (session player), 354–355
batteries, 15
The Beatles, 19, 32, 163, 193, 287–289, 292,
    294–297, 301–302, 304–306, 355
Beatles style genre, 19
beats
  backbeat, 154
  as chunks of notes, 84–85
  counting in odd meter, 257
  division of, 79–80
  downbeat, 244–245
Beck, Roscoe (blues bassist), 214
Béla Fleck and the Flecktones, 33, 229, 356
Benjamin, Benny (drummer), 358–359
Bikutsi grooves, 251–252
Blaine, Hal (drummer), 359–360
blending bass lines, 282–285
blending groove, 282–285
blues progression
  blues rock, 196–198
  jazz, 211–214

blues rock, 196–198. *See also* rock grooves;
  rock styles
blues shuffle
  bassist, 214
  groove in minor tonality using chromatic
    tone, 217
  groove using major chord, 215
  groove using minor mode, 216
  groove using Mixolydian mode, 215–216
  groove using Mixolydian mode with
    chromatic tone, 216–217
  groove using only root, 215
  triplet figure, 217
body, bass guitar
  anatomy of, 14–15
  cleaning, 340
bold groove, 282–285
Bonham, John (drummer), 359
boogie bass line, 102–103
bossa nova
  groove, 239
  groove for half-diminished chord, 238
  groove for major, minor, or dominant
    chord, 238
  style, 237–238
box groove
  blues rock, 198
  country rock, 200
  hard rock in minor tonality, 193
  pop rock in dominant tonality, 195
  rock 'n' roll, 188
Brazilian style. *See* bossa nova
bridge
  middle section of song, 269
  pickups inside, 14
  raising and lowering, 346–348
  restringing bass, 332–334
Brown, Ray (upright bassist), 205
buying a bass
  budget for, 313
  choosing, 19
  custom-made, 317–318
  fretless, 312–313
  from music store, 314–316
  needs assessment, 309–313
  from newspaper ad, 316
  online, 316–317

• **C** •

C major scale, 35
cable, 320, 324
calypso style, 245–246
Cameroon styles, 249–252
Caribbean calypso style, 245–246
Carter, Ron (upright bassist), 205
cases, 323–324
Chambers, Paul (upright bassist), 205
changing strings. *See also* strings
  frequency, 20, 329
  need for, 20
  removing strings, 330–331
  restringing procedure, 332–337
  when to change, 330
Chappell, Jon
  Guitar For Dummies, 10
Cheat Sheet (this book), 5
chord changes
  chord chart, 146–147
  setting up, 11
  in solos, 174, 176
chord chart
  chord changes, 146–147
  reading notation, 70
  for solos, 176
chord progression
  calypso groove, 245
  pivoting notes, 162
  rock, 201–202
  song notation with, 272
chord symbols, 70
chord tone, 101, 148
chords. *See also specific chords*
  augmented, 100
  basic description, 16–17
  diminished, 100
  fingerboard diagram, 34–36
  groove using, 121
  suspended, 100
  triad, 95–99
  vocal chart, 73
chord-tone concept, 208–209
chorus unit, 325
chromatic leading tones, 295

chromatic tone
  in blues shuffle, 216–217
  within the box, 115–116
  in funk, 230
  groove using, 122
  hard rock groove, 192
  leading, 206
  notation, 88
  as note for supplementing modes, 114
  outside the box, 116–117
  in pop rock, 195
  in R & B, 224
  in rock 'n' roll, 188
Clarke, Stanley (Return to Forever), 33, 228, 353
Clayton, Adam (U2), 12, 191, 288
cleaning
  body, 340
  cloth, 324, 340–341
  fingerboard, 341
  frets, 341
  hand washing, 339
  hardware, 340
  neck, 340
  pickups, 340
  polish, 340–341
  strings, 341–342
  tool bag, 348–349
  wood, 341
clef, 70
closed-hand pick playing, 30–31
closing strings, 55–56
Cogbill, Tommy (session player), 222
Collins, Bootsy (bassist), 357–358
color, scales, 109
combo amplifier, 320–321
"Come Together" (The Beatles), 297
common tone, 225
constant structure, 147–149, 208, 225
control panel, amplifier, 322–323
controls, bass guitar body, 14
countermelody method, 301–303
country rock, 199–201. *See also* rock grooves; rock styles
custom-made bass, 317–318
cutting strings, 330–331, 334–335

• D •

D major scale, 35
"Day Tripper" (The Beatles), 297
dead note
  in groove, 118
  groove using, 123
  playing, 118
  in R & B, 224
  raking, 119
designer grooves, 151–153
diatonic leading tone, 206, 295
digital delay device, 327
diminished chord, 100, 208
distortion device, 327
dominant chord
  in 5/4 meter, 259
  in 7/4 meter, 264
  7th chord structure, 101
  in Afro-Cuban music, 240–242
  in bossa nova, 238
  in calypso, 246
  in funk, 229–232
  in funk shuffle, 219–220
  in fusion, 226–228
  groove, 134
  in hip-hop, 233–234
  in Motown, 225–226
  in pop rock, 194–195
  in R & B, 223–224
  in reggae, 243–244
  in rock, 187–190
  scales, 102, 110
  in ska, 246–247
  in South African style, 248–249
  in waltz, 256
dominant groove, 136–139
dominant leading tone, 206, 295
Dorian mode
  harmonically ambiguous groove, 125
  minor scale relation, 112
  origin, 113, 124
  in R & B, 223
dot
  on fingerboard diagram, 35
  on neck of bass guitar, 38

octave marker, 38
  subdivision of note, 82
downbeat, 244–245
Dream Theatre, 191
driving sixteenth notes, 191
drop-one technique, 244
drum
  backbeat, 154
  bass, 154, 156
  hi-hat, 155–156
  snare, 154–156
drummer
  Al Jackson Jr. (R & B), 358
  Benny Benjamin (Motown), 358–359
  Bernard Purdie (session player), 361–362
  David Garibaldi (Tower of Power), 361
  Hal Blaine (session player), 359–360
  Jab'o Starks (James Brown band), 357–358
  John Bonham (Led Zeppelin), 359
  locking in with, 11
  Peter Erskine (Weather Report), 360
  Sly Dunbar (reggae), 362
  Zig Modeliste (Meters), 360–361
Drums For Dummies (Strong), 154
Dunbar, Sly (drummer), 362
Dunn, Donald "Duck" (blues bassist), 196,
    214, 285, 358
dynamics, 27

● **E** ●

effects, gadgets, 325
effects pedals, 327–328
eighth note
  combination, 267–268
  fills, 179
  pumping, 288–290
  R & B/Soul genre, 277–278
  in rock, 273–274
  rock style, 276
  subdivision of note, 81
  triplets, 82
electric guitar, 9
electronic tuner, 41–42, 324
electronics, 15
end pin, 15, 23
Entwistle, John (The Who), 12, 191, 354
envelope filter, 327
envelopes, coiled strings with, 333

Erskine, Peter (drummer), 360
etude, 208

● **F** ●

Fender Jazz bass, 314
Fender Precision bass, 191, 314
5th note, 135
5th-fret tuning method, 46–48
fill. *See also* solos
  connecting to groove, 177
  purposes, 176–177
  symmetry of bass, 17–18
  timing a, 177–178
finger
  permutation, 63–65
  position for groove, 134
fingerboard
  cleaning, 341
  neck components, 13–14
fingerboard diagram. *See also* grids
  basic description, 33
  elements, 34–35
  finding notes on neck, 37–39
  intervals, identifying, 39–40
  major scale, 36–37
  minor scale, 36–37
  open-string scales, 37
finger-style playing, 27–29
finish, wood, 343
5/4 meter, 258–260
flanger/phase shifter, 327
flash, 18
flat symbol, 38
Flea (Red Hot Chili Peppers), 33, 229
4/4 meter, 261
4th note, 135
frequency, 57–58
fretless bass, 228, 312–313
frets
  cleaning, 341
  half steps, 14
  neck components, 13–14
  number of, 22
  use of, 22
fretting hand. *See* left hand
funk
  generic groove, 234–236
  sixteenth note feel, 278–279

Funk Brothers, 225
funk shuffle
  generic shuffle, 220
  groove for dominant and minor chords,
    219–220
  groove using notes from dominant or
    minor modes, 219
  groove using only root, 218
funk style
  finger-style for major tonality, 232
  finger-style for minor or dominant
    tonality, 231–232
  groove for dominant and minor tonality,
    229–230
  groove for major or dominant tonality,
    230–231
  groove for major tonality, 230
  groove for minor tonality, 230–231
  groove in slap-style, 229
  heavy groove for major or dominant
    tonality, 230–231
  hip-hop, 233–234
  musical genres, 18
  neutral note choice, 229
fusion style
  groove for dominant chord, 227
  groove in major or dominant chord, 226–227
  groove over four strings on dominant
    chord, 228
  history, 228
  rock and jazz combination, 226

• *G* •

Garibaldi, David (Tower of Power), 361
genre
  Beatles, 19
  blending bass lines, 282–285
  funk, 18, 278–279
  Latin, 279–280
  odd meters, 19
  pop/singer-songwriter, 273
  R & B/Soul, 274–278
  rock, 18, 273–274
  shuffle, 280–281
  standard chord progression, 272
  style differentiation, 271
  swing, 18
  world beat, 19

gig bags, 323–324
Graham, Larry (slap-style bassist), 33
grids. *See also* fingerboard diagram
  elements, 34–35
  how to use, 2
  major scale structure, 93
  minor scale structure, 95
  showing open-string scales, 37
groove. *See also specific styles*
  altering, 163–165
  ambiguous, 218
  apex, 151–153, 162–163
  with bass drum, 154
  blending, 282–285
  bold, 282–285
  chord tone, 148
  connecting fill to, 177
  constant structure, 147–149
  content, 17
  creativity with, 162–166
  dead note in, 118–120
  designer, 151–153
  dominant, 136–139
  with eighth-note fill, 179
  elements, 129–136
  guidelines for creating, 133–134
  harmonically ambiguous, 124–126
  with hi-hat, 155–156
  lower apex, 152–153
  major, 142–145
  minor, 139–142
  mobile, 134, 148–150
  note selection for, 133–136
  paring down, 165–166
  scales, commonly used, 134–136
  shape, 98
  simplifying, 165–166
  with sixteenth-note fill, 181
  with snare drum, 154–155
  with triplet fill, 180
  upper apex, 151–152
  using 7th chord, 121
  using chords, 121
  using chromatic tone, 122
  using dead note, 123
  using Mixolydian mode, 122
groove skeleton, 17, 130–133, 162–163
groove tail, 145–146, 162–163, 225

Guitar For Dummies (Phillips and Chappell), 10
guts, bass guitar, 15

• H •

half note, 81
half step
  frets, 14
  interval, 92
  major and minor scale diagram, 36
  order of notes, 38
half-diminished chord
  7th chord structure, 101
  in Afro-Cuban music, 241
  in bossa nova, 238
  scale/chord combination, 111
  scales, 102
Hamilton, Tom (Aerosmith), 191
hand position. _See also_ left hand; right hand
  left hand, 26–27
  right hand, 27–33
  while sitting, 25
  while standing, 24
handspun-plus-two-frets method of finding notes, 77
hard rock, 191–193. _See also_ rock grooves; rock styles
hardware, cleaning, 340
harmonic minor scale, 114
harmonically ambiguous groove, 124–126
harmonics
  beating or wavering sound, 53
  location of, 50
  playing technique, 51
  relationships between, 52
  root and 5ths, 292–293
  tuning method, 50–53
harmony, linking with rhythm, 10–11
headphone amp, 326–327
headstock, 13, 336
high string, hand reaching for, 29
hi-hat, 155–156
Hinton, Milt (upright bassist), 205
hip-hop style, 233–234
holding a bass
  compromising the position, 22
  sitting position, 25
  standing position, 24
  strapping on, 23

• I •

I-IV-V progression, 196
index finger, 58
inlays, 55
input jack, 15
international styles
  African, 248–252
  Afro-Cuban, 240–242
  bossa nova, 237–239
  Caribbean calypso, 245–246
  reggae, 242–245
  samba, 239–240
  ska, 246–247
  world beat, 19, 252–253
interval
  chunks of notes, 85–86
  half step, 92
  identifying, 39–40
  names and configurations, 39–40
intonation, 346–347
inversion
  basic description, 103–104
  major chord, 104–107
  minor chord, 107–109
Ionian mode, 112–113

• J •

jack, on body of bass guitar, 15
Jackson, Anthony (session player), 311
Jackson Jr., Al (R & B drummer), 358
jam session
  creative collaboration, 156
  notes, listening for, 157–159
  notes, pivoting, 160–161
  preparing the ear, 157
Jamerson, James (bassist)
  with Benny Benjamin (drummer), 358–359
  finger-style playing technique, 27
  history, 354
  Motown sound, 225
jazz
  blues walking pattern, 211–214
  walking bass line, 205–214
Johnson, Louis (slap-style bassist), 33
Jones, John Paul (Led Zeppelin), 191, 359

• K •

Kaye, Carol (studio musician), 32, 354
keeping time, 11–12
key of C, 35
key of D, 35
key signature, 88

• L •

Latin style, 240, 279–280. *See also* Afro-Cuban music
leading tone
  diatonic, 295
  dominant, 295
  sound, 206
Led Zeppelin, 191, 359
Lee, Geddy (Rush), 191, 268
Lee, Will (session player), 354–355
left hand
  conventions used in this book, 3, 21
  coordinating with right hand, 16, 63–66
  finger permutation, 63–65
  moving up and down neck, 3
  muting strings, 65
  sitting with bass, 25
  standing with bass, 24
licks, 169
locking in with the drummer, 11
Locrian mode, 112–113, 238
long-term bass use, 310–311
low string, 29
lower groove apex, 152–153
luthier, 317–318
Lydian mode, 112–113
lyrics, vocal chart, 73

• M •

maintenance
  adjustments, 344–347
  bridge, 346–348
  cleaning, 339–341
  electronics, 343
  of finish, 343
  repair tool bag, 348–349
  repairs, minor, 342–343
  screws, tightening, 342–343
  storage, 349–350
  string changes, 20, 338

major chord
  7th chord structure, 101
  in Afro-Cuban music, 240–242
  in blues shuffle, 215
  in bossa nova, 238
  in calypso, 246
  in funk, 230–232
  in fusion, 226–227
  in hip-hop, 234
  inversions, 104–107
  in Motown, 225
  in pop rock, 194
  in R & B, 222–224
  in reggae, 243–244
  in rock, 187–190
  scales, 102, 110
  in ska, 246–247
  sounds, 16, 70
  in South African style, 248–249
  in waltz, 256
major groove, 142–145
major pentatonic scale, 174–176
major scale
  fingerboard diagram, 36–37
  groove, 134
  notation, 88
  structure, 93–94
  tonal center, 91
major triad, 95–98
Makossa style, 249–250
marker method of finding notes, 77
McCartney, Paul (The Beatles), 19, 32, 163, 193, 287–289, 294–297, 301–302, 304, 355
measures (bars), 79–80
melodic minor scale, 114
metronome
  exercise, 79
  gig bag contents, 324
  keeping time, 12
  setting the, 78
Mid knob, 322
middle finger, 58
Miller, Marcus (solo bassist), 33, 229, 355
minor chord
  in 5/4 meter, 259
  in 7/4 meter, 264
  7th chord structure, 101
  in Afro-Cuban music, 240–242
  in blues shuffle, 216–217
  in bossa nova, 238

in calypso, 246
in funk, 229–232
in funk shuffle, 219–220
in hard rock, 192
in hip-hop, 233–234
inversions, 107–109
in Motown, 226
in R & B, 223–224
in reggae, 243–244
in rock, 187–190
scales, 102, 111
in ska, 246–247
sounds, 16, 70
in South African style, 249
in waltz, 256
minor groove, 139–142
minor pentatonic scale, 169–173
minor scale
  Aeolian mode, 124
  fingerboard diagram, 36–37
  groove, 134
  harmonic, 114
  melodic, 114
  natural, 94, 124
  structure, 94–95
  tonal center, 91
minor triad, 95–98
Mixolydian mode
  in blues rock, 198
  in blues shuffle, 215–216
  in fusion, 226–227
  groove using, 122
  harmonically ambiguous groove, 125
  major scale relation, 112
  origin, 113
  in pop rock, 195
  in R & B, 223
  in rock 'n' roll, 187–188
  in swing style, 204–205
mobile groove, 148–150
Modeliste, Zig (Meters), 360–361
modes. *See* scales
modulation, 14
Motown style, 225–226
multi-effects unit, 328
Murray, Dee (bassist), 193
music notation, 70–71. *See also* notation
music stand, 326
music store, 314–316

musical interval, 16
musical staff, 70
muting strings, 65
Myung, John (Dream Theatre), 191

• N •

natural minor, 124
natural sign, 88
neck, bass guitar
  anatomy of, 13–14
  attachment to body, 315
  bass guitar compared to other guitars, 10
  cleaning, 340
  finding notes on, 37–39
neutral note, 136, 249
newspaper ad, 316
notation
  chord chart, 70
  chromatic scale, 88
  key signature, 88
  major scale, 88
  music, 70–71
  regular music, 70
  right-hand accents, 61
  scale, 92
  with standard chord progression, 272
  tablature, 71–73
  triad accompaniment, 99
  triple, 3
  vocal chart, 73
notes. *See also specific notes*
  accenting, 60–61, 262
  chunks of, 84–85
  finding on neck, 37–39
  fingerboard diagram, 34–35
  handspan-plus-two-frets method of
    finding, 77
  listening for, 157–159
  looking for specific, 162
  music notation, 70–71
  neutral, 136
  number representation, 3
  octave method of finding, 73–78
  passing, 135–136
  pivoting, 160–161
  selecting for groove, 133–136
numbers, note representation, 3
nut, 13–14

• O •

Oakley, Berry (Allman Brothers), 196
octave
  major scale structure, 93
  notation of scale, 92
  octave method of finding notes, 73–78
  scale representation, 34
octave marker, 38
octave pedal, 327
odd meter
  4/4 meter, 261
  5/4 meter, 258–260
  7/4 meter, 262–265
  counting beats in, 257
  generic song, 270
  musical genres, 19
  syncopation and subdivision, 266–268
  waltz style, 255–257
one-string chromatic approach, finding
    notes, 162
online, buying a bass, 316–317
open strings, 54
open-hand pick playing, 30–31
open-string scales, 37
Osborn, Joe (studio musician), 32, 359–360

• P •

Palladino, Pino (pop rock bassist), 193
passing note, 135–136
passing tone, 168
passive electronics, 15
Pastorius, Jaco (Weather Report)
  finger-style playing technique, 27
  fretless bass use, 228
  history, 355
  with Peter Erskine, 360
  sign-offs, 285
pedal
  effects, 327–328
  volume, 325
"Penny Lane" (The Beatles), 294–297
percussive sound, 32
phase shifter, 327

Phillips, Mark
  Guitar For Dummies, 10
phrases
  groove representation, 120
  measures and beats, 79
  rhythmic notes, 80
Phrygian mode, 112–113
piano, reference pitch from, 43–44
pick
  closed-hand pick playing, 30–31
  how to hold, 30
  open-hand pick playing, 30–31
  size, 29, 112
pick-style playing
  bassist, 32
  closed-hand, 30–31
  open-hand, 30–31
  right-hand position, 29–31
pickups
  cleaning, 340
  modulation, 14
  thumb resting on, 28
  translation of string vibration, 58
pitch. *See also* tone
  bass guitar compared to other guitars, 10
  string tension, 58
  string vibration, 57–58
pivoting notes, 160–161
playing space, 273
plucking hand. *See* right hand
P-Nut (modern bassist), 243
polish, 340–341
pop rock, 193–195, 273. *See also* rock
    grooves; rock styles
Porter Jr., George (Meters), 360–361
pots (potentiometers), 15
Prestia, Francis Rocco (Tower of Power),
    27, 229, 361
progressive rock, 192–193. *See also* rock
    grooves; rock styles
pulse
  groove skeleton element, 130
  keeping time, 11
pumping eighth note, 288–290
Purdie, Bernard (drummer), 361–362

• Q •

quarter note
in rock, 273–275
subdivision of note, 80

• R •

R & B (rhythm and blues)
groove using dead notes and chromatic
tones, 224
groove using dominant mode, 223
groove using major mode, 222–223
groove using minor mode, 223
history, 221
session player, 221–222
syncopation, 222
R & B/Soul genre, 274–278
Rainey, Chuck (session player), 222,
361–362
raking
dead note, 119
string crossing, 62
reading music. *See also* notation
beats, 79–80
chord chart, 70
in chunks, 84–86
learning how, 2
measures (bars), 79–80
musical notation types, 69
note location, 73–78
phrases, 79–80
playing while, 89
regular music notation, 70–71
tablature notation, 71–73
vocal chart, 73
Red Hot Chili Peppers, 33, 229
reference pitch, 41–45
reggae
bass trademarks, 242
drop-one groove, 244–245
groove for major, minor, or dominant
chord, 244
groove for major or dominant chord, 243
groove for minor chord, 243
relative tuning, 42

restringing procedure, 332–337
rests
as chunks of notes, 84–85
note values, 83
Return to Forever, 228, 353
rhythm
feel of, 130
linking with harmony, 10–11
music notation, 70–71
triplet, 203
rhythm and blues. *See* R & B
rhythm sections
Bootsy Collins and Jab'o Starks, 357–358
Chuck Rainey and Bernard Purdie, 361–362
Donald "Duck" Dunn and Al Jackson Jr., 358
Francis Rocco Prestia and David
Garibaldi, 361
George Porter Jr. and Zig Modeliste,
360–361
Jaco Pastorius and Peter Erskine, 360
James Jamerson and Benny Benjamin,
358–359
Joe Osborn and Hal Blaine, 359–360
John Paul Jones and John Bonham, 359
Robbie Shakespeare and Sly Dunbar, 362
rhythmic syncopation. *See* syncopation
riff, 17
right hand
accents, 60–61
conventions used in this book, 3, 21
coordinating with left hand, 16, 63–66
finger-style playing, 27–29
pick-style playing, 29–32
same-string strokes, 59–60
sitting with bass, 25
slap-style playing, 32–33
standing with bass, 24
string crossing, 62–63
warm-ups, 58–63
rock grooves
blending or bold grooves, 284
blues rock box groove, 198
blues rock using notes from chord, 197
blues rock using notes from chord and
mode, 198
blues rock using only root, 197

rock grooves *(continued)*
  country rock box groove, 200
  country rock using mode, 200
  country rock using notes from chord,
    199–200
  country rock using only root, 199
  generic, 201–202
  hard rock box groove in minor tonality, 193
  hard rock using minor chord, 192
  hard rock using notes from minor chord
    and mode, 193
  hard rock using only root, 192
  pop rock box in dominant tonality, 195
  pop rock using major tonality, 194
  pop rock using notes in dominant
    tonality, 194–195
  pop rock using only root, 194
  rock box groove, 188–189
  rock 'n' roll box groove, 189
  rock 'n' roll in major tonality, 190
  rock 'n' roll in minor tonality, 189
  rock 'n' roll in minor using notes from
    chord, 187
  rock 'n' roll using notes from chord, 187
  rock 'n' roll using notes from chord and
    mode, 188
  rock 'n' roll using only root, 186
rock 'n' roll. *See* rock grooves; rock styles
rock styles
  blues rock, 196–198
  country rock, 199–200
  difference between, 185
  hard rock, 191–193
  history, 186, 191
  musical genres, 18
  pop rock, 193–195
  progressive rock, 191–193
  quarter or eighth note, 273–274
  rock 'n' roll, 186–191
root
  basic description, 34
  chord symbols, 70
  fingerboard diagram representation, 35
  groove, 134
  groove skeleton element, 130
  playing, 292–293
  as tonal center, 93
  in two-note relationship, 158

root position, 104
root-5 concept, 207–208, 292–293
rubbing alcohol, 324
Rush, 191

• *S* •

Saadiq, Raphael (hip-hop bassist), 233
saddle, 336–337, 346
salsa, 240. *See also* Afro-Cuban music
samba style, 239–240
scale tone, 93
scales. *See also* major scale; minor scale
  Aeolian mode, 112–113
  basic description, 16–17
  color, 109
  dominant chord, 102, 110
  Dorian mode, 112–113
  fingerboard diagram, 34–36
  half-diminished, 102, 111
  intervals, 92
  Ionian mode, 112–113
  Locrian mode, 112–113
  Lydian mode, 112–113
  major chord, 102, 110
  minor chord, 102, 111
  Mixolydian mode, 112–113
  notation, 92
  open-string, 37
  Phrygian mode, 112–113
  tonal center, 92
scale-tone concept, 210–211
screwdriver, 324
screws, tightening, 342–343
service agreement, 317
session player, 221–222
7/4 meter, 262–265
7th chord
  groove using, 121, 135
  structures, 101–102
7th-fret tuning method, 48–50
Shakespeare, Robbie (reggae bassist),
  243, 362
Shannon, Tommy (blues bassist), 214
sharp symbol, 38
short-term bass use, 311
shuffle genre, 280–281
sign-offs, 285–286

sitting with bass, 25
six-note blues scale, 168
six-string bass, 311–312
sixteenth note
  in 5/4 meter, 260
  in 7/4 meter, 266
  fill, 181
  in funk, 278–279
  R & B/Soul genre, 278
  subdivision of note, 81
6th note, 136
ska style, 246–247
skeleton, groove, 17, 130–132, 162–163
slap-style playing
  funk groove in, 229, 279
  right-hand position, 32–33
snapping the string, 32–33
snare drum, 154–156
solid state amplification, 321
solos. *See also* fill
  blues scale, 168–169
  challenges, 167
  chord changes, 174, 176
  chord chart, 176
  major pentatonic scale, 173–175
  minor pentatonic scale, 169–173
  symmetry of bass, 17–18
sonic space, 154–155
South African style, 248–249
speakers
  basic description, 319
  cable, 320
  combo amp, 320–321
  size, 321–322
stand, bass, 326
standing with bass, 24
Starks, Jab'o (drummer), 357–358
stool, 326
storage, bass, 349–350
straight rhythmic style, 288
strap pin, 14, 23–24
strapping on bass, 23
straps, 324
striking hand. *See* right hand
string crossing, 62–63

string retainers, 336
strings. *See also* changing strings
  bass guitar compared to other guitars,
    9–10
  cleaning, 341–342
  coiled, 333
  cost, 337
  cutting, 330–331, 334–335
  dull, 330
  envelopes, 333
  extra, 324
  fingerboard diagram representation, 35
  length, 10, 334
  maintenance, 338
  muting, 65
  neck components, 13–14
  needs assessment, 311–312
  raking, 62
  ring (ball), 333
  tension, 58
  vibration, 57–58
Strong, Jeff
  Drums For Dummies, 154
style, 18
subdivision, 266–268
suspended chord, 100
swing style
  groove using major pentatonic scale, 204
  groove using Mixolydian mode, 204–205
  musical genres, 18
sympathetic vibration, 65
syncopated rhythmic style, 288–292
syncopation
  in Afro-Cuban music, 240–242
  in calypso, 245
  in R & B, 222
  and subdivision, 266–268

• *T* •

tablature
  notation, 71–73
  reading, 2
tail, groove, 145–146, 162–163, 225
TalkBass website, 313

technical support, 374
tension
  creation and release by bass guitarist, 11
  groove tail, 145–146
  string, 58
3rd note, 135
three-quarter time, 256
thumb rest, 28
thumb-style playing
  funk groove in, 229, 279
  right-hand position, 32–33
tie, 83
time, keeping, 11–12
timing fills, 177–178
tonal center, 35, 91–93. *See also* root
tonality, 91
tone. *See also* pitch
  common, 225
  leading, 206
  string vibration, 57–58
Tower of Power, 229
Treble knob, 322
triad, 95–99
triple notation, 3
triplet feel/rhythm
  blues shuffle, 214–217
  counting beats in measure, 203
  funk shuffle, 218–220
  groove skeleton elements, 130
  jazz, 205–214
  swing styles, 18
triplet figure, 217
triplet fill, 180
triplet rhythm, subdivision of note, 82
truss rod, 15, 344–345
tube amplification, 321
tuner, electronic, 41–42, 324
tuning bass guitar
  5th-fret method, 46–48
  7th-fret method, 48–50
  harmonics method, 50–53
  importance, 16
  to itself, 41, 46–53
  with reference pitch from guitar, 43, 45
  with reference pitch from piano, 43–44
  with reference pitch when playing
    alone, 41–43

with reference pitch when playing with
    others, 43–45
  relative tuning, 42
tuning fork, 43
tuning head, 330, 336–337
tuning machines, 13
tuning post, 330, 332, 334–335
turnarounds, 285–286
two-strings/two-frets method of finding
    notes, 76

• *U* •

U2, 12, 288
unison accompaniment, 299–301
unison riff, 191
upper groove apex, 151–152
up-tempo, 246

• *V* •

vibration
  string, 57–58
  sympathetic, 65
video clips, 374
vocal chart, 73
voice leading, 302
Volume knob, 322
volume pedal, 325

• *W* •

walking bass lines, 205–214, 294–297
waltz, 255–257
Weather Report, 228, 355
website
  ActiveBass, 313
  TalkBass, 313
The Who, 12, 191, 354
whole note, 82
whole step, 36
Wiley Product Technical Support, 374
Wooten, Victor (Béla Fleck and the
    Flecktones), 33, 229, 356
world beat style, 19, 252–253. *See also*
    international styles
wrench, 324

About the Author

Patrick Pfeiffer is a professional bassist, composer, clinician, author, and bass educator in New York City. He earned his bachelor's degree in music from Arizona State University and his master's in jazz studies (with distinction) from the prestigious New England Conservatory of Music. Pfeiffer's solo CD *Fruits and Nuts* earned stellar reviews and a recommendation from *Bass Player Magazine* as well as from *Jazz Improv Magazine*. Besides performing and recording, Pfeiffer teaches bass guitar in New York City and often conducts clinics alongside such bass luminaries as Will Lee, John Patitucci, Gerald Veasley, Michael Manring, Bakithi Kumalo, Adam Nitti, and many more.

His former students include Adam Clayton of U2, Jean-Louis Locas of Cirque du Soleil, Mark Wike of The Bogmen, Alec Such of Bon Jovi, and Nick diPierro of Her & Kings County. Other former clients include Red Ant Records, PolyGram, and Arista Records.

Pfeiffer has played and/or recorded with George Clinton, Jimmy Norman, Phoebe Snow, Slam Stewart, Paul Griffin, Bernard Purdie, Babatunde Olatunji, Sheila Jordan, George Russell, Margaret Whiting, Joe Lovano, Carlos Alomar, Hernan Romero, Katie Agresta, the Marvelettes, the KMA Allstars, the Gary Corwin Dream Band, and many others. Pfeiffer was featured artist and adjudicator in the Jazz on the Great Plains festival in South Dakota and repeatedly one of the featured performers and instructors at Gerald Veasley's famous Bass Boot Camp in Reading, Pennsylvania.

Besides the bestselling *Bass Guitar For Dummies* editions, which have been translated into seven languages to date, Pfeiffer also authored *Bass Guitar Exercises For Dummies* (published by Wiley), *Improve Your Groove: The Ultimate Guide for Bass* (published by Hal Leonard), and *Daily Grooves for Bass* (published by Carl Fischer).

Pfeiffer is endorsed by Aguilar Amplification and by the elite bass companies MTD and Fodera. In 2011, Fodera Guitars honored him with a "Pfeiffer Signature" 6-string fretless electric bass. His latest basscapades can be found at www.PatrickPfeifferBass.com.

Dedication

This book is dedicated to the love of my life, my beautiful wife, Lisa Ann Herth Pfeiffer.

I am buoyed by your love, balanced by your Reiki, and awed by your spirit.

Author's Acknowledgments

My love and heartfelt gratitude to Lisa Pfeiffer for her love, wisdom, honesty, and support whenever I find myself immersed in yet another bass project. A huge thank you to my wonderful friends: To my tireless pre-editor Crissy Walford; to Nicolas diPierro for the nightly bombing runs of art; to Lawrence Green for the beautiful Finale files and tutorials; and to Steven Schlesinger for the great photos. It's my privilege to have an amazing group of musicians on the recording of this book's tracks: David B. Meade and Michael D'Agostino on drums, Sean Harkness on guitar, and Lou DiNatale on keyboards. A big thank you to the amazing Taylor Ryan of AM Studios in New York City for expertly recording, mixing, and mastering the tracks. Special thanks to Shawn Setaro for proof-playing my musical examples. I am very grateful for the love and support I've always gotten from my parents, Ursula and Wilhelm Pfeiffer. Parents everywhere should help their kids follow their dream. Mine did, even though they often worried about my single-mindedness toward becoming a musician.

My utmost respect and thanks to the *For Dummies* crew, Tracy Boggier, David Lutton, Tim Gallan, Jennette ElNaggar, Rebekah Brownson, the amazing video crew of Paul Chen, Shelley Lea, Kathleen Jeffers, Eric Hurst, and all the people behind the scenes I never got to meet. You all are an incredible team, and I am grateful for the long hours you've put into making sure this book is the best it can possibly be. Thank you! It was a great privilege and a real pleasure to work with you. A special thanks to Marla Marquit Steuer for pointing the right folks into the right (my) direction, and a big thank you to my agent Bill Gladstone and all the folks at Waterside. I'd also like to thank the great Will Lee for the beautiful foreword and the continuing support and inspiration you give me, and also special thanks to Gerald Veasley for including me as part of your incredible commitment to the bass community. A big nod of respect and thanks goes to Chris Scialfa for keeping my repertoire fresh and to bassist extraordinaire Danny Morris for using my books at Berklee. To my students: I'm grateful for every lesson you teach me and every lesson you take with you. A special thanks goes to my brothers Andreas and Mark for your encouragement and support. I can always count on you (I just wish sometimes you'd remember I'm your older brother).

I'm very grateful to my teachers, Hilmar Stanger, Bruce Amman, Robert Miller, Dennis Sexton, Frank Smith, Chuck Marohnic, Jeff Andrews, and Miroslav Vitous. I carry your lessons with me. Also kudos and a big thanks to Ed Friedland for his excellent book *Reggae Bass* (Hal Leonard) and Aladji Touré for his equally excellent book *Les Secrets de la Basse Africaine* (Lemoine). Both books were a great help for the world beat section of my book and I'd recommend them to any bassist who would like to delve deeper into these two styles. A special thank you goes to Michael Tobias for building my precious MTD basses, and to Jason DeSalvo, Joey Lauricella, and Vinny Fodera of Fodera for the amazing "Pfeiffer Signature" bass. Also special thanks to Dave Boonshoft and Justin Huth of Aguilar amplification for the excellent amplifier. I'm extremely grateful to Michael Carolan for giving my music a chance to be heard and to Katie Agresta for so many things and, not the least, for giving me the opportunity to be in this great country. You are incredible friends. Thank you, Adam Clayton — you never cease to amaze me. Thanks to Julie Hanlon, Dee Behrman (my coach), Loys Green, and Mike Visceglia.

With every new book, this is the section I dread most . . . I am grateful to the beautiful people who are no longer with me, but whose love and support continue to see me through: Marjorie Herth, Sandy Green, Mike Kissel, Paul Griffin, Gary Corwin, Lance Berry, Bill Evans (the bass player), Robert Mast, and Reiner Hoffmann, without whom I may never have become a bass player in the first place.

And a very special thanks to LuLu for being a source of unconditional love and to Juba Muktananda (who thinks I am the world's greatest hunter every time I come back from the grocery store).

A special thanks to Gurumayi Chidvilasananda of the Sidha Yoga Foundation and to Daisaku Ikeda and the SGI family.

Publisher's Acknowledgments

Acquisitions Editor: Tracy Boggier

Associate Editor: David Lutton

Senior Project Editor: Tim Gallan

Copy Editor: Jennette ElNaggar

Technical Editor: David Murray

Project Coordinator: Rebekah Brownson

Cover Image: ©iStockphoto.com/RapidEye